Student Study Guide

to accompany

EDUCATIONAL PSYCHOLOGY
Windows on Classrooms

Seventh Edition

Paul Eggen
University of North Florida

Don Kauchak
University of Utah

PEARSON

Merrill
Prentice Hall

Upper Saddle River, New Jersey
Columbus, Ohio

Vice President and Executive Publisher: Jeffery W. Johnston
Assistant Vice President and Publisher: Kevin M. Davis
Development Editor: Autumn Benson
Editorial Assistant: Sarah Kenoyer
Production Editor: Sheryl Glicker Langner
Design Coordinator: Diane C. Lorenzo
Cover Design: Ali Mohrman
Cover Image: Fotosearch
Production Manager: Laura Messerly
Director of Marketing: David Gesell
Marketing Manager: Autumn Purdy
Marketing Coordinator: Brian Mounts

Pearson Prentice Hall™ is a trademark of Pearson Education, Inc.
Pearson® is a registered trademark of Pearson plc
Prentice Hall® is a registered trademark of Pearson Education, Inc.
Merrill® is a registered trademark of Pearson Education, Inc.

Pearson Education Ltd.   Pearson Education Australia Pty. Limited
Pearson Education Singapore Pte. Ltd.   Pearson Education North Asia Ltd.
Pearson Education Canada, Ltd.   Pearson Educación de Mexico, S.A. de C.V.
Pearson Education–Japan   Pearson Education Malaysia Pte. Ltd.

10 9 8 7 6 5 4 3 2 1
ISBN: 0-13-173615-9

TABLE OF CONTENTS

CHAPTER SIXTEEN: Assessment Through Standardized Testing

INTRODUCTION TO THE STUDENT STUDY GUIDE TO ACCOMPANY EGGEN AND KAUCHAK'S

EDUCATIONAL PSYCHOLOGY: WINDOWS ON CLASSROOMS

TO THE STUDENT

As with our revision of the text and earlier editions of your study guide, we have prepared this supplement to *Educational Psychology: Windows on Classrooms* (7th ed.) with you in mind. This study guide is intended to complement and reinforce the content in the text, and if you use it conscientiously, it will help you develop a deep and thorough understanding of the *nature of learning*, and how factors such as *learner development* and *individual differences, motivation, classroom management, instruction,* and *assessment* all affect how much students of all ages learn. Our goal is for this guide to contribute to your success as you study educational psychology.

ORGANIZATION OF THE STUDY GUIDE

Each chapter of the study guide includes the following parts:
- **Chapter Outline:** The Chapter Outline presents the organization of each chapter. All section headings are identified in the outline.
- **Chapter Objectives:** The Chapter Objectives specify what you are expected to achieve as you study each chapter.
- **Chapter Overview:** The Chapter Overview summarizes the content of each chapter. You can use the overview in different ways. You may want to read it before you begin your detailed study of the chapter in the text to provide you with a frame of reference, you may want to read it after completing your study to help you identify the most important elements of each chapter, or you may combine the two.
- **Application Exercises:** The Application Exercises ask you to apply the content of each chapter to a real-world classroom situation. Feedback immediately follows the exercises. We encourage you to respond to the exercises in writing, and then compare your answers to the feedback. Your study will be more effective if you follow this procedure than if you merely read the exercises and then read the feedback.
- **Self-Help Quiz:** Each chapter concludes with a quiz. Answers to all the items are provided at the end of each quiz. As with the Application Exercises we recommend that you first answer all the questions on the quiz before looking at the feedback.

COMPANION WEBSITE

Additional practice opportunities are available on the website that accompanies this text. Go to www.prenhall.com/eggen. The following modules are available for each chapter on the site.
- **Knowledge Extensions:** This module includes questions designed to deepen your understanding of the topics in each section of the chapter and integrate them with topics you've studied in earlier sections and chapters.
- **Practice Quiz and Essay Questions:** These exercises provide self-assessment questions and feedback to help you study for quizzes and exams.
- **Practice for Praxis:** This module provides feedback for the short answer questions that follow the case studies in the "Developing as a Professional: Praxis Practice" section that appears at the end of each chapter.
- **Online Cases:** This module provides additional practice in applying your knowledge to genuine classroom scenarios.
- **Online Portfolio Activities:** The activities are designed to help you develop your teaching portfolio.
- **Exploring Further:** This module allows you to study topics presented in the text in more depth.
- **Web Links** take you to selected educational psychology sites on the Web.

Good luck in your study. We hope you find this Study Guide useful and meaningful.

CHAPTER 1: EDUCATIONAL PSYCHOLOGY: DEVELOPING A PROFESSIONAL KNOWLEDGE BASE

Chapter Outline_____

I.   Educational psychology and becoming a professional
    A. Characteristics of professionalism
        1. Commitment to learners
        2. Decision making
        3. Reflective Practice
        4. Professional knowledge
II.   Professional knowledge and learning to teach
    A. Knowledge of content
    B. Pedagogical content knowledge
    C. General pedagogical knowledge
        1. Instructional strategies
        2. Classroom management
    D. Knowledge of learners and learning
        1. Knowledge of learners
        2. Knowledge of learning
    E. The INTASC standards: States respond to the need for professional knowledge
    F. Changes in education: Reform and accountability
        1. The Praxis Exam
    G. Learning contexts: Teaching and learning in urban environments
III. The role of research in acquiring knowledge
    A. Descriptive research
        1. Evaluating descriptive studies
    B. Correlational research
        1. Evaluating correlational research
    C. Experimental research
        1. Evaluating experimental research
    D. Action research
    E. Conducting research in classrooms: Action research principles
    F. Research and the development of theory
IV.   The use of case studies in educational psychology

Chapter Objectives_____

- Describe the characteristics of professionalism, and identify examples of the characteristics in teachers' actions.

- Describe the different kinds of knowledge professional teachers possess, and identify examples of professional knowledge in teachers' actions.

- Describe different types of research, and analyze applications of these types.

- Explain how using case studies makes educational psychology meaningful.

Chapter Overview_____

This chapter introduces you to educational psychology, which focuses on learning and factors that influence it. As you examine the contents of your text, you will study–in addition to the nature of learning itself–learner development, individual differences, and motivation, together with the impact that teachers have on learning as a result of their instruction, management, and assessment.

Research that has examined the processes involved in learning to teach focuses on two factors–teachers' knowledge and teachers' thinking. Studying educational psychology is designed to help you develop both.

Researchers have found that skilled professionals are committed to learners, are able to make decisions in ill-defined contexts, reflect on their practice, and possess a body of specialized knowledge. Professional teachers possess four types of specialized knowledge: knowledge of the content they're teaching; knowledge of how to represent topics in ways that learners can understand, called pedagogical content knowledge; general pedagogical knowledge, such as questioning skills and the ability to organize and manage classrooms; and knowledge of learners and learning, such as understanding that most students, including those in middle, junior high and high school, tend to think about the world in concrete ways.

Knowledge is acquired through experience and research. Descriptive research uses surveys, observations, and interviews to describe opinions, attitudes, and events, such as a survey asking teachers what they believe are the most important problems in education. Correlational research looks for relationships between two or more variables, such as examining the relationship between the amount of time students spend studying and their academic achievement. Experimental research systematically manipulates variables in an attempt to determine cause and effect, such as training one group of teachers to call on all students equally, and comparing the achievement of their students to the achievement of students taught by untrained teachers. Action research, which is applied research designed to answer specific school- or classroom-related questions, is intended to produce results that are immediately applicable to the improvement of practice.

As research accumulates, patterns emerge and theories are gradually formed. The theories are then used to help us explain and predict events in the world. Learning theory helps us explain, for example, why students learn more when they're actively involved in learning activities than when they passively listen to teachers.

As teachers we use our understanding of research and theory to make decisions designed to help our students learn as much as possible. For example, research indicates that we should call on our students as equally as possible, but we must make decisions about the order in which we call on them, how much time we give them to answer, and how we intervene if they answer incorrectly. Making decisions is part of being a professional.

Self-Help Quiz_____

TRUE/FALSE QUESTIONS. Write T in the blank if the statement is true and write F if the statement is false.

_____ 1. Professions, such as medicine, are based on theory, while education is developed primarily on the basis of classroom experience.
_____ 2. Research is of little value if the results of different studies are conflicting.
_____ 3. A body of knowledge must be complete in order to apply it to classrooms.
_____ 4. Research results and theories are essentially unrelated to each other.
_____ 5. Education is virtually the only profession that has conflicting research results.

MULTIPLE-CHOICE ITEMS. Circle the best response in each case.

6. Of the following, the best description of a theory is:
    a. the information known about a particular field of study.
    b. the knowledge and facts that people in professions know.
    c. classroom applications of principles in the real world of teaching.
    d. combinations of related patterns.

7. Which of the following statements are true of theories?
    1. They are based on the results of patterns identified by research.
    2. They serve as a basis for predicting the outcome of future events.
    3. They serve as a basis for explaining events.
    4. Once developed, they are not modified.

a. 1, 2, 3, 4   b. 1, 2, 3   c. 1, 2, 4   d. 2, 3, 4   e. 1, 4

Use the following description for items 8-12.

Karen Adcox was having a difficult time getting her students involved in her lessons. She would begin by telling them that the content they were studying was important, but the students were unresponsive.

She thought a lot about the problem, talking to colleagues and looking for ideas. In reading an article in one of her professional journals one evening, she saw a report indicating that students are often curious when teachers begin their lessons with a question or problem that doesn't have an apparent solution. It sounded like it might help her in her frustration with her students, but she asked herself, "How am I going to do this in language arts? That's where the students are the most listless."

Then she hit on an idea. She began her next class by telling the students, "Look, kids, when we have one baby we spell it b a b y, but when we have more than one we spell it b a b i e s. On the other hand, we spell boy, b o y, but when we have more than one we spell it b o y s rather than b o i e s. Why do you suppose we have the difference?"

She then made it a point to call on her minority students as much as she called on those who were not minorities. She was pleased to discover that all her students were more interested in what she was doing, so much so that whenever possible, she began her lessons with a problem or question.

8. Of the following, which characteristic of professionalism is best illustrated when Karen ". . . thought a lot about the problem, talking to colleagues and looking for ideas"?
    a. Commitment to learners
    b. Decision making
    c. Reflective practice
    d. A body of specialized knowledge

9. Of the following, which characteristic of professionalism is best illustrated when Karen ". . . saw a report indicating that students are often curious when teachers begin their lessons with a question or problem that doesn't have an apparent solution"?
   a. Commitment to learners
   b. Decision making
   c. Reflective practice
   d. A body of specialized knowledge

10. The type of knowledge best illustrated in Karen's strategy of beginning her learning activity with a question designed to arouse her students' curiosity is:
   a. knowledge of content.
   b. pedagogical content knowledge.
   c. general pedagogical knowledge.
   d. knowledge of learners and learning.

11. Karen read her professional journal and learned about the effects of beginning lessons with a question or problem. She then figured out an original way that this information could be applied with her language arts students. Which type of professional knowledge is best illustrated by the way she began her lesson?
   a. Knowledge of content
   b. Pedagogical content knowledge
   c. General pedagogical knowledge
   d. Knowledge of learners and learning

12. In the episode we saw that Karen ". . . made it a point to call on her cultural minority students as much as she called on those who were not minorities." She did so because she read a research article indicating that students are more involved in lessons when teachers call on all of them as equally as possible. Based on the information we have, the type(s) of research best illustrated in the article Karen read, is/are:
   a. descriptive research.
   b. correlational research.
   c. experimental research.
   d. action research.
   e. both correlational and experimental research.

Self-Help Quiz Answers_____

1. f
2. f
3. f
4. f
5. f
6. d Theories are defined as sets of related principles based on observations that in turn are used to explain additional observations. Principles are patterns. Some of the information in a field goes beyond theory (choice a), and some of the information that professionals "know" goes beyond theories (choice b). Theories don't necessarily result in classroom applications (choice c).
7. b Theories are based on the results of patterns identified by research; they do serve as a basis for predicting the outcome of future events; and they serve as a basis for explaining events. They are, however, modified if they are unable to adequately explain observations.
8. c Thinking about our professional practice illustrates the process of reflection.
9. d Studying research articles and reports helps professionals develop their body of specialized knowledge.
10. d Karen demonstrated all four types of knowledge in the case study, but knowledge of learners and learning was most prominent. She knew that students' interest is increased when lessons are introduced with a question or problem that doesn't have an obvious answer. She capitalized on that idea in the way she introduced her topic.
11. b Being able to present information in a way that arouses curiosity or makes information understandable to learners demonstrates pedagogical content knowledge.

12.   b   ". . . A research article indicating that students are more involved in lessons when teachers call on all of them as equally as possible," implies a correlation. Two variables–student involvement and questioning patterns–are being related to each other. There is, however, no evidence in the description indicating that one variable–the questioning pattern–is being consciously manipulated to determine cause and effect, which would be the case in an experimental study.

CHAPTER 2: THE DEVELOPMENT OF COGNITION AND LANGUAGE

Chapter Outline_____

I.   What is development?
      A. Principles of development
      B. The human brain and cognitive development
          1. The learning physiology of the brain
          2. Putting brain research into perspective
II.   Piaget's theory of intellectual development
      A. The drive for equilibrium
      B. Organization and adaptation: The development of schemes
          1. Achieving equilibrium: The process of organization
          2. Maintaining equilibrium: The process of adaptation
      C. Factors influencing development
          1. Experience with the physical world
          2. Social experience
      D. Stages of development
          1. Sensorimotor (0 to 2 years)
          2. Preoperations (2 to 7 years)
              a. Conservation
              b. Egocentrism
          3. Concrete operations (7 to 11 years)
              a. Classification and seriation
          4. Formal operations (11 to adult)
              a. Characteristics of formal thought
              b. Adolescent egocentrism
              c. Formal operations: Research results
      E. Applying Piaget's work in classrooms: Instructional principles
      F. Putting Piaget's theory into perspective
III. A sociocultural view of development: The work of Lev Vygotsky
      A. Social interaction and development
      B. Language and development
      C. Culture and development
      D. The relationship between learning and development
      E. Vygotsky's work: Instructional principles
          1. Zone of proximal development
          2. Scaffolding: Interactive instructional support
      F. Piaget's and Vygotsky's views of knowledge construction
IV.   Language development
      A. Theories of language acquisition
          1. Behaviorist views
          2. Social cognitive perspectives
          3. Nativist theory
          4. Sociocultural theory
      B. Stages of language acquisition
          1. Early language: Building the foundation
          2. Fine-tuning language
          3. Increasing language complexity
      C. Promoting language development: Suggestions for teachers

Chapter Objectives_____

- Describe the principles of development, and identify examples of the principles in children's behaviors.

- Use concepts from Piaget's theory of intellectual development to explain both classroom and everyday events.

- Use Vygotsky's sociocultural theory to explain how language, culture, and instructional support can influence learner development.

- Explain language development using different theories of language acquisition.

Chapter Overview_____

As students progress through our schools, their development exerts a powerful influence on learning. Development refers to the orderly, durable changes in a learner resulting from learning, maturation, and experience. As our students develop, they not only acquire new abilities but also come to view the world in different ways.

Research on the human brain indicates that rapid brain growth occurs during early development, resulting in critical periods for the development of processes such as perception and language growth. However, brain growth isn't specific and it doesn't provide educators with suggestions about how and when to capitalize on it.

Jean Piaget described cognitive development as caused by an individual's drive for equilibrium. He suggested that we organize our experiences into schemes or patterns, and we use these schemes to interpret our environment. When new events can be interpreted using existing schemes, they are assimilated; when new events don't fit into existing schemes, disequilibrium occurs; the schemes are modified and new schemes are created–a process he called accommodation. Through the reciprocal processes of assimilation and accommodation, development occurs.

Piaget found that the way children respond to the world and process information can be described in patterns which he called stages. As they move through the stages their thinking progresses from processing information primarily through the senses to logically processing abstract information. Piaget's theory has had important influences on the way we think about teaching and learning. Curriculum developers now emphasize the importance of experiences that proceed from concrete to abstract. Instruction is more learner-centered, with increased emphasis on hands-on experiences.

A second important view of development is based upon the work of Lev Vygotsky, a Russian psychologist. This sociocultural view of development emphasizes the central role that social interaction, language, and culture lay in development. Teachers utilize Vygotsky's theory when they design learning activities within the learner's zone of proximal development, which represents a range of instructional tasks which students can accomplish with assistance. Teachers provide this assistance through instructional scaffolding that supports students' efforts.

Language development coincides with and complements other aspects of development. As students develop, their ability to talk about their world, and their ability to think about it, also develops. Increased vocabulary and increasingly complex sentence structures reflect students' growing ability to think about the world using language as a tool. Teachers can further this growth by encouraging students to use existing language patterns as the basis for future growth.

Application Exercises_____

We encourage you to first write your responses to each of the exercises below, and then check your answers with the feedback that immediately follows the exercises.

Exercise 2.1

For items 1-4, explain the individual's behavior by using the following concepts: *accommodation, adaptation, assimilation, development, equilibrium,* and *scheme.* The person you focus on is the one whose name is italicized. In each case, use as many of the concepts as necessary to form a full and complete explanation.

1. Mrs. Andre's class has completed a unit on the multiplication of fractions and is now working on division. *Tim*, when faced with the problem

    $2/3 \div 1/3 =$____ , gets 2/9 as an answer.

2. *Celena* commented to her friend Jane in the teachers' lounge one morning, "Susan really puzzles me. You never know how to take her. One day she's your best friend, and the next she barely squeaks out a hello."

3. *Kathy's* English class has been assigned to write a paper making a persuasive argument. "I was initially confused, but I think I know how to do it now," she commented to her dad, who was helping her with it. "It's like making and defending a position, except you have to include a suggestion or a plan of action."

4. *"Malivai's* spelling has improved dramatically since the beginning of the year," Mrs. Stone enthusiastically told Malivai's mother in a conference in May. "At first he approached spelling as if every new word was completely new. Then he started seeing patterns in the words and his spelling performance took a jump."

5. Karin Dunlop is a ninth-grade English teacher. She knew that students take the PSAT (Preliminary Scholastic Aptitude Test) as tenth graders, and she wanted to prepare them as well as possible, so she did extensive work with antonyms and analogies. She gave her students the following words with brief definitions.
    relic–keepsake
    ordain–officially appoint
    acuteness–sharpness
    dawdle–waste time
    superfluous–more than needed
    She directed students to learn the words, and the next day she gave them an exercise involving antonyms for the words in the left column. Even through students vigorously claimed that they had studied the words carefully, the results were disappointing.
    Using Piaget's work as a basis, provide a specific explanation for why the students did so poorly, and then specifically suggest what Karin might have done differently to get better results.

6. James Washington has been working with his fifth graders on a unit involving air and air pressure. He has discussed air and air pressure in detail, and the children read about it in their books. In a demonstration, he adds a cup of water to an empty can, heats the can to drive out some of the air inside, caps the can, and watches while the atmospheric pressure crushes the cooling can. To speed up the cooling, however, he pours cold water on the can. To his dismay, students suggest that the water crushed the can.
    Based on the research results discussed in this section, explain specifically why students would conclude what they did.

Exercise 2.2

Classify the behavior of the person whose name is italicized in the following examples into one of Piaget's four stages of development. Then explain your classification based on information from the example.

1. Conchita Martinez is discussing the causes of World War I in her junior high American history class. "It started with the assassination of the archduke," Brad suggested. "But," *Karen* added, "there was also a rising spirit of nationalism all over Europe at the time."

2. *Cher* knows that the word *horse* represents horses.

3. *Tim* is 5 minutes late for class and jokingly says,"I have minus 5 minutes to get there."

4. *Susan* didn't understand the fulcrum of a simple lever until the teacher used a meterstick to pry up a stack of books.

5. *Luis* is playing somewhat roughly with the family cat, and his mother, concerned that he might be scratched, puts the cat around the corner. Luis's attention quickly turns to something else.

6. *Ann's* teacher is working on numbers in base 6. She shows the students bundles of six sticks and individual sticks. After a series of examples, she displays two bundles of six sticks each and three more sticks and asks the class to write the number in base 6 that represents the 15 sticks. Ann correctly responds with the numeral 23. She can't do this without the bundles of sticks.

Exercise 2.3

Read the following example and answer the questions that follow.

Delores Robles is trying to help her eighth-grade students understand how to write narrative stories. They have read several and have broken into groups to discuss the settings, characters, and plots in short stories. The students are now writing their own stories, and Delores helps them develop their characters, plots, and settings and how each of the elements interacts with the other two. They also share their stories with each other and get feedback.

Jason, Dana, Elena, and David are having trouble developing characters with depth. Delores shows them stories written by students the previous year that illustrated different levels of character development. With periodic reference to the stories, Jason and Dana are making progress. Elena and David continue to struggle with expressing themselves in writing, and Delores encourages them to simply "say it silently to yourself," and then write it just as you would say it.

1. Identify two aspects of the lesson in which Delores used social interaction to promote learning.

2. Provide a complete description of the zones of proximal development for Delores' students. Explain how you know in each case.

3. How did Delores use scaffolding to help her students understand character development?

Exercise 2.4

Identify whether each of the following more emphasizes Piaget's or Vygotsky's view of development.

1. A pre-school class has a sand table set up in which students can put sand into different-shaped containers. Students are encouraged to experiment and measure with these containers.

2. In a pre-school corner different costumes and outfits are available. Students are encouraged to put these on and pretend, creating mini-skits with each other.

3. A second grade teacher places students into groups to create dioramas that depict ideas from their study of different Native American Indian tribes. As they work the teacher encourages them to discuss the ideas behind the art.

4. A fourth grade teacher has developed a learning center on electricity. Students go to the center and pick up "Brain Teasers." These contain a box of batteries, wires, and bulbs, and students are encouraged to experiment with them to find out how electricity works.

5. A high school physical education teacher notices that some of her students are still having trouble learning how to score volleyball games. To help these students she pairs these students up with "experts" and has the pair score a videotaped game.

Exercise 2.5

In items 1-3, identify the theory of language acquisition best illustrated by each.

1. "Me toy," says 2-year-old Tanya, holding out her hand.
    "Oh, Tanya wants the toy. Say, 'I want the toy.'"
    "Want toy," replies Tanya.
    "Good girl!"

2. An eager dad was playing with his daughter and working on her vocabulary. He had a small box of toy animals. As he held each one up, he asked, "What is it?"
    When the child responded correctly, he replied, "Good! . . . Now, here's another one. What is it?" When the response was incorrect, he'd say, "No, that's not a rhino. That's a hippo. You say it."

3. Mom was walking through the park with her 1-year-old on her back. People looked at her a little strangely as she carried on the following monologue: "Look at the dog. What a funny-looking dog. Look at his legs. They're so short.
    "Oh, there's some water ahead. It looks like a pond. See the ducks swimming in the pond. The one with the green head is the daddy. Should we go feel the water?"
    The child listened with wide-eyed detachment.

Read the following sentences/phrases and classify them as reflecting early (E) (0-2) or later (L) (beyond 2) stages in language development. Explain why in each case.

4. He was there.

5. Was he there?

6. The boy brought the toy because he thought he would be bored.

7. Me go.

8. The car that was skidding slid off the icy road.

Feedback for Application Exercises_____

Exercise 2.1

1. Tim has a "multiplying fractions" scheme. Rather than adapting by accommodating the scheme to allow the formation of a division of fractions scheme, he assimilated (incorrectly) the problem into his already existing scheme, which allowed him to remain at equilibrium.

2. Susan's unpredictable behavior disrupts Celena's equilibrium, which makes her uneasy and uncomfortable. Her "Susan scheme" does not allow her to understand or predict Susan's behavior.

3. Kathy is demonstrating adaptation through the process of accommodation. She has a "making and defending a position" scheme, and she now is accommodating the scheme to form a "persuasive argument" scheme. Her writing is developing as a result.

4. This example illustrates year-long development, and as a result, Malavai now has schemes that he didn't have earlier.

5. The words were presented only in the abstract, so the students merely memorized the brief definitions. As a result they performed poorly on the antonym exercise, which is a form of application. Karin needed to develop the words beginning with concrete experiences, much as Carol Barnhart had done earlier in the chapter.

6. While James has discussed air and air pressure with the students and has also had them read about it, there is no indication in the example that James has provided any concrete experiences for the children. As a result, they remain dominated by their perception, and perceptually they see water pouring on the can and the can collapsing. Given the students' limited experience, their conclusion is not surprising.

Exercise 2.2

1. Karen is demonstrating formal operational behavior. She is able to simultaneously consider two variables. Further, she appears to comfortably deal with abstract concepts, such as nationalism. It is important to note that merely because she is at least 12–13, and therefore chronologically fits the stage of formal operations, doesn't mean that her thinking is necessarily formal operational. Without prerequisite experience, learners' thinking might be concrete operational at best.

2. Cher is displaying preoperational characteristics. Knowing that the word *horse* represents the category horses is a form of symbolic thought.

3. Tim is indicating formal operational thinking. He is applying an abstract concept (negative numbers) in an even more abstract way by referring to "negative time."

4. Susan is displaying concrete operational thinking. She could handle the concept of fulcrum when shown the concrete materials.

5. Luis is demonstrating sensorimotor behavior. The example suggests that he hasn't acquired the concept of object permanence.

6. Ann's thinking was concrete operational. She was able to perform a logical operation when she had concrete materials to manipulate.

Exercise 2.3

1. In addition to the social interaction that occurred in whole-group activities, she broke students into groups twice. The first time they identified setting, characters, and plot; the second time they shared their stories with each other.

2. The zones of proximal development for most of Delores' students are at the stage of describing the interaction of plot and character in writing, since they're able to do so with Delores' help. Jason and Dana's zones are at the development-of-character level; they aren't yet at the point of being able to describe the interplay of character and plot. Elena's and David's zones are at the point of simply being able to express themselves in writing. Their development is the least advanced of the class.

3. Delores used scaffolding by providing examples of characters at different stages of development. The examples could be thought of as prompts or models that were designed to support the students in their efforts to write their own stories. She also provided ongoing support for all the students in their respective zones of proximal development.

Exercise 2.4

1. Piaget's view. This typical Piagetian task is used to help students form conservation of volume.

2. Vygotsky's view. Note how the teacher encourages social interaction through the dialogues in the skits.

3. Vygotsky's view. The combination of group work and encouragement to discuss ideas promotes learning from a social constructivist perspective.

4. Piaget's view. Cognitive constructivism suggests that teachers encourage students to tinker around with concrete manipulatives while they're learning. Note that no mention was made of social interaction.

5. Vygotsky's view. Working in pairs and discussing authentic, meaningful tasks are characteristics of teaching based on social constructivism.

Exercise 2.5

1. This parent was using social cognitive theory to teach language. She modeled the desired language ("Say, 'I want the toy.'") and she reinforced Tanya for her reply. Behaviorism doesn't account for the importance of modeling.

2. This dad applied behavioral views of language acquisition to improve his daughter's vocabulary. When the child correctly identified an animal she was reinforced with praise. When the child was incorrect, she was corrected and provided with the correct answer.

3. Psycholinguists believe that children acquire language by being exposed to it in its varied forms. The text says, "When children are exposed to language, this program [the language acquisition device] analyzes speech patterns for the rules of grammar . . . that govern a language." The results of this analysis can explain why children have the ability to produce novel and unique sentences. Neither behaviorism nor social cognitive theory can explain this ability.

4. (E) This is an example of past irregular which usually occurs around the age of 2.

5. (E/L) The ability to ask questions (reordered sentences) usually occurs around age 3.

6. (L) This is a very complex sentence structure expressing cause and effect relationships. These usually appear around first grade.

7. (E) One- and two-word utterances are the first stage of language acquisition.

8. (L) Embedded sentences (i.e., The car was skidding. The car slid off the road.) are usually found in pre-school and kindergarten children.

Self-Help Quiz_____

TRUE-FALSE QUESTIONS: Write T in the blank if the statement is true, and F if the statement is false.

_____ 1. Development and learning are coordinate concepts, both describing similar types of changes in a learner.

_____ 2. When a child modifies his idea of a football and a tennis ball so that both fit into his previously formed concept of "ball", this is an example of assimilation.

_____ 3. A major theme in Vygotsky's work is that children frequently use language to describe problem solving or goal-reaching steps to themselves, especially on difficult tasks.

_____ 4. Children pass through Piaget's stages of development in distinct steps, although some may skip a stage if they are intellectually mature.

_____ 5. Most junior high students typically have reached the stage of formal operations and are able to think and reason in the abstract.

MULTIPLE CHOICE QUESTIONS: Circle the best response in each case.

6. A child is shown two sponges and identifies them as identical. One sponge is then cut up while the child watches so that it is now in twelve smaller pieces. When asked which has more sponge, the child says the amounts of sponge are the same. The concept best illustrated by the child's actions is:
    a. egocentrism.
    b. centration.
    c. transformation.
    d. conservation.

Use the following example to respond to items 7 and 8.

Mrs. Park has taught her students the process of subtracting one-digit from two-digit numbers without regrouping and is now teaching them subtraction with regrouping. Jimmy, a boy big for his age from an upper-income family, is having trouble with the process, however. When given the problems

    64   32
    -7 and -5   Jimmy gets 63 and 33 as results.

7. Of the following, the Piagetian concept most closely related to Jimmy's tendency is:
    a. accommodation.
    b. centration.
    c. reversibility.
    d. maturation.

8. Of the following the best explanation for why Jimmy got 63 and 33 as answers is:
    a. Jimmy is accommodating his subtraction without regrouping schema to the new problems.
    b. Jimmy's maturation isn't advanced enough to allow him to solve problems with regrouping.
    c. Jimmy is reversing the process from problems with regrouping to problems without regrouping.
    d. Jimmy remained at equilibrium by getting the results that he did.

9. You're teaching the concept of *noun* to your third graders. Using Piaget's theory as a basis for making your decision, the best example of the following to use in illustrating the concept would be:
    a. a soccer ball.
    b. a drawing of a house.
    c. a colored picture of an oak tree.
    d. a picture of a girl with the word "girl" written underneath it.

10. Mr. Kenna's chemistry students are having a difficult time understanding how a solid and a liquid can be at the same temperature when the material is the same (such as an ice cube turning to water). Mr. Kenna explains that it takes energy to change the "state" from solid to liquid without changing the temperature. This change in state is the result of changing the arrangement of the molecules from a solid to a liquid and it takes heat to do that. The kids still don't get it. Based on Piaget's work, which of the following is the best explanation for the students' difficulty?
   a. The students are not yet chronologically at the age of formal operations and this is a formal operational task.
   b. The students' maturation isn't to the point where they are ready to handle this topic.
   c. The students are among the 50% who don't reach the stage of formal operations.
   d. The students lack the concrete experiences needed to understand the ideas involved.

11. Of the following, the best solution to Mr. Kenna's problem in item 10, according to Piaget would be to:
   a. describe the process of the change in molecular motion between a solid and a liquid in more detail, so they see the difference.
   b. show them a model illustrating the molecular motion of the substance in each state and the change in motion as it melts.
   c. melt a piece of ice in front of them and have them describe it as it melts.
   d. have them explain their ideas about melting (instead of describing the process for them).

12. Of the following four concepts the one conceptually least related to the other three in Piaget's theory is:
   a. accommodation.
   b. assimilation.
   c. schema.
   d. adaptation.

13. Jackie puts a pencil and ruler together because they are both straight. The stage of development that this behavior best illustrates is:
   a. sensorimotor.
   b. preoperational.
   c. concrete operational.
   d. formal operational.

14. In item 13 The characteristic Jackie is demonstrating is:
   a. identifying cause-effect relationships.
   b. grouping on the basis of a functional relationship.
   c. seriation of objects.
   d. grouping on the basis of a perceptual feature.

Use the following case study to help in answering Items 15-17.

Mrs. Wilson breaks her first graders into groups of three and gives each group 12 plastic cubes and a container the cubes will fit into (2 x 2 x 3). They identify the pieces as cubes and conclude that they're all the same size. She has them put cubes into the container. They remove the cubes and she asks them how much space the cubes took up, and leads them to conclude "12 cubes." She asks them what they call the space, and when they're unable to say "Volume," she tells them they have a volume of "twelve cubes." To reinforce the idea, she then asks them what the volumes of their boxes are, and leads them to say "twelve cubes."

15. Based on this information and Piaget's work, which of the following is the best assessment of Mrs. Wilson's teaching of the concept volume?
    a. Her instruction was effective because the students had a concrete illustrations for both cube and volume.
    b. Her instruction was effective because she reinforced the concept by having them say they had a volume of "twelve cubes."
    c. Her instruction was ineffective, because she should have used actual units (such as twelve cubic inches) instead of "twelve cubes."
    d. Her instruction was ineffective, because she shouldn't have told them they had a volume of twelve cubes.

16. Consider the students' understanding of *cube* compared to their understanding of *volume*. Which of the following is the most valid description of their understanding?
    a. Their understanding of cube and volume will be similar, since they saw concrete examples of each.
    b. Their understanding of volume will be more complete than their understanding of cube, since the lesson focused on volume.
    c. Their understanding of volume will be more complete than their understanding of cube since Mrs. Solomon reinforced the idea at the end.
    d. Their understanding of cube will be more complete than their understanding of volume, since volume requires concrete operations and cube doesn't.

17. The next day Mrs. Wilson has her students again make a stack of blocks (2 x 2 x 3) and count the cubes, and she then has them make another one (1 x 2 x 6) by putting the blocks in two rows of 6, side by side. They again count the cubes. She then asks them if the two volumes are the same or if they are different. Based on Piaget's work, if the students' behaviors are typical for children their ages, which of the following is the most likely response?
    a. The students will conclude that the volumes are the same, since they can see 12 cubes in each case.
    b. The students will conclude that the volumes are the same since they actually counted the cubes.
    c. The students will conclude that the volumes are different, since their understanding of volume is likely to be incomplete.
    d. The students will conclude that the volumes are different, since they look different.

Use the following case study to answer Items 18 and 19.

The second grade team at Crystal Lake Elementary school is trying to increase their second graders' understanding of the need to pay attention.

Mr. Winthrop says to his students, "Now listen everyone. It is very important to pay attention, so that we can all learn more." He reminds the students about the need for attention every day.

Mrs. Grimley says to her students, "Attention is very important. Let's see what we mean by attention," and she has Mrs. Myers, a parent volunteer, talk to her while she keeps her eyes focused on Mrs. Myers's face as Mrs. Myers talks. Mrs. Grimley then makes comments such as, "Jeanna is doing a very good job of paying attention," whenever she sees them demonstrating attentive behaviors.

Mr. Minchew has a rule that says, "Pay attention at all times when the teacher is talking." When students don't pay attention, he first reminds them, and after three infractions, they're isolated from the class.

Mrs. Patterson makes comments, such as, "David has been very attentive for this whole lesson. He has kept his eyes focused on the front of the all the time while I've been talking. That's excellent," whenever she sees students who are particularly attentive.

18. Based on research, the teacher's approach likely to be most successful is:
    a. Mr. Winthrop
    b. Mrs. Grimley
    c. Mr. Minchew
    d. Mrs. Patterson

19. Based on research, the teacher's approach likely to be least successful is:
    a. Mr. Winthrop
    b. Mrs. Grimley
    c. Mr. Minchew
    d. Mrs. Patterson

Use the following information for Items 20-22.

Karen Skram, a third-grade teacher, is working with four of her students on solutions to word problems in math. She gives the students a problem, tells them to try it and watches their progress.

Tanya sits, stares at the problem, puts some numbers on the paper, but makes little progress. Karen sits with her, offers a suggestion, Tanya tries it, Karen offers another, Tanya tries again, but Tanya is not able to grasp the solution to the problem.

Felice looks at the problem briefly, grumbles, "Mrs. Skram, I can't do this," writes a few things down on the paper after Karen responds, "Oh yes, I think you can. Give it a try." She then asks, "What are they asking us for in the problem?" Felice reads the problem aloud, concludes that they must subtract, and then successfully solves the problem..

Billy also grumbles that he can't solve the problem. "What does this tell you?" Karen asks, pointing to the problem. Billy looks at the question for several seconds and then solves the problem.

Leroy mumbles, "I don't see this problem," he stares at it for a few seconds, almost inaudibly mumbles again, "add these, . . . no, subtract, I think," as he scratches on his paper, and after a couple minutes he solves the problem.

20. Based on this information and Vygotsky's work, which of the following is the most valid conclusion?
    a. Solving word problems is within the zone of proximal development for Tanya, but the other students' zones are beyond the solutions of simple subtraction word problems.
    b. Solving word problems is within the zone for Felice and Billy, but Tanya's zone is not to this level of development, and Leroy's is beyond the solutions of simple subtraction word problems.
    c. Solving word problems is within the zone for Leroy, but Tanya's Felice's and Billy's zones are not to this level of development.
    d. Solving word problems is within the zones for Felice, Billy, and Leroy, but Tanya's zone is not to this level of development

21. The student(s) that demonstrated private speech was/were:
    a. Felice and Billy
    b. Felice, Billy, and Leroy
    c. Felice
    d. Leroy

22. The students that were provided scaffolding were:
    a. Tanya
    b. Felice and Billy
    c. Tanya, Felice, and Billy
    d. All the students were provided scaffolding, since Karen carefully monitored their progress.

23. Consider Piaget's and Vygotsky's views of development. Of the following, the most valid conclusion is:
    a. Vygotsky emphasizes the role of social interaction in development, whereas social interaction is not important for Piaget.
    b. Vygotsky's view provides for the teacher a more prominent role in guiding learning than does Piaget's view.
    c. Piaget views learners as active, whereas Vygotsky views them as passive recipients of guidance through scaffolding.
    d. Language is critical in Vygotsky's view of development, whereas it is irrelevant in Piaget's view, since, according to Piaget, manipulation of concrete materials is the primary cause of development.

Use the following short case study to answer Items 24 and 25.

Kevin and Linda are working on a science activity in Mrs. Lake's class. "Magnets pick up iron, and other metal stuff," Kevin says. "See," and he demonstrates how a paper clip is attracted to a magnet.

"Ohh, neat," Linda responds. "So, what do we write down ? . . . Magnets . . . pick . . . up . . . metals," she writes carefully on her paper.

Mrs. Lake, who has been watching their progress, comments briefly, "Maybe try this," as she points to the aluminum foil on the desk where they're working.

"Hey, it doesn't work," Linda responds, as she tries the magnet and aluminum foil.

"Uh huh," Kevin, who didn't notice Mrs. Lake's suggestion, argues. "Does too. . . . See?" and he shows how a metal spoon is attracted to the magnet.

"Nope, . . . look," Linda retorts. "Look, it doesn't work on this (the aluminum foil), and she demonstrates for Kevin how the aluminum foil is not attracted to the magnet.

After several more minutes, Mrs. Lake calls for the students' attention. "What kinds of patterns did we find?" she asks.

The students volunteer their findings, the class discusses them in detail, and they summarize the results.

24. Specifically identify the aspects of the activity that are consistent with implications for instruction that would be based on Piaget's theory.

25. Specifically identify the aspects of the activity that are consistent with implications for instruction that would be based on Vygotsky's theory.

Self-Help Quiz Answers_____

1.   f
2.   t
3.   t
4.   f
5.   f
6.   d   Understanding that the "amount" stays the same regardless of the number of pieces is best described as conservation.
7.   b   Jimmy is centering on the large and small numbers and is ignoring the fact that the small one is on top and the larger one is on the bottom. He subtracts the smaller from the larger regardless of their position.
8.   d   Subtracting the smaller from the larger number allowed Jimmy to remain at equilibrium.
9.   a   The soccer ball is the most concrete example. Also, there would be no point in showing a picture of a girl when the class has several "real" girls in it.
10.   d   When learners are unable to understand information, assuming they have the ability, lack of experience is usually the cause.
11.   b   The model is the only one that actually illustrates the process. Melting the ice merely illustrates change of state and doesn't illustrate anything about the motion of the molecules.
12.   c   Assimilation and accommodation are types of adaptation.
13.   b   Jackie is classifying on the basis of a perceptual feature, which is characteristic of preoperations.
14.   d   Jackie is classifying on the basis of a perceptual feature.
15.   a   The students had concrete illustrations of both the concept cube and the concept volume. Experiences with the physical world are important according to Piaget's theory. Piaget's theory doesn't call for using language to reinforce ideas (choice b), and her instruction helped the students understand the concept volume regardless of whether or not she used conventional units (choice c). She merely supplied a label by saying the word "volume." They were able to understand the concept based on her instruction.
16.   d   "Cube" is perceptual, i.e., learners can "see" the characteristics of cube. Understanding "the amount of space" something takes up goes beyond mere perception. (For example, a 5-year-old will recognize a cube, whereas he or she is unlikely to have a clear concept of volume; in fact many children in elementary school have difficulty with the concept volume.)

17. d   The students are likely to base their understanding on their perceptions and conclude that the volumes are different.

18. b   Mrs. Grimley used a combination of modeling and positive reinforcement to help her students understand the need to pay attention.

19 c   Mr. Minchew didn't actually teach his students what paying attention means, and second graders may not understand the concept of attention merely from stating it in a rule. Further, he used punishment when they were inattentive rather than reinforcing attentive behaviors.

20. b   Felice and Billy were able to solve the problem with Karen's help. Tanya was unable to solve the problem, even with Karen's assistance, so solving word problems was beyond her zone. Leroy was able to solve the problems without help, so his zone was beyond the solutions to simple subtraction problems.

21. d   Private speech is "self-talk that guides thinking and action." This is what Leroy demonstrated. Merely grumbling that they were unable to do the problem, as Felice and Billy did, is not private speech.

22. c   Karen made comments intended to help Tanya, Felice, and Billy solve the problems. She was successful with Felice and Billy, but not with Tanya.

23. b   Vygotsky's view of development provides an important role for a teacher or more knowledgeable peer in promoting development.

24.   The children are involved in a direct experience with the physical world. Also, according to Kevin's scheme for magnetic materials, all metals are attracted to magnets. Linda demonstrated that his scheme wasn't adequate, when she showed that the aluminum foil was not attracted to the magnet. According to Piaget, social interaction provides an avenue for allowing learners to test their schemes against the schemes of others.

     You might note that–other than providing the materials and creating the environment–Piaget's theory doesn't actually provide a role for the teacher in the process.

25.   Three aspects of Vygotsky's view of development are demonstrated in the activity. First, the children were faced with the problem of finding out what kinds of materials are attracted to magnets. Second, the students were involved in a discussion of what was happening. According to Vygotsky, discussions of this type are critical for learning and development. Third, in contrast with Piaget, Vygotsky's theory provides an important role for the teacher. We saw in the activity that Mrs. Lake briefly intervened by suggesting that they try the aluminum foil. According to Vygotsky this role is critical in learners' development. In contrast, a strict application of Piaget's work would suggest that the students be allowed to "discover" on their own that the aluminum foil wasn't attracted to the magnet.

CHAPTER 3: PERSONAL, SOCIAL, AND EMOTIONAL DEVELOPMENT

Chapter Outline_____

I.   Personal development
    A. Heredity
    B. Parents and other adults
    C. Peers
II.   Social development
    A. Perspective taking: Understanding others' thoughts and feelings
    B. Social problem solving
    C. Violence and aggression in schools
    D. Promoting social development: Instructional principles
III.   The development of identity and self-concept
    A. Erikson's theory of psychosocial development
        1. Putting Erikson's work into perspective
        2. Supporting psychosocial development
            a. Early childhood
            b. The elementary years
            c. Adolescence
    B. The development of identity
        1. Patterns in identity development
        2. Sexual identity
    C. The development of self-concept
        1. Self-concept and self-esteem
        2. Self-concept and achievement
    D. Promoting psychosocial, identity, and self-concept development: Instructional principles
    E. Ethnic pride: Promoting ethnic identity and positive self-esteem
        1. Ethnicity and self-esteem
        2. Ethnic pride and identity formation
IV.   Development of morality, social responsibility, and self-control
    A. Increased interest in moral education and development
    B. Piaget's description of moral development
    C. Kohlberg's theory of moral development
        1. Level I: Preconventional ethics
            a. Stage 1: Punishment-obedience
            b. Stage 2: Market exchange
        2. Level II: Conventional ethics
            a. Stage 3: Interpersonal harmony
            b. Stage 4: Law and order
        3. Level III: Postconventional ethics
            a. Stage 5: Social contract
            b. Stage 6: Universal principles
        4. Putting Kohlberg's theory into perspective
            a. Gender differences: The morality of caring
    D. Emotional factors in moral development
    E. Promoting moral development: Instructional principles
    F. Learning contexts: Promoting personal, social, and moral development in urban environments

Chapter Objectives_____

- Describe the factors influencing personal development, and explain how differences in parenting and peer interactions can influence this development.

- Describe characteristics that indicate advancing social development, and explain how social development relates to school violence and aggression.

- Use descriptions of psychosocial, identity, and self-concept development to explain learners' behaviors.

- Use descriptions of moral reasoning to explain differences in people's responses to ethical issues.

Chapter Overview_____

This chapter examines the process of development from three perspectives–personal, social, and moral–and asks how schools can help children develop in healthy ways. Influenced by heredity, parents and other adults, and peers, personal development describes the growth of personality traits and how they influence the ways we respond to our physical and social environments. Social development describes advances young people make in their ability to get along with others; perspective taking and social problem solving are two indicators of these advances.

Eric Erikson focused on students' psychosocial development. Like Piaget, he believed that development occurs in stages and that these stages influence how the individual interprets and interacts with the world. Unlike Piaget, Erikson's theory focuses on social and emotional development and describes how people use psychosocial challenges, which he called crises, to grow and develop.

The three important stages that students face during the school years are initiative versus guilt, industry versus inferiority and identity versus confusion. Teachers influence psychosocial development directly through their interactions with students and indirectly through the academic tasks they ask students to perform.

An important area of psychosocial development is a child's self-concept. Successful experiences with instructional tasks help build a healthy academic self-concept, which in turn has a positive influence on later achievement.

A third area of development examined in this chapter describes the growth of moral and ethical reasoning. Piaget's work in this area suggests that moral development relates to a shift from external to internal control. Kohlberg also studied moral development and described it in terms of orderly stages or steps in response to the environment. As children progress through these stages, they first think of right and wrong based on the consequences for them; later move to considering others, rules, and order; and finally progress to viewing ethics as a matter of social contracts.

Moral development also includes emotional components. Experiencing shame and guilt, while unpleasant, marks advances in moral development. The development of empathy indicates additional development.

Application Exercises_____

We encourage you to first write your responses to each of the exercises below, and then check your answers with the feedback that immediately follows the exercises.

Exercise 3.1

In Items 1 through 6, classify the person whose name is italicized into one of Erikson's eight stages of psychosocial development.

1. *Carmella* washes her hair every day. Her mother says she is going to wash it out of her head. "But, Mom," Carmella protests, "I'll look so gross if I don't wash it."

2. *Deon* is small for his age, and schoolwork isn't quite his "thing." He loves sports, though, and puts a lot of his energy into competition. He's the fastest runner in his grade. He pitches for his Little League team, even though he's a year younger than most of the other kids, and he set a team record by striking out 10 batters in one five-inning game.

3. "Guess what happened today?" Kathy's dad asked her mother as she walked in the door from work. He laughed. "*Kathy* scratched some stuff on some papers–she called them pictures–and glued them to the wall of her bedroom. It ruined the wallpaper."
   "Did you get after her?"
   "I thought about it, but then she said, 'Look at the pictures I made for you, Daddy.' That did it. I told her that the pictures were very nice. We'll talk to her later and push the dresser in front of the marks."

4. *Mr. Thomas* is raving to his wife about the present national administration's apparent lack of concern about the environment. "Those S.O.B.'s are trying to ruin the parks," he yells. "If there isn't a policy change, there will be nothing left for our kids or anyone else's kids to see and enjoy when they grow up."

5. "Are you getting serious about Joyce?" *Tom* was asked. "I could be, but I'm not going to allow myself to," he answered. "I've been through two relationships that didn't work out, and I've hurt two people. I'm beginning to wonder about my ability to feel strongly about someone else. I was fascinated with Sheri's great looks, and it was nice having Jan chase me like that, but now I don't know what to think."

6. "Guess what I found under *Mike's* mattress," his mother said somewhat uneasily to her friend as they were jogging. "Playboy magazine opened to the centerfold."
   Her friend laughed. "Not to worry. He's a boy. He isn't even sure himself what he's feeling. Relax. He's normal," she said with an unconcerned wave of her hand.

7. *Emmitt* is an eighth grader who you can't seem to "get going." He never volunteers answers in class and does only the minimum required on homework assignments and projects. However, the work he turns in is always acceptable, and he has been an above-average student throughout his schooling. In other ways, he seems to be a typical, "normal" youngster for his age.
   Analyze the boy's behavior using Erikson's theory as a frame of reference. Then suggest what you might do to help change his behavior.

Exercise 3.2

Classify the following statements as indicating one of the following: General self-concept, academic self-concept, social self-concept, physical self-concept, or subject-specific self-concept. The example may indicate a positive self-concept or it may indicate a somewhat negative self-concept.

1.   I hate it when I look in the mirror. I'm fat and my face has zits.

2.   I guess I'm basically an OK person. I try my best and it seems to work.

3.   School is fine. I would like to have more friends though.

4.   I do pretty well in school. I'm not the smartest kid there, but I'm not the dumbest either.

5.   If I could only pass chemistry. I hate that subject and I just don't get it.

6.   I wish I would start growing. I hate always being the shortest kid in the class.

7.   I like school. I have to study, but when I do, I can do pretty well.

Exercise 3.3

Look at the following examples and classify each as illustrating either external morality or autonomous morality. Then classify the same statements as demonstrating preconventional reasoning, conventional reasoning, or postconventional reasoning.

Students found that a Coke machine could be "tricked" by hitting two selections at the same time to get a free drink. Three students responded as follows:

1.   "I don't think it's right. What about the guy who runs this business? It's like stealing from him."

2.   "I'm not taking one. We talked about this stuff in class, and we agreed that we should only take what we've earned."

3.   "I'd take one, but what if somebody saw us and reported us to the office?"

Middle school students are standing around the playground talking about a new student who has a speech impairment. Some of the students have been making fun of his speech. The following are some student comments:

4.   "Hey, quit that. How would you feel if that was you?"

5.   "If Mrs. Janek finds out, they're gonna be in big trouble. She wants us to be nice to each other."

6.   "What about Mrs. Janek's rule that she keeps reminding us about? She's always saying, 'Treat each other with respect.'"

Exercise 3.4

For the following items, consider each of the stated reasons for not using drugs. Classify each description into one of Kohlberg's first five stages.

1.   If I'm caught using drugs, my reputation will be ruined.

2.   If everyone used drugs, our society would disintegrate.

3.   It's expensive, and I don't get that much out of it.

4.   If I get caught, I could go to jail.

5.   If my parents found out I used drugs, they would be crushed.

6.   My dad drinks, and alcohol is a drug, so who are they to tell me not to use them?

7.   If my parents knew I used drugs, I'd be grounded.

8.   Freedom to choose is critical, and drug use results in the loss of that freedom.

Feedback for Application Exercises_____

Exercise 3.1

1. Carmella is in the identity-confusion stage. Her concern for her appearance and what others think of her is typical of this stage.

2. Deon is in the industry-inferiority stage. While he isn't a strong student, he is developing a sense of accomplishment and competence through his success in sports, and through them should positively resolve the crisis.

3. Kathy is in the initiative-guilt stage of development. She is past doing things on her own and has taken the initiative to make the pictures for her father. Her parents' supportive attitude in the face of a potentially aggravating experience should help her positively resolve the crisis.

4. Mr. Thomas is in the generativity-stagnation stage. His concern for the next generation is an indicator of a positive resolution of the stage.

5. Tom is in the intimacy-isolation stage. His superficial relationships and his inability to feel strongly about someone indicates that he is having difficulty with the crisis, which at this point is not being positively resolved.

6. Mike is in the identity-confusion stage. He is experiencing the normal feelings of an adolescent boy beginning his search for identity as he moves toward manhood.

7. The case study indicates that Emmitt has a problem with initiative, indicating that he didn't fully resolve the initiative-guilt crisis, which in turn left him with this problem. On the other hand, he appears to be resolving the identity-confusion crisis acceptably as indicated by him being a typical "normal" youngster for his age. The best the teacher can do is to provide him with opportunities to take initiative and then strongly reward any activities that result. Also, make it a point to encourage initiative in all his work and then be careful not to penalize him in any way for taking it.

Exercise 3.2

1. This example refers to physical self-concept. Students in the middle, junior high, and high schools are often preoccupied with their looks.

2. This is a case of general self-concept. This statement suggests general satisfaction with who she is.

3. This example refers to social self-concept. Wanting friends suggests concerns in this area.

4. This example illustrates academic self-concept. Concerns about schoolwork in general reflect academic self-concept.

5. This example refers to subject-specific self-concept. The individual has a poor self-concept with respect to chemistry.

6. This illustrates physical self-concept. This is a common concern of late-developing adolescent boys.

7. This refers to academic self-concept. Studying and doing well suggest an academic orientation.

Exercise 3.3

1. Piaget would describe this as illustrating autonomous morality. Autonomous morality views justice as a reciprocal process of treating others as they would want to be treated.
   Kohlberg would describe this as conventional ethics. The student is expressing views based on concern for the owner of the Coke machine.

2. Autonomous morality. The student is demonstrating a rational idea of fairness and is relying on himself to make the decision.
   Postconventional ethics. The statement, "We talked about this stuff in class, and we agreed that we should only take what we've earned," suggests that the student views taking only what we've earned as a social contract.

3. External morality. External morality views rules as fixed and enforced by others.
   Preconventional ethics. Concerns about being reported to the office reflects thinking that emphasizes consequences to the individual.

4. Piaget would describe this as illustrating autonomous morality. Autonomous morality sees justice as a reciprocal process of treating others as they would want to be treated.
   Kohlberg would describe this as conventional ethics. The student is expressing views based on concern for the feelings of the student being taunted.

5. External morality. External morality views rules as fixed and enforced by others.
   Preconventional ethics. Concerns about being reported to Mrs. Janek reflects thinking that emphasizes consequences to the individual.

6. External morality. External morality focuses on rules.
   Conventional ethics. Conventional ethics is based upon concern for others and adherence to rules.

Exercise 3.4

1. Stage 3. The focus is on the individual's reputation, or the opinion of others. Although there is an element of the self involved, since it is his or her reputation, the primary focus is on others, making it conventional ethics.

2. Stage 4. The concern is for the general orderliness of society.

3. Stage 2. The focus here is on the self. The individual is not getting in return what the cost requires. No concern for others or principled ethics is indicated in the example.

4. Stage 1. The concern is strictly related to punishment.

5. Stage 3. The person's concern is for the feelings of family.

6. Stage 3. This example isn't as obvious as the others, but the individual is basing the decision on the ethical example of others. There is no evidence of fear of punishment, and no exchange, as in Stage 2, is implied.

7. Stage 1. Grounding is a form of punishment.

8. Stage 5. A principle is being stated. It could be argued that the statement exists in the form of a general principle, and is therefore more appropriately Stage 6, but as indicated in the text of the chapter, the description of Stage 6 isn't completely clear. Further, in Kohlberg's early work, he suggested that Stage 6 was a "universal" principle. It could be argued that all principles are grounded in specific cultures, such as the preeminence of the individual which is grounded in western culture.

Self-Help Quiz_____

TRUE-FALSE QUESTIONS: Write T in the blank if the statement is true, and F if the statement is false.

_____ 1. Teachers can help children overcome severe obstacles later in life by challenging them and giving them opportunities in which they can succeed in the elementary grades.

_____ 2. Personal development is influenced primarily by parents and other adults, but social development is influenced primarily by peers.

_____ 3. According to Kohlberg, an effective way to teach moral behavior is to explain ethical laws and principles.

_____ 4. One criticism of Kohlberg's work on moral development is that moral behavior cannot be predicted from his descriptions.

_____ 5. Self-concept tends to be a general characteristic. If people "feel good about themselves" in one area, they tend to feel good about themselves in most other areas as well.

MULTIPLE CHOICE QUESTIONS: Circle the best response in each case.

6. "C'mon in here and tell me about school," Hannah's dad says to her as she comes in the door.
      They talk for several minutes about school, social activities, and life in general. They have a drink, and her dad finally says, "Better get started with your homework."
      "Aww, Dad," Hannah grumbles.
      "No, get going. I'm working in here, so let me know if you get stuck on any of it, and I'll try and help you. . . . I want to see it when you're finished."

Based on the information above, the best description of Hannah's dad's parenting style is:
   a. authoritarian, because he demanded that Hannah get started on her homework; he had high expectations for her.
   b. authoritative, because he offered to help her if she had problems; he was responsive to her.
   c. authoritative, because he spent time talking with her but also expected her to conscientiously do her work.
   d. permissive, because her dad allowed her to talk about topics that didn't relate to school and learning.

7. "How about you getting some stuff from the Internet," Kathy suggests to Jeremy, one of her group mates as they discuss a science project. "You've said you like working on the Internet and finding stuff there."
      Of the following, which is the best description of Kathy's behavior?
   a. She is demonstrating perspective taking, since she appears to understand how Jeremy feels.
   b. She is demonstrating social problem solving, since there appears to be a problem with their project, and she is attempting to solve it.
   c. She is demonstrating an authoritative leadership style since she appears to be leading the group.
   d. She is demonstrating postconventional ethics, since she appears to be operating on a principle.

8. Erikson's work is based on which of the following ideas?
   a. People from different cultures have different basic needs.
   b. A person must resolve the crisis at each stage of psychosocial development in order to move to the next stage of psychosocial development.
   c. Movement from one stage of psychosocial development to another is characterized by a change in individuals' motivations.
   d. A crisis is a point in a person's psychosocial development that is characterized by a loss of personal identity.

Ron, 24, is in a conversation with his fiance, Kathy. "What are you doing?" Kathy queries.

"I want to give the boss a call to see what he thinks of this."

"It bothers me when you do that all the time," Kathy responds. "You're so capable. Why do you want him looking over your shoulder all the time? It hurts me to see you operate like this."

"Don't worry about it, Kat. I know what kind of a guy I am and how I operate best. And, it seems to be working. My last raise was a good one."

9. Based on Erikson's work and the information in the case study, which of the following would Kathy conclude Ron has least well resolved?
   a. Trust vs. distrust
   b. Autonomy vs. shame and doubt
   c. Industry vs. inferiority
   d. Identity vs. confusion

10. Based on the information in the case study, which crisis has Ron best resolved?
   a. Trust vs. distrust
   b. Autonomy vs. shame and doubt
   c. Industry vs. inferiority
   d. Identity vs. confusion

11. Mrs. Hanson is a teacher making an effort to apply Erikson's theory to classroom practice. Whenever the opportunity arises in a social studies lesson to discuss prominent figures and their accomplishments, she discusses them thoroughly in an effort to present them as models for the students. Based on this information, which of the following would be best prediction of Mrs. Hanson's students' ages?
   a. 6
   b. 10
   c. 13
   d. 21

12. Cliff is very self accepting. He acknowledges his assets and limitations. He takes people at face value and in a reflective mood says, "Well, I've done pretty well. Anyway, I did my best, and that's all anyone can ask." Of the following, Cliff best fits which stage according to Erikson's theory?
   a. Identity vs. confusion
   b. Intimacy vs. isolation
   c. Generativity vs. stagnation
   d. Integrity vs. despair

13. If an individual decides not do so something because his father and his mother will be disappointed in him, he would best be describe as reasoning at the:
   a. interpersonal harmony stage.
   b. law and order stage.
   c. social contract stage.
   d. universal principles stage.

14. One way to teach ethics and morals is for teachers to:
   a. give students opportunities to discuss moral dilemmas with each other which provides opportunities to hear other points of view.
   b. emphasize topics that involve values encouraged by the school and avoid those that don't.
   c. state explicit guidelines for school behavior and strictly enforce them.
   d. reinforce positive behaviors and punish negative ones.

15. We've heard of the moral ethic "Don't bite the hand that feeds you." This notion best fits which one of Kohlberg's Stages?
   a. 1
   b. 2
   c. 3
   d. 4

16. Joey tends to be a bit of a bully on the playground, shoving the smaller boys down and making them cry. You take him aside and say, "Joey, how do you think the other kids feel when you treat them like this?" together with other related statements. Amazingly, this seems to help, and Joey's behavior has improved. In the absence of any other information, based on this anecdote, we would judge Joey's age to be no younger which of the following?
   a. 4
   b. 8
   c. 13
   d. 16

In the following case study identify the stage of moral reasoning best illustrated by each of the numbered paragraphs.

A group of people were sitting at a party discussing tax time with the same concerns most people have at that time of the year.

"I'm taking a trip this summer," Nick declared with a wry grin. "I plan to see my brother. He's a teacher too. We are really going to talk teaching. In fact my kids are going to talk teaching.

"My trip is going to cost only 65% of what it would have," he finished with a sly look.

17. "You talk tough now," Judy replied seriously. "You won't be cute when you get audited."

18. "Well, my brother and I are very close emotionally, my folks are getting older, they'll be there, and they really want to see the kids," Nick responded.

19. "Shoot, I'd do it in a second," John added. "Besides, everyone does it, and no one would react to your little indiscretion."

20. "On the other hand," Frances responded pensively. "Nick is technically breaking the law."

"Ahh, you're a lawyer," Betty responded with a tongue-in-cheek sneer.

21. "True," Frances responded, though not defensively. "Change the law and I'll go along with it. In effect, it amounts to an agreement to pay our fair share to make the system work."

"It's a bad law and a piece of crap," Sharon responded emotionally.

22. "Well, we can't just go around doing as we please," Tony added cautiously. "I mean what would the world be like if everyone thought like Sharon does. It would be chaos."

"I'm sorry I brought it up," Nick said with a placating grin.

Four teachers were having coffee one day after school, and as their conversation went on, they began talking about the negative self-concepts of some of their disadvantaged students, particularly with respect to academic work. They then began to discuss the different ways that the students' academic self-concepts could be improved. As they were talking, Mrs. Ivanisevich commented, "I try to give my students some independence, and I let them help me decide on the learning activities that we're going to conduct."

Mr. Lilyquist added, "I try to provide an environment where the students know I care for and trust them."

Mr. Henderson continued, "I try to attack the problem formally. I have a series of activities in which we discuss how important it is feel good about ourselves. The activities help the students to see that they're all worthwhile people and valuable to the world."

Mrs. Gomez countered, "I think the primary thing is that the students accomplish something, so I try to be sure that they're successful on the learning activities we do. Then they feel good about what they've accomplished."

23. Based on research and these descriptions, the teacher *most* likely to be successful is:
    a. Mrs. Ivanisevich
    b. Mr. Lilyquist
    c. Mr Henderson
    d. Mrs. Gomez

24. Based on research and these descriptions, the teacher *least* likely to be successful is:
    a. Mrs. Ivanisevich
    b. Mr. Lilyquist
    c. Mr Henderson
    d. Mrs. Gomez

25. Jason, a capable student, loves animals and wants to work for the government in an environmental protection program. His parents, fearing that he wouldn't make much money in a career of that sort, pressure Jason into considering engineering. Jason acquiesces and enrolls in an engineering program at his state university.
    Of the following, Jason's decision best illustrates:
    a. Identity diffusion
    b. Identity foreclosure
    c. Identity moratorium
    d. Identity achievement

Self-Help Quiz Answers_____

1. t
2. f
3. f
4. t
5. f
6. c   Hannah's dad demonstrates authoritative parenting, which can lead to healthy personal growth. He is responsive as indicated by his interest in talking to her about "school, social activities, and life in general." He also has high expectations; he expects her do her work and do it correctly ("I want to see it when you're finished.").
7. a   In saying, "You've said you like working on the Internet and finding stuff there," Kathy demonstrates an ability to see the project from Jeremy's point of view. No evidence of a problem exists in the example (choice b); the term *authoritative* is used in reference to a parenting style (choice c); and no evidence exists indicating that Kathy is operating based on a principle (choice d).
8. c   Each of Erikson's stages presents a psychosocial challenge to individuals, and individuals are motivated to meet the challenge, or in other words, resolve the crisis. None of the other choices is a true statement, according to Erikson.
9. b   Kathy would suggest that Ron has not developed into an autonomous individual.
10. d   Ron's comment, "I know what kind of a guy I am . . ." suggests that he has a clear sense of his identity. Admittedly, he commented that he got a good raise (choice c), but this is very indirect evidence of industry, and we have little other evidence about his sense of industry.
11. c   Role models can provide powerful assistance in helping adolescents resolve the identity versus confusion crisis.
12. d   People characterized as having integrity look back on their lives with few regrets.
13. a   People at the interpersonal harmony stage are concerned with living up to the expectations of others.
14. a   Discussion of dilemmas provides opportunities for students to compare their views with the views of others.
15. b   At the market exchange stage people are concerned about reciprocity for their actions.
16. c   Responding to concerns for others' feelings indicates that Joey is at the interpersonal harmony stage. This stage is part of conventional ethics, which is characteristic of 10-20 year olds.

17.   Concern about being audited is a form of being caught which suggests the punishment obedience stage.

18.   Living up to the expectations of parents suggests interpersonal harmony.

19.   Being caught up in majority opinion or behaving in a certain way because "everybody does it" is characteristic of interpersonal harmony.

20.   Emphasis on obeying laws and rules for their own sake is characteristic of a law and order orientation.

21.   Frances's comment, "In effect, it amounts to an agreement to pay our fair share to make the system work," describes a social contract.

22.   Tony's concern about chaos suggests a moral view describing the need for an orderly society, which is characteristic of the law and order stage.

23.   d   Research suggests that ensuring success on meaningful tasks is the most effective way to influence self-concept.

24.   c   Activities focusing on self-concept (or self-esteem) in the absence of genuine accomplishment are unlikely to be successful.

25.   b   Identity foreclosure occurs when students adopt the ready-made decisions of others.

CHAPTER 4: GROUP AND INDIVIDUAL DIFFERENCES

Chapter Outline_____

I. Intelligence
   A. Intelligence: One trait or many?
      1. Gardner's theory of multiple intelligences
         a. Applications of Gardner's theory
         b. Criticisms of Gardner's theory
      2. Sternberg's triarchic theory of intelligence
         a. Improving intelligence
   B. Intelligence: Nature versus nurture
   C. Ability grouping
      1. Ability grouping: Research results
      2. Ability grouping: Implications for teachers
   D. Learning styles
      1. Learning preferences: Research results
      2. Learning styles: Implications for teachers
II. Socioeconomic status
   A. Influence of SES on learning
      1. Basic needs and experience
      2. Parental involvement
      3. Attitudes and values
   B. SES: Some cautions and implications for teachers
III. Culture
   A. Ethnicity
   B. Culture and schooling
      1. The cultural basis of attitudes and values
      2. Cultural differences in adult-child interactions
      3. Classroom organization and culture
      4. Culture and schooling: Some cautions
   C. Language Diversity
      1. English dialects: Research findings
      2. Dialects in the classroom: Implications for teachers
      3. English Language Learners
      4. Types of ELL programs
         a. Maintenance ELL programs
         b. Transitional ELL programs
         c. ELL pullout programs
         d. Sheltered English
      5. Evaluating ELL programs
   D. Teaching culturally and linguistically diverse students: Instructional principles
IV. Gender
   A. Differences in the classroom behavior of boys and girls
   B. Gender stereotypes and perceptions
   C. Responding to gender differences: Instructional principles
V. Students placed at risk
   A. Resilience
      1. Schools that promote resilience
      2. Teachers who promote resilience
   B. Teaching students placed at risk: Instructional principles

Chapter Objectives_____

- Describe differences in the way intelligence is viewed, and explain how ability grouping can influence learning.

- Define socioeconomic status and explain how it can affect school performance.

- Describe cultural, ethnic, and language diversity and explain how each can influence learning.

- Explain gender role identity and describe steps for eliminating gender bias in classrooms.

- Describe characteristics of schools and qualities of teachers that promote student resilience.

Chapter Overview_____

The students we teach differ in several ways, each of which can affect their school achievement. To best meet the needs of all students, we must be aware of these differences and capitalize on the richness that they bring to our learning activities.

One of the most powerful of these differences lies in the area of intelligence, defined as the ability to solve problems, reason abstractly, and acquire knowledge. A second is socioeconomic status (SES), which is a measure of a family's relative position in the community, determined by a combination of income, occupation, and education level. Culture, or the combination of attitudes, values, beliefs, and ways of acting characteristic of different groups, influences learning in a similar way. Ethnicity, an important part of culture, refers to a student's ancestry or national reference group. Members of an ethnic group share a common history, language, value system, and set of customs and traditions. Gender differences also impact the effectiveness of our instruction. Though research suggests that boys and girls are quite similar in aptitude, it also reveals differences in how they are treated as well as the type of careers they pursue. Teachers can do much to minimize these differences by communicating high expectations for all students, by interacting with students equally, and by encouraging girls to explore careers in math and science, areas often believed to be male domains.

Students placed at-risk are in danger of failing to complete their education with the skills necessary to survive in a technological society. Resilient youth develop coping strategies that increase their likelihood of success in challenging environments. Parents and teachers promote resilience through caring and maintaining high expectations that help develop student self-esteem and feelings of self control.

Application Exercises_____

Exercise 4.1

Tony, a third grader, was feeling both excited and a little nervous. He had just been moved to a new math group, and he knew that it would now be harder. At the same time, he felt good because Ms. Lemar had told him that he was doing so well that he needed an additional challenge. But, fourth grade math!

He hoped everything would be all right. He went to Mrs. Anderson's second grade class for reading, and he stayed in homeroom for the afternoon. "I think I'll be okay," he decided.

Ms. Lemar interrupted his thinking. "Okay, everybody, look up here. . . . We have three new members here today, and we want to welcome them. Celia, we're glad you're here. You too, Tony and Kareem. Welcome to our class. We're glad you're all with us.

"Now, each of you in this class is a good math student. You can all do the work. I'm going to expect a lot from you during the next nine weeks, and I'm sure you'll do super. Let me know if you have any problems. . . . Now, let's see where we were before vacation."

Think about the practice of ability grouping, and using ability grouping as the context, identify at least four positive characteristics or practices illustrated here.

Exercise 4.2

You are a teacher with a class of 24 students, 17 of whom are members of cultural minorities. Describe specifically what you might do in your teaching to help overcome the concept of *cultural inversion* in your class.

Exercise 4.3

Classify each of the following as maintenance, transitional, or ESL bilingual programs.

1.   Pablo Suarez spends his day in a self-contained fifth-grade classroom. In that class he learns primarily in English. When he has a problem or doesn't understand something he can raise his hand and an aide will come over and talk to him in Spanish, explaining the content or directions he doesn't understand.

2.   Jacinta Escobar is a first-grade student at Woodrow Wilson Elementary School. When she arrives in the morning her teacher greets her in Spanish. Jacinta is learning to read and write in both Spanish and English, and many of the songs the class sings are in Spanish.

3.   Abdul Hakeem has recently moved to New York from his old home in the Middle East. He is in the seventh grade and attends most of the regular classes like the other students. Though his speaking skills in English are limited, he can read enough to get by in most classes. During fourth period every day he goes to a special class that focuses on English vocabulary and oral communication skills.

4.   You are a fourth-grade teacher with 8 non-native English-speaking students in your class of 26. You're beginning a unit on adjectives and adverbs with your students in language arts. Based on the information in this section, describe specifically how you would teach the topic, taking into account the special needs of your non-native English speakers and capitalizing on the information in this section.

Exercise 4.4

In your text you saw the example where Marti Banes, an advanced-placement chemistry teacher, had very few girls in her class, and the girls who were enrolled sat passively during her learning activities.

1.   What is the best explanation for the low number of girls in her class?

2.   What short- and long-term strategies might she pursue to correct this problem?

Exercise 4.5

Read the following case study and then answer the question that follows.

When students entered Elaine Higby's classroom, they saw a review assignment written on the board. As Elaine took roll and prepared for the lesson, they routinely started on the assignment.

The bell rang at 9:05, and at 9:06 Elaine began with a brief review of integers. She had the students identify several integers on a number line that she displayed on the overhead, and she had the students identify examples of negative integers, such as -2 being a hole two feet in the ground or a room two floors below ground level. Because the students were quickly able to identify the integers and produce the examples, she believed they were ready to move on to adding and subtracting integers.

"Adding and subtracting integers is challenging," she commented. "But I know you can do it."

She then gave the students packets of cubes, telling them that the black cubes represented positive numbers and the white cubes represented negative numbers. She had the students solve several addition and subtraction problems, such as $6 + (-3)$, $-4 – (+5)$, and $5 – (-2)$ using the cube. As they worked with the cubes under Elaine's guidance, they could see that $6 + (-3) = 3$, $-4 – (+5) = -9$, and $5 – (-2) = 7$. As they worked, she placed special emphasis on the link between the manipulatives (the cubes) and the numerals she wrote on the board.

When the students were getting correct solutions using the cubes, she then assigned a series of additional problems as seatwork. She told the students they could draw the cubes on their papers if necessary, but that they would later be required to quickly solve problems without the aid of the cubes.

As the students worked, she closely monitored them, providing brief periods of assistance when students struggled. When she saw that Jeremy, Tanya, and Calvin continued to have trouble, she had them move to the back of the room, and she guided them through several more problems with the cubes.

The following are principles of instruction for students placed at risk:
- Create and maintain an orderly learning environment with predictable routines.
- Combine high expectations with frequent feedback about learning progress.
- Use teaching strategies that actively involve all students and promote high levels of success.
- Use high-quality examples that provide the background knowledge students need to learn new content.
- Stress self-regulation and the acquisition of learning strategies.

Assess the extent to which Elaine implemented the principles in her lesson.

Feedback for Application Exercises_____

Exercise 4.1

Some positive practices identified in the episode include:

1. *Flexible grouping.* Tony was in one math group and was moved to a higher achieving group in the middle of the year.

2. *Different groupings for different subjects.* Students are often successful in different subjects and having alternate grouping arrangements for different content volumes allows teachers to match instruction to student needs.

3. *Heterogeneous homeroom grouping.* This was only implied in the episode, but the fact that Tony stayed in his homeroom in the afternoon suggested that subjects like science, social studies, art, and health were taught in groups with mixed abilities. This minimizes some of the negative affective consequences of grouping.

4. *Positive expectations.* Regardless of what group students are in they should be made to feel that they can and will succeed. Mrs. Lemar did a nice job of communicating this at the beginning of her math class.

Exercise 4.2

First, one of the most important things you can do is try to establish a climate where all students feel accepted and valued. One way to accomplish this is to carefully practice equitable treatment of your students. This means call on all the students in your class approximately equally, prompt each one when they're unable to answer, give each similar feedback, and use the same body language with each.

Second, provide high quality examples and representations of the topics you study. For example, Karen Johnson and Jenny Newhall, in Chapter 2, and Diane Smith, at the end of this chapter, used high-quality examples to teach density, the properties of air, and comparative and superlative adjectives, respectively. Diane also did an excellent job of using open-ended questions to help her students be successful. Each of the teachers used a very effective approach for students who would be called involuntary minorities.

Third, keep all grades and other performance records private, and tell the students to avoid sharing their grades with anyone else in the class. This is designed to take the pressure off the students who want to perform well, but feel peer pressure to avoid doing so. (Many will probably share their grades anyway, but telling them not to gives the student who would rather avoid sharing his or her grades a "way out.")

Finally, you may even tell them to not raise their hands in class (again to keep some students from "standing out" in front of their peers). Then be sure to call on all students equally, and be certain that you give them enough support to be certain that each is able to answer.

Exercise 4.3

1. Pablo attends a transitional program. In transitional programs the first language (Spanish) is used until English proficiency is reached. Then it is used as an aid or supplement to English to help students when they have problems with English instruction.

2. Jacinta's class is a maintenance program, designed to develop expertise in both Spanish and English.

3. Abdul's fourth period class is a pull-out ESL program designed to supplement his regular instruction.

4. The most effective strategy is to build on the students' experiences. One way to begin would be to label several objects in the room in both Spanish and English as Tina Wharton did in the example in your text. Then describe the objects, writing the descriptions on the board and discussing the descriptions in detail. In the discussion, point out that each of these describing words are adjectives. Then, follow a similar procedure with adverbs. Have the students describe the action of something, such as the way you walk across the floor. Again, write the description on the board and discuss it thoroughly, pointing out that the description of the action is an adverb in each case.

Exercise 4.4

1. Research indicates that female students take fewer elective and fewer advanced science classes. Probably the strongest explanation is cultural; female students don't perceive science as an appropriate field for them to major in nor do they view science-related careers as positively as do male students.

2. In the short term she should do everything she can to make the females in her class comfortable, modeling her interest in science and communicating positive expectations for them in the class. Long-term solutions might include recruiting in lower-level classes, working with other science teachers to make sure the science curriculum is gender friendly, and actively talking with parents and counselors about careers in science.

Exercise 4.5

The following is an assessment of the extent to which Elaine implemented each of the principles.

Elaine effectively implemented the first four principles. The following is an assessment of each.

She implemented the first: "Create and maintain an orderly learning environment with predictable routines" by having an assignment waiting for them when they entered the room. Expectations for the lesson were clearly stated. The students began the assignment without being told, suggesting that doing a beginning-of-class assignment was part of their daily routine.

She also began her instruction one minute after the bell rang, which further indicated that Elaine was well organized—organization helps promote an orderly learning environment.

Elaine implemented the second principle: "Combine high expectations with frequent feedback about learning progress" by saying, "Adding and subtracting integers is challenging, but I know you all can do it," which communicated her expectations; she provided ongoing feedback during the learning activity. She also provided feedback as she monitored the students during the learning activity.

She implemented the third principle: "Use teaching strategies that actively involve all students and promote high levels of success" by ensuring that all the students were involved as they worked with the cubes. Her guidance ensured that they were successful.

The fourth principle: "Use high-quality examples that provide the background knowledge students need to learn new content" was implemented when she provided the students with concrete examples of negative numbers, such as -2 being two floors below ground level, and by ensuring that the students understood the solutions to the problems.

While Elaine's instruction was generally effective, there was little evidence that she stressed self-regulation and the acquisition of learning strategies (the fifth principle) in her lesson. She could have increased the emphasis on learning strategies by modeling strategies with "think alouds" during the lesson, and she could have also asked successful students to share their strategies. She could have also modeled strategies, such as "The first thing I think about is whether we are adding or subtracting. . . . Then, I look at the sign of the number."

Self-Help Quiz_____

TRUE/FALSE QUESTIONS: Write T in the blank if the statement is true, and write F if the statement is false.

_____ 1. Lack of experience is a major factor contributing to poor performance on intelligence tests.
_____ 2. Gardner's theory of multiple intelligences adds dimensions to intelligence that help explain how a person selects effective problem solving strategies.
_____ 3. Homogeneous ability grouping has had little effect on the expectations of teachers and the motivation of low ability students.
_____ 4. Lower SES parents place greater emphasis on conformity and obedience than do their middle and upper SES counterparts.
_____ 5. Effective teachers of students placed at risk use qualitatively different teaching strategies than do those who teach their more advantage counterparts.

MULTIPLE CHOICE QUESTIONS: Circle the best answer for each question.

6. Experts most commonly define intelligence as:
    a. the ability to achieve in school and get along with others.
    b. the ability to learn, reason in the abstract, and solve problems.
    c. the ability to adapt to unique environments.
    d. the ability to think clearly and make decisions after adequate deliberation.

7. Which of the following most accurately describes intelligence according to Sternberg?
    a. Intelligence is made up of fluid and crystallized abilities uninfluenced by school and culture.
    b. Schools should use more time and resources to address divergent thinking, the search for relationships and memorization of important content.
    c. Schools should treat intelligence not as a single trait, but as a complex series of interacting components.
    d. Nature is more important than nurture in shaping intelligence.

8. According to Gardner's theory of multiple intelligences:
    a. the curriculum should be broadened to include emphases on alternate subjects and topics.
    b. schools should renew their focus on basic skills
    c. teachers should use teaching strategies linked to students' learning styles.
    d. female students should be taught to think like male students and vice versa.

9. Individual teachers can accommodate different reading abilities in a classroom by dividing students into subgroups for teaching reading. This is best described as:
    a. between-class ability grouping.
    b. within-class ability grouping.
    c. the Joplin Plan.
    d. heterogeneous grouping.

10. According to research, which of the following tends to be the most common problem associated with ability grouping?
    a. Teachers tend to have inappropriately high expectations for students in low groups.
    b. Students in low groups tend to be stigmatized by both teachers and peers.
    c. Students are frequently moved from one ability group to another, which disrupts the continuity of their schooling.
    d. Low groups are often given work that is too difficult.

11. Which of the following statements best describes the way low SES parents tend to interact with their children? Low SES parents tend to:
    1. explain ideas to their children.
    2. give vague directions.
    3. be encouraging and cooperative.
    4. use simple language.
    5. identify causes of events.

a. 1, 3, 4   b. 1, 2, 3   c. 2, 3, 4   d. 2, 4   e. 1, 5

12. Cultural conflict most often occurs when:
    a. schools embrace a philosophy of acceptance toward cultural diversity.
    b. there is a disparity between school and home language or language patterns.
    c. competition is used as a motivational tool.
    d. children from different cultures mix in one school.

13. According to research, of the following, which is most likely to be a problem in programs for at-risk students?
    a. Expectations for students are inappropriately high.
    b. Emphasis on higher level thinking is lacking.
    c. Teacher warmth and enthusiasm tends to be excessive and artificial.
    d. Too much emphasis is placed on assessment and feedback.

14. According to research examining gender issues, which of the following statements best explains the difference in achievement scores in math between boys and girls in middle, junior high, and high schools?
    a. Societal expectations influence boys' and girls' behaviors with respect to math.
    b. Math is more innately appealing to boys, so they tend to be more motivated to study math than are girls.
    c. Boys are more naturally talented in math because of their better visual and spatial abilities.
    d. The physical differences between boys and girls at the junior high and high school level are more apparent.

Use the following case study to answer Items 15-19.

Gabriella is a fourth grader at Oakridge Elementary School—a suburban school populated mostly by children whose parents are teachers, middle management personnel from insurance companies and other businesses, and naval officers who are stationed at a nearby naval air station. Gabriella, whose native language is Spanish, lives with her divorced mother—a minimum wage housekeeper who left school after the 10th grade. Gabriella has limited experience with school-related activities. In a discussion of American westward expansion, for example, she asked what a bridle was as Mrs. Petschonek talked about the gear the cowboys used. Also, she had never heard of the country Hungary, confusing it with being hungry. However, Gabriella learns new ideas in class more quickly than many of her classmates, and she periodically asks questions atypical of fourth graders, such as "Why are there so many movies about cowboys if there weren't really that many of them?"

15. Based on the information in the case study, which of the following is the best prediction?
    a. Gabriella will get a lower score than will her typical peers on some sections of typical intelligence tests.
    b. Gabriella will score about the same as typical fourth graders on most sections of typical intelligence tests.
    c. Gabriella will score higher than typical fourth graders on most sections of typical intelligence tests.
    d. We can't make any predictions about Gabriella's performance on intelligence tests based on the information in the case study.

16. Based on the information in the case study and researchers' conceptions of intelligence, which of the following is the best description?
    a. Gabriella is less intelligent than most of her peers.
    b. Gabriella's intelligence is about comparable to that of her peers.
    c. Gabriella is more intelligent than most of her peers.
    d. We don't have any evidence one way or the other about Gabriella's intelligence based on the information in the case study.

17. Based on the information in the case study, of the following, which is the best conclusion we can make about Gabriella's socioeconomic status?
    a. It is lower than that of her peers.
    b. It is about the same as that of her peers.
    c. It is higher than that of her peers.
    d. We don't have enough information from the case study to make a conclusion about Gabriella's socioeconomic status.

18. Based on information in the case study and research on school dropouts, if Gabriella fits patterns typical for students with her background and socioeconomic status, which of the following is the best prediction?
    a. She is much less likely to drop out of school than is a typical classmate.
    b. She is slightly less likely to drop out than is a typical classmate.
    c. The likelihood of Gabriella dropping out is about the same as that of a typical classmate.
    d. Gabriella is about twice as likely to drop out as is a typical classmate.

19. When Gabriella came to Oakridge at the beginning of the year, she was placed in a low ability reading group. Based on research examining ability grouping, which of the following is the most likely outcome?
    a. Gabriella will be moved to a higher ability group before the end of the year.
    b. Gabriella will remain in the low group until the end of the year but will be placed in a higher ability group the following year.
    c. Gabriella will remain in a low ability group for the remainder of the year and will be placed in a low ability group again the following year.
    d. We can't predict what is likely to happen based on research examining ability group placements.

Use the following information for Items 20-23.

Verna Maxwell teaches in an inner city school near some government funded housing projects. In her class of 27 fifth graders, she has 14 students who are cultural minorities. Among them are Henry, a Native American, Kim, a Cambodian refugee, Lu, a second-generation Chinese American, and Rom, who has recently moved to the United States from India. Twenty of her 27 students are boys.

20. Based on Ogbu's work, which of the four is most likely to experience cultural inversion?
    a. Henry
    b. Kim
    c. Lu
    d. Rom

21. According to research examining effective teaching for cultural minorities, in working with her minority students in question and answer activities, which of the following is the best advice we can give Verna?
    a. Call on the minority students only when they volunteer, because teachers often don't understand students' preferred learning styles.
    b. Call on students such as Henry and Lu, because they are Americans, but don't direct questions to Kim and Rom, because they may not be comfortable in an American classroom.
    c. Use typical questioning patterns with Henry and Lu, but ask Kim and Rom open-ended questions.
    d. Treat all the students, including the cultural minorities, as equally as possible in both the type and number of questions asked.

22. Which of the following statements most accurately describes Verna's class?
    a. The majority of her class will probably have the characteristics of at-risk students, since many are cultural minorities and come from low income families.
    b. The majority of her class will probably have the characteristics of at-risk students since most of them are boys.
    c. The majority of her class will not be at-risk since most of them do not experience cultural inversion.
    d. We don't have enough information in the case study to make a conclusion about the at-risk characteristics of Verna's students.

23. According to research, which of the following would be the most effective assessment practice in Verna's class?
    a. Increase the number of assessments to provide the opportunity for frequent feedback to students.
    b. Decrease the number of assessments, since frequent assessments discriminate against cultural minorities.
    c. Give the students more independent work to accommodate their different learning styles.
    d. Decrease the emphasis on higher-order thinking, since many of her students probably lack background experiences.

Use the following case study to answer Items 24-25.

Mrs. Parker has 14 girls and 15 boys in her fifth grade class. She says, "The Battle of Gettysburg is believed to be the turning point of the Civil War. In what state is Gettysburg?" Then she asks, "What do you suppose would have happened if the South had won the battle instead of the North?"

24. If Mrs. Parker's questioning is typical of the types of questions directed to boys and girls, which of the following is most likely?
    a. She will direct both her questions to girls.
    b. She will direct both her questions to boys.
    c. She will direct the first question to a girl and the second question to a boy.
    d. She will direct the first question to a boy and the second question to a girl.
    e. There will be no pattern in her questioning behavior.

25. If Mrs. Parker's questioning is typical of the number of questions addressed to boys and girls, which of the following is most likely?
    a. She will direct more questions to boys.
    b. She will direct more questions to girls.
    c. She will direct about the same number of questions to boys as to girls.

Self-Help Quiz Answers

1. t
2. f
3. f
4. t
5. f
6. b   Experts generally agree on these three components of intelligence.
7. c   Sternberg thinks of intelligence as having several components that can be influenced by instruction.
8. a   Gardner's theory suggests many different kinds of intelligence that need to be addressed in the schools.
9. b   Within-class ability grouping addresses differences in ability by grouping within the same classroom.
10. b   Lowered teacher expectations and negative reactions from peers are both problems with ability grouping.
11. d   Low SES parents tend to use simplified language and not give clear directions to their children.
12. b   Language differences are the biggest source of cultural discontinuities in the schools today.
13. b   Too much emphasis is placed on "basic skills" resulting in a "dumbing down" of the curriculum.
14. a   Societal forces explain gender differences in math and science better than any genetic reason.
15. a   Intelligence tests don't measure "pure" aptitude; instead they are heavily influenced by experience.
16. c   Given her poor experiential background, the fact that she learns quickly and asks precocious questions suggests higher intelligence.
17. a   Both her mother's occupation and level of education suggest lower SES than her peers.
18. d   The combination of background factors suggests she is considerably more likely to drop out of school than her peers.
19. c   Research on ability grouping suggests that these placements tend to be stable over time.
20. a   Cultural inversion, or the tendency to reject majority values and behaviors, is most likely to occur in minorities that have a history of discrimination and separation, such as Native Americans.
21. d   Equal treatment and equitable distribution of questions are two of the best ways to communicate positive expectations.
22. a   The combination of being a cultural minority and coming from low SES students places many of her students at risk.
23. a   Frequent feedback is one of the characteristics of effective instruction for at-risk students.
24. c   Teachers are more likely to address high level questions to boys and low level ones to girls.
25. a   Research indicates that boys are called on more frequently than girls.

CHAPTER 5: LEARNERS WITH EXCEPTIONALITIES

Chapter Outline_____

I.   Changes in the way teachers help students with exceptionalities
    A.   Individuals with Disabilities Education Act (IDEA)
        1.   A free and appropriate public education (FAPE)
        2.   Least restrictive environment: The evolution towards inclusion
            a.   Collaborative consultation: Help for the classroom teacher
            b.   Putting inclusion into perspective
        3.   Protection against discrimination in testing
        4.   Due process and parents' rights
        5.   Individualized education program
    B.   Amendments to the Individuals with Disabilities Education Act
II.   Students with learning problems
    A.   The labeling controversy
    B.   Mental retardation
        1.   Levels of mental retardation
        2.   Programs for students with mental retardation
    C.   Learning disabilities
        1.   Characteristics of students with learning disabilities
        2.   Identifying and working with students who have learning disabilities
            a.   The use of classroom-based information for identification
            b.   Adaptive instruction
    D.   Attention deficit/hyperactivity disorder
    E.   Behavior disorders
        1.   Kinds of behavior disorders
        2.   Teaching students with behavior disorders
            a.   Behavior management strategies
            b.   Teacher sensitivity
    F.   Communication disorders
        1.   Helping students with communication disorders
    G.   Visual disabilities
        1.   Working with students who have visual disabilities
    H.   Hearing disabilities
        1.   Working with students who have hearing disabilities
    I.   Assessment and Learning: Assessment trends in special education
        1.   Curriculum-based assessment
        2.   Adaptive behavior
III. Students who are gifted and talented
    A.   Creativity
    B.   Identifying students who are gifted and talented
    C.   Teaching students who are gifted and talented: Instructional principles
IV.   The teacher's role in inclusive classrooms
    A.   Identifying students with exceptionalities
    B.   Teaching students with exceptionalities: Instructional principles
        1.   Provide additional instructional support
        2.   Adapt seatwork and homework
        3.   Supplement reading materials
        4.   Teach learning strategies
    C.   Social integration and growth
        1.   Developing classmates' understanding and acceptance
        2.   Helping students learn acceptable behaviors
        3.   Strategies for promoting interaction and cooperation

Chapter Objectives_____

- Describe the provisions of and amendments to the Individuals with Disabilities Education Act (IDEA).

- Describe the most common learning problems that classroom teachers are likely to encounter.

- Identify characteristics of learners who are gifted and talented, and describe methods for identifying and teaching these students.

- Explain the roles of classroom teachers and teaching strategies that are effective for working with students having exceptionalities.

Chapter Overview_____

Learners with exceptionalities are those who require special help to reach their full potential. Students with exceptionalities fall at both ends of the ability continuum, including students who are mildly retarded and others who are gifted and talented. Most of the exceptional students in regular classrooms have mild learning problems. These include students who are intellectually handicapped, students with learning disabilities, students with attention deficit/hyperactivity disorder (AD/HD), and students who are behaviorally disordered (sometimes described as emotionally handicapped).

The way that students with exceptionalities are helped in our schools changed when Public Law 94-142, the Individuals with Disabilities Education Act (IDEA), was passed. It provides for: (1) due process through parental involvement, (2) protection against discrimination in testing, and (3) an individualized education program (IEP). Inclusion advocates a total, systematic, and coordinated web of support services; it has changed the classroom teacher's role in working with these students.

Effective teaching practices for students with exceptionalities provide extra support so that students can experience high rates of success. Pre-referral assessment strategies emphasize classroom-based data gathering for instructional problem solving. Support for classroom teachers often occurs in the regular classroom through the use of pre-referral teacher assistance teams, site-based teams, or collaboration consultation teams. These teams often bring special educators into the classroom to help the regular teacher adapt instruction. Other strategies for working with students with exceptionalities in the regular classroom include cognitive strategy instruction and strategies to promote social integration and growth.

Application Exercises_____

Exercise 5.1

Examine the following list of descriptors and decide whether they apply to all three types of learning problems (G = General) or whether they are more characteristic of a specific learning problem (MR = Mental Retardation; LD = Learning Disability; BD = Behavior Disorder).

_____ 1.   Problems functioning in regular classrooms.

_____ 2.   Below-average performance on intelligence tests.

_____ 3.   Learning problems often involving language.

_____ 4.   Management problems often interfering with learning.

_____ 5.   Discrepancies between two measures of achievement.

_____ 6.   Students sometimes withdrawn and extremely shy.

_____ 7.   Failure and frustration often interfering with learning.

Exercise 5.2

Read the following classroom episode and identify in it the different functions that the classroom teacher performs in working with students having exceptionalities.

Toni Morrison had been working with her class of second graders for a week trying to get them into reading and math groups that matched their abilities. Marisse, a transfer student, was hard to place. She seemed to understand the material but lost attention during different parts of lessons. When Toni worked with her one-on-one, she did fine, but Toni often noticed her staring out the window.

One day as Toni watched the class work in small groups, she noticed that Marisse held her head to one side when she talked. Toni wondered . . . She spoke to the principal, who recommended that Marisse be referred to the school psychologist for possible testing.

Two weeks later, the school psychologist came by to discuss her findings. Marisse had a hearing problem in one ear that would require a hearing aid as well as special help from Toni.

In a few days, Marisse came to school with her hearing aid. She obviously felt funny about it and wasn't sure if this was a good idea. Toni moved her to the front of the room so she could hear better, made sure to give directions while standing in front of Marisse's desk, and double-checked after an assignment was given to ensure that the directions were clear to her.

After a couple of days, Toni took Marisse aside to talk about her new hearing aid. Marisse could hear better, but she still felt a little strange with it. Some of the kids looked at her curiously, and that made her uneasy. Toni had an inspiration: Why not discuss the hearing aid in class and let the others try it? This was a risky strategy, but Marisse reluctantly agreed to it.

It worked. During show-and-tell, Marisse explained about her new hearing aid and gave the class a chance to try it out themselves. The strange and different became understandable, and Marisse's hearing aid became a normal part of the classroom.

1.   Explain how *least restrictive environment* was illustrated in the case.

2.   Define *adaptive fit* and explain how it was illustrated in the case.

3.   What did the school do to meet the legal requirements of IDEA?

4.   What specifically did Toni do to facilitate *social integration and growth*?

Exercise 5.3

Read the following description of a team developing an IEP.

Pablo Martinez, a second grader at Lake Park Elementary, one of the schools in the Northern Burlington District, had been falling further and further behind in math and reading. Mrs. Henderson, his teacher, felt it was time to act. She talked with the special education teacher, who called a meeting with Pablo's parents. At the meeting, the special education teacher explained why they were there and what they hoped to accomplish. English as a second language was explored as one possible source of Pablo's problems. Mrs. Henderson shared Pablo's reading and math scores with them as well as his standardized achievement scores from the previous year. Everyone concurred that Pablo was having troubles, and his parents agreed to have the school psychologist test him for possible placement in a special program. Fortunately, the school psychologist was bilingual and was able to administer his tests in Spanish.

At the next meeting, the results of the tests were shared with the parents. They showed that Pablo had normal intelligence but that he performed poorly on the verbal parts of the scale. Everyone agreed that Pablo should remain in the regular classroom but that he would benefit from a resource program that was taught in his native language. In addition, the group developed a number of specific learning goals for Pablo, some of which would be met in Mrs. Henderson's classroom, some in resource, and some in both. The group was especially concerned about links between the two rooms and ways to reinforce learning activities at home.

Using information from the case, describe how each of the following provisions of IDEA was met:

1.   Free and appropriate public education (FAPE)

2.   Least restrictive environment

3.   Protection against discrimination in testing

4.   Due process through parental involvement

5.   Individualized education plan

Feedback for Application Exercises_____

Exercise 5.1

1. (G) Problems functioning in regular classrooms is characteristic of all three types of learning problems. These problems are typical of most students with exceptionalities and often require special, supplementary help for these students.

2. (MR) Below average performance on intelligence tests is a distinguishing characteristic of mental retardation.

3. (LD) Learning problems often involving language is common for students with learning disabilities.

4. (LD, BD) Management problems often interfering with learning tends to exist for students with exceptionalities in general to a greater extent than for those not having exceptionalities. However, it is most characteristic of students with learning disabilities and behavior disorders.

5. (LD) Discrepancies between two measures of achievement often indicates a learning disability and this discrepancy is commonly used to identify the disability.

6. (BD) Students who are sometimes withdrawn and extremely shy is most characteristic of students with an internalized behavior disorder (although it could be found in all students with exceptionalities).

7. (G) Failure and frustration that often interferes with learning is characteristic of all three types of learning problems.

Exercise 5.2

1. By retaining Marisse in the regular classroom and adapting that classroom to fit Marisse's learning needs, Toni tried to create a least restrictive learning environment.

2. Adaptive fit is the degree to which a student is able to cope with the requirements of a school setting and the extent to which the school accommodates the student's special needs. Toni attempted to insure adaptive fit by moving Marisse to the front of the room, giving directions in front of her desk and double-checking to make sure directions were clear.

3. The legal requirements of IDEA include:
- due process through parental involvement.
- protection against discrimination in testing.
- a least restrictive environment.
- individualized education programs.

The case study illustrated all of these except *discrimination in testing* which was not directly addressed.

4. To facilitate social integration Toni had Marisse explain and share her hearing aid. A major classroom obstacle to social acceptance is lack of understanding or ignorance on the part of other students.

Exercise 5.3

1. *Free and Appropriate Public Education (FAPE):* Pablo is attending an elementary school in the Northern Burlington District, which suggests that Lake Park is a public school.

2. *Least Restrictive Environment:* The general thrust of this provision is to keep children, as much as educationally possible, in the regular classroom. Research suggests that mainstreaming students like Pablo in the regular classroom has both academic and social advantages.

3. *Protection Against Discrimination in Testing:* This is an especially critical component of IDEA because of the growing number of non-native English speaking students in our schools. Because of this problem, and in response to a court case (*Diana v. State of Education*, 1970), one state, California, agreed to test all children whose primary language was not English in both their primary language and English (Salvia & Ysseldyke, 1991). Because of the close interrelationship between language and intelligence testing, this provision is essential to accurate testing.

4. *Due Process Through Parental Involvement:* Pablo's parents were consulted from the beginning of the process, and their approval for testing was obtained. If they hadn't given their approval, the process would have stopped there. In addition, their input was further solicited in the development of the I.E.P. as well as the decision to keep him in the regular classroom with resource help. If they had not approved of these decisions, they had the right to an external independent review of the process.

5. *Individualized Education Plan:* The individualized education plan specified goals for both the regular and resource classrooms. In addition, it outlined ways to coordinate efforts within the school and between the school and home.

Self-Help Quiz_____

TRUE/FALSE QUESTIONS: Write T in the blank if the statement is true, and write F if the statement is false.

_____ 1. One of the classroom teacher's main responsibilities is to help students with exceptionalities overcome negative attitudes of others toward them.

_____ 2. To maintain consistency in identification of children with exceptionalities, results of IQ and achievement tests should be given more weight than less objective information like classroom performance and adaptive behavior.

_____ 3. Students with mild handicaps can usually learn well enough to remain in the regular classroom without special help if they are accepted by their peers.

_____ 4. A student with a learning disability is typically below "normal" intelligence.

_____ 5. Research on mainstreaming reveals that knowledge and strategies that teachers use effectively with regular students need to be qualitatively changed in order to reach special education students.

MULTIPLE CHOICE QUESTIONS: Circle the best answer for each question.

6. The component of PL 94-142 that guarantees parent involvement in the classification and placement of their children, as well as access to their children's school records, is called:
    a. due process.
    b. protection against discrimination in testing.
    c. provision for the least restrictive environment.
    d. mainstreaming.

7. Which of the following is the most accurate description of inclusion as it is conceptualized by experts?
    a. Placing students with exceptionalities in regular classrooms full-time with the support of special education experts.
    b. Placing students with exceptionalities in regular classrooms whenever possible with the support of special education experts.
    c. Placing students with exceptionalities in regular classrooms for all their academic work except basic skill areas, such as reading and math.
    d. Providing instruction by special education specialists for students when they are pulled out of mainstream classes, but not providing special education support for teachers when students with exceptionalities are mainstreamed in regular classrooms.

8. Of the following, the best description of the purpose of curriculum-based measurement is:
    a. measure intelligence of the special education student in comparison to the rest of the regular class.
    b. assess achievement of the special education student in comparison to the rest of the regular class.
    c. identify specific areas that are encountered in the regular classroom in which the special education student needs help.
    d. identify long-term curriculum goals for the special education student.

9. Which of the following choices is the most accurate description of students with learning problems?
    a. These students can be mentally retarded, learning disabled, or behaviorally disordered.
    b. These students make up about 20% of the total school population.
    c. These students usually have other physical handicaps such as sight or hearing impairments.
    d. These students usually have average to above average IQ's.

10. Of the following, the best description of the reason children with learning disabilities can be difficult to identify is:
    a. they have many of the same characteristics of the educable mentally retarded.
    b. they are easily confused with developmentally slow children or students with behavior problems.
    c. discrepancies between IQ and achievement tests do not show up when testing the learning disabled.
    d. high levels of creativity often compensate for problems in other areas.

11. Of the following, the most difficult kind of behavioral disorder to identify typically is:
    a. the student displaying hyperactivity.
    b. the child who is defiant and hostile.
    c. the child who does not respond to regular rules and consequences.
    d. the shy, timid, depressed child.

12. When teachers and other students overreact to a physical handicap by doing everything for the student, an unhealthy dependence upon others can result. This is best described as:
    a. negative self-concept.
    b. learned helplessness.
    c. a behavioral disorder.
    d. a communication disorder.

13. Which of the following is a symptom of a language disorder?
    a. Tuning out when information is presented on the chalkboard
    b. Poorly articulating words, especially consonants
    c. Using few words or very short sentences
    d. Stuttering

14. Which of the following is NOT considered a trait of a student who is gifted and talented?
    a. Highly organized and focused on details
    b. Unconventional and nonconforming
    c. Likes to work alone
    d. Talented in one specific area

15. Which of the following is NOT true of accelerated programs for the gifted and talented?
    a. They challenge students by increasing the pace.
    b. They broaden student interests by introducing them to other topics.
    c. They result in improved achievement in accelerated areas.
    d. They sometimes work by allowing students to skip grades or test out of classes.

16. The development of "meta" skills such as meta-attention and meta-communication are a part of:
    a. strategy training.
    b. effective feedback.
    c. cooperative learning.
    d. an accelerated curriculum.

Use the following case study to answer Items 17-21.

Jerry Griffin, a 5th grade teacher, in observing Samone Duvalier, one of his students–originally from Haiti–thinks that Samone may have a specific learning disability. Samone, a native French speaking child who speaks competent English, is given the WISC-III, an individually administered intelligence test (in English) by certified special education officials. He scores very low on the vocabulary section of the test compared to the other sections, and he is diagnosed as having a specific learning disability. Jerry and exceptional student specialists from the school prepare and implement an IEP. Part of the IEP calls for Samone being placed in a resource reading program for one hour a day. (He is mainstreamed the rest of the day.) Mrs. Duvalier, Samone's mother, after meeting with the school officials, objects to the placement, and asks for Samone's school records and test results. The school offers the name of a person who could do an independent evaluation of Samone but will not release their own test results, only saying that Samone's score was very low in the vocabulary section.

17. According to PL 94-142, the school's refusal to release the records was:
    a. against the law, because of the provision guaranteeing parental involvement.
    b. against the law, because of the provision guaranteeing minority protection, since Samone is a cultural minority.
    c. within the law since Samone was found to have a disability. It would have been against the law if no disability was found.
    d. within the law since Samone was mainstreamed for most of the school day (only in a resource program for an hour a day).

18. The school officials violated a specific provision of PL 94-142 in their handling of Samone's case. Of the following, the best description of the violation is:
    a. placing Samone in a resource reading program.
    b. officials offering the name of an independent evaluator.
    c. mainstreaming Samone for most of the day.
    d. giving Samone the test in English.

19. Consider the school officials' use of the WISC-III as a basis for making their assessment of Samone. Based on PL 94-142, which of the following is the most accurate statement?
    a. Officials' use of the test was within the law, since the WISC-III is validated and widely used.
    b. Officials' use of the WISC-III was not within the law since it is an intelligence test.
    c. Officials' use of the WISC-III was within the law, but should have been supplemented with another measure before Samone was placed in the resource program.
    d. The use of the WISC-III was within the law, since the test was given by certified personnel.

20. Consider the school officials' offering of an independent evaluator to diagnose Samone's possible exceptionality. Based on PL 94-142, which of the following is the most accurate statement?
    a. The offer was within the law.
    b. The offer is prohibited by the law.
    c. The law doesn't speak to the offer of an independent evaluation.

21. Consider the development and implementation of Samone's IEP. Based on PL 94-142, which of the following is the most accurate statement?
    a. The development and implementation of the IEP was done according to the law.
    b. The development of the IEP was against the law, since Mr. Griffin–a regular teacher rather than a certified special education expert–was involved in the process.
    c. The development and implementation of the IEP was against the law, since it called for Samone being removed from the regular classroom for part of the day.
    d. The development and implementation of the IEP was against the law, since Samone's mother didn't sign it.

22. Alfredo, an Hispanic student, and Ken, a white student in Mrs. Evans 4th grade class both do consistently above average work. Alfredo's homework periodically reflects a lack of care, but he has a good imagination, and often makes comments in class discussions of problems and issues that indicates insight atypical for a fourth grader. He is periodically a bit disruptive, although he wouldn't be classified as a serious management problem.

Ken, in contrast, is every teacher's ideal. He follows directions, his work is extremely neat, and he is never a management problem. Ken and Alfredo scored similarly on achievement tests in the 3rd grade.

Based on this information, if Mrs. Evans's class is consistent with patterns identified by research, which of the following is most likely?
   a. Ken is more likely to be identified as gifted than is Alfredo.
   b. Alfredo is more likely to be identified as gifted than is Ken.
   c. Ken and Alfredo are equally likely to be identified as gifted.
   d. Neither Ken nor Alfredo are likely to be identified as gifted, since we have no evidence that either has taken an intelligence test.

23. Which of the following are classified as students with exceptionalities?
   1. Students who have an intellectual handicap
   2. Students who have learning disabilities
   3. Students who have behavioral disorders (emotional handicaps)
   4. Students who are gifted and talented
   5. Students who have hearing and visual impairments

a. 1, 2, 3, 4, 5   b. 1, 2, 3, 5   c. 1, 2, 5   d. 2, 3, 5   e. 1, 2

24. Donna and John are two students in your second grade class. If they are consistent with patterns identified by research, which of the following is the most accurate statement?
   a. Donna and John are about equally likely to be diagnosed as having AD/HD (attention deficit/hyperactivity disorder).
   b. Donna is slightly more likely than John to be diagnosed as having AD/HD.
   c. Donna is much (three to nine times) more likely than John to be diagnosed as having AD/HD.
   d. John is slightly more likely than Donna to be diagnosed as having AD/HD.
   e. John is much (three to nine times) more likely than Donna to be diagnosed as having AD/HD.

25. Which of the following statements most accurately describes effective teaching for students with exceptionalities?
   a. Students with exceptionalities should be taught using methodology that is qualitatively different from the methodology used with regular students.
   b. Students with exceptionalities should be taught primarily in an individualized format with heavy emphasis placed on drill and practice with basic skills.
   c. Students with exceptionalities should be placed in special facilities that are geared to their individual needs.
   d. The effective methods used for teaching students with exceptionalities are the same methods that are effective with regular students.

Self-Help Quiz Answers_____

1.   t
2.   f
3.   f
4.   f
5.   f
6.   a   Due process guarantees parents' involvement at critical points in the placement process.
7.   b   Inclusion emphasizes the concept of adaptive fit–making sure instructional adjustments meet the needs of students.

8. c Curriculum-based measurement is designed to ensure that adaptations fit the needs of students in the classroom.
9. a Mild learning handicaps can include students who are mentally retarded, learning disabled, or behaviorally disordered.
10. b Many of the characteristics of a learning disability, such as shortened attention span and distractibility, are also symptoms of children who are developmentally slow.
11. d Internalized behavior disorders often are undetected because the child does not act out or stand out in the classroom.
12. b Learned helplessness is a negative by-product of well-intentioned overhelping.
13. c Language or expressive disorders involve problems with understanding or using language to express ideas.
14. a Gifted and talented students are often quite bright and creative but they are often uninterested in details.
15. b Acceleration programs emphasize depth versus breadth.
16. a Strategy training attempts to develop students' awareness of their own mental processes.
17. a Parents are guaranteed access to all tests and test results by IDEA.
18. d Students for whom English is not their first language should be tested in their native language.
19. c Sole use of only one test, such as an intelligence test, is forbidden by the provisions of IDEA.
20. a An independent evaluation is guaranteed by IDEA.
21. d Not only should Samone's parents sign the IEP, they should have been involved in its design.
22. a Teachers often mistake neatness and conformity for being gifted and talented.
23. a All of these are considered students with exceptionalities.
24. d Boys are much more likely to be diagnosed as AD/HD than girls.
25. d Basically the same methods and strategies that work in the regular classroom are also effective with students with exceptionalities.

CHAPTER 6: BEHAVIORISM AND SOCIAL COGNITIVE THEORY

Chapter Outline_____

I.   Behaviorist views of learning
    A.   What is behaviorism?
    B.   Classical conditioning
        1.   Classical conditioning in the classroom
        2.   Generalization and discrimination
        3.   Extinction
    C.   Operant conditioning
        1.   Reinforcement
            a.   Positive reinforcement
            b.   Negative reinforcement
            c.   Shaping
            d.   Reinforcement schedules
            e.   Extinction
            f.   Satiation
        2.   Punishment
            a.   Using punishment effectively
            b.   Ineffective forms of punishment
        3.   The influence of antecedents on behavior
            a.   Environmental conditions
            b.   Prompts and cues
            c.   Generalization and discrimination
    D.   Behaviorism in the classroom: Applied behavior analysis
        1.   Steps in applied behavior analysis
            a.   Identify target behaviors
            b.   Establish a baseline
            c.   Choose reinforcers and punishers
            d.   Measure changes in behavior
            e.   Reduce frequency of reinforcers
        2.   Functional analysis
    E.   Putting behaviorism into perspective
II. Social cognitive theory
    A.   Comparing behaviorism and social cognitive theory
        1.   Definition of learning
        2.   The role of expectations
        3.   Reciprocal causation
    B.   Modeling
        1.   Cognitive modeling
    C.   Vicarious learning
    D.   Nonoccurrence of expected consequences
    E.   Functions of modeling
        1.   Learning new behaviors
        2.   Facilitating existing behaviors
        3.   Changing inhibitions
        4.   Arousing emotions
    F.   Processes involved in learning from models
    G.   Effectiveness of models
    H.   Self-regulation
        1.   Setting goals
        2.   Monitoring progress
        3.   Self-assessment
        4.   Self-reinforcement
        5.   Cognitive behavior modification

Chapter Objectives

- Identify examples of classical conditioning concepts in events in and outside of classrooms.

- Identify examples of operant conditioning concepts in classroom activities.

- Use social cognitive theory concepts, such as the nonoccurrence of expected consequences, reciprocal causation, and vicarious learning, to explain examples of people's behaviors.

- Identify examples of social cognitive theory concepts, such as types of modeling, modeling outcomes, effectiveness of models, and self-regulation in people's behaviors.

- Identify examples of behaviorist and social cognitive theory concepts in teachers' work with students having diverse backgrounds.

Chapter Overview

The first section of your text focused on the learner and learner characteristics. We now turn to the first of four chapters devoted to the learning process itself. As you study your text and work your way through this study guide, keep the following question in mind: "How does the information I'm studying explain the way people learn and how they behave?" This question can serve as a reference point or "hook" to which the ideas you study can be attached.

Behaviorism is a view of learning that focuses on the relationships between observable behavior and experience. It doesn't consider internal processes, such as expectations, beliefs, insight, or perception; nor does it consider needs such as self-esteem or belonging to social groups. Classical and operant conditioning are two parts of behaviorism.

Social cognitive theory explains how watching others' behaviors influences our own thoughts, emotions, and behavior. Social cognitive theory differs from behaviorism in its emphasis on mental processes, such as beliefs and expectations, and in recognizing that learners both influence and are influenced by their environments.

Modeling refers to behavioral, cognitive, and affective changes derived from observing the behavior of others. People are likely to imitate the behavior of models that have high status or models they perceive as competent or similar to themselves.

Vicarious conditioning is the process of observing the consequences of another person's behavior and adjusting our behavior accordingly. For instance, when a student is openly praised for diligent work, other students' diligence is likely to increase; the first student is positively reinforced and serves as a model for the others, and the others are vicariously reinforced.

Application Exercises_____

We encourage you to first write your responses to each of the exercises below, and then check your answers with the feedback that immediately follows the exercises.

Exercise 6.1

Look at Items 1 through 3. If the behavior described in the italicized portion of the example is primarily the result of learning, put an L in the space in front of the example. Otherwise leave the space blank.

_____ 1. Mrs. Smith is doing a demonstration with air pressure and blows up a balloon. The balloon bursts, and Cathy, sitting in the front row, *jerks her head back.*

_____ 2. Ronnie, age 8, is going in for some booster shots. He *cries* when he sees the nurse with the needle.

_____ 3. Donnell, a senior, wants to be a good football player. He was a bit slow last year, running a 5.4 sec 40 yd dash. He lifted weights all summer, and to his pleasure, he now runs a *4.9-sec 40-yd dash.*

Read the following case study.

Duranna is a conscientious and good student, although she is a bit unsure of herself. She's typically very attentive in class, and her classmates regard her as someone who will usually be able to answer questions.

One day, Mr. Harkness, her American history teacher, was conducting a question and answer session, and Duranna jerked when she heard her name called, suddenly realizing that she hadn't heard the question. A couple of the boys giggled as Mr. Harkness stared at her. Her stomach clenched, and she felt her face turn red. She started to stammer, then fell silent.

Now Duranna is uneasy whenever Mr. Harkness starts calling on students in class, and she doesn't like geometry as well as she did either, because she never knows when Mrs. Drake might call on her. She's relieved when she's in the safe confines of Spanish class, where Mrs. Lopez always calls on students in order up and down each row.

Consider this scenario as an example of classical conditioning and identify each of the following from it.

4. Unconditioned stimulus

5. Unconditioned response

6. Conditioned stimulus

7. Conditioned response

8. Generalization

9. Discrimination

10. Think about the concept of extinction. Describe how Mr. Harkness could help Duranna eliminate her conditioned response, that is, help it become extinct.

Exercise 6.2

Read the following scenario and answer the questions that follow it.

Miguel is an inquiring student who asks good, probing questions in class, and the other students seem to appreciate him because his questions often help clear up some of their uncertainties. However, Miguel's questioning periodically makes Mr. Orr uneasy because he doesn't always have the answers.

One day when Miguel started to ask his fourth question in a row, Mr. Orr responded derisively: "Well, look at the brain. He's at it again."

Miguel stopped in mid-sentence.

During class a couple days later, Miguel asked one question and raised his hand to ask another. Mr. Orr looked at him and sneered, "Let's hear from the brain again."

The following day, Miguel quietly took notes the entire period.

1.   Explain Miguel's behavior (his question asking). Use information from the case study to defend your answer.

2.   Explain Mr. Orr's behavior (his sarcasm). Use information from the case study to defend your answer.

3.   A teacher says to her students, "All right, as soon as you've finished identifying the longitude and latitude of the five cities I've given you, you can begin your map projects." For the Premack Principle to be in effect, what must be true about the students' attitudes toward map work compared to longitude and latitude problems?

Exercise 6.3

Read each of the following short case studies. For each, select from the concepts—*generalization, discrimination, potency, punishment, fixed-interval reinforcement, variable-interval reinforcement, variable-ratio reinforcement, satiation, extinction,* and *shaping*—the one that is most clearly illustrated in the example. In each case, explain the illustration.

1.   Mrs. Thornton arrives at the door of her classroom at 7:35 a.m. She takes out her key, puts it in the lock, and attempts to open the door. The door won't budge. "Hmm," she says to herself. "That's never happened before." She jiggles the key a couple more times, and then heads for the workroom to try and find a janitor.

2.   Mrs. Green's fifth grade class is studying insects. They've examined grasshoppers, beetles, a roach, and a water strider. "Hey!" Mary exclaimed while looking at a spider. "This isn't an insect."

3.   Ken, a senior, wants to be as well prepared as possible for college. He's taking analytic geometry, even though math is not his strong suit, and he plans to major in a foreign language in college. He studied very hard for his first analytic geometry test and got a low C. He tried hard on the second test too, but it came back a D. He's having a difficult time trying now and is spending less time on the homework. He studied only haphazardly for his last test.

4.   "I always give partial credit at the beginning of the year," Jane Howe, a geometry teacher, commented. "The kids have so much trouble with proofs. As time goes on, I make them do more to earn points on the problems, and by the end of the year, they have to get the whole thing right for any credit."

5.   "I'm quitting sending notes home to parents," Mrs. Starke, a fourth grade teacher, commented to a colleague in the teachers' lounge one day. "We had a workshop in which we were encouraged to write positive notes to send home when the kids are good. I tried it, and the children responded for a while. Now they hardly react, and the notes don't seem to affect their behavior. I even saw one child throw the note away rather than take it home."

6.   Steve Weiss, a chemistry teacher, gives his students one problem each day when they come to class that counts five points on their overall quiz grade for the 9 weeks. "Generally, they're doing well," he noted. "I always give back their papers the next day, and they're about to the point where they like it. They ask me stuff like, 'Is this going to be another easy one today?'"

Exercise 6.4

1.   Think about the children's story about the three little pigs. What form of modeling—*direct, symbolic,* or *synthesized*—is demonstrated in the story? What happens to the reader when the two lazy little pigs are eaten by the wolf? Explain. When the conscientious little pig outwits the wolf, what effect on behavior is this intended to have on the reader? Explain.

2.   Think about the book *A Tale of Two Cities*. We described it in Chapter 3 as a piece of literature that has a moral dilemma embedded in it. Explain the dilemma in its effect on readers using the concepts of *vicarious reinforcement* and *vicarious punishment* when the character Sidney Carton chooses to die in his friend's place. What form of modeling is demonstrated by Sidney Carton?

Exercise 6.5

Read the following case study and answer the questions that follow.

Juanita Holmes was working with her seventh grade geography students on specifying geographical locations. They knew the concepts of longitude and latitude and could read the numbers on a map. She stood next to a large world map.

"Look at the map, everyone," she began. "Today we're learning an important skill that we'll use throughout the course. To start, let's find ourselves. Where do we look first? Jody?"

"We're in the United States," Jody responded. "It's right there," she continued, pointing.

"Good," Juanita smiled. "Now let's be more precise."

She had the students locate their state and city and went on.

"Next we're going to locate another city. Name a famous city."

Several examples were suggested, and she decided on Mexico City.

"Now watch," she commanded. "I'm looking at these numbers up here. They're what? Karen?"

". . . Longitude."

"Excellent, Karen. Now look, everyone. I'm going to find one that runs as close to Mexico City as possible. Here we go," and she traced a line from the top of the map through Mexico City with her finger.

"It's very close to 100 degrees," she noted, pointing to the number at the top. "We see we're west of England, where we said the zero line of longitude is, so Mexico City is 100 degrees west longitude."

She repeated the process to find Mexico City's latitude.

"Give me another city," she continued. Settling on Chicago, she said, "Okay. Put your own maps on your desk." After waiting a few seconds, she asked, "What is its longitude? Joanie?"

". . . It looks like it's about 88^0."

She smiled at Joan. "Okay. West or east? . . . Jack?"

". . . West."

Juanita continued the process, helping the students locate Chicago's latitude and then the location of Paris. Finally, she had them work independently to locate three more cities, saying that they would get five points on their homework grade for correctly identifying all three.

Analyze Juanita's lesson as an example of applying social cognitive theory in the classroom by identifying each of the four processes involved in learning from models.

1.   Attention

2.   Retention

3.   Reproduction

4.   Motivation

Exercise 6.6

Read the following case study and answer the questions that follow.

  Joe, a junior high teacher, has a faculty meeting every Wednesday at 2:00 p.m. One week, Karen, the assistant principal, arrived for the meeting at 1:55 p.m. with overheads and handouts, ready to go. Joe got up from his classroom desk at 1:55, prepared for the meeting. As he stepped out into the hall, he glanced through the lounge doorway and saw four faculty members sitting and working. "I'll wait for them to walk by," he said to himself, and he sat back down and scored some more tests. The four walked by at about 2:10, so he went to the meeting. Everyone was there and settled by 2:15, and the meeting began.
  The next week, the meeting again got started at about 2:15, and the following week at about 2:20.
  The fourth week, Joe was in his office at 2:15 on Wednesday when his friend Sue walked by. "Aren't you coming to the meeting?" she asked.
  "I'll be there in a minute," Joe responded with a smile, as he always did in response to a question. He came to the meeting at 2:25.

1.   Identify an example of modeling in the scenario.

2.   We see that Joe started going to the meetings later and later. Which concept from operant conditioning—*positive reinforcement, negative reinforcement, presentation punishment* or *removal punishment*—best explains why he is going later? How do you know it is that concept?

Feedback for Application Exercises_____

Exercise 6.1

1. Cathy jerking her head back in response to the bursting balloon is an example of a reflex, and therefore is not a learned behavior.

2. Ronnie's crying is a learned behavior, based on previous negative experiences with needles or other experiences associated with needles. (People are not instinctively or reflexively afraid of needles.)

3. Donnell's increased speed is primarily the result of his improved strength and physical conditioning rather than the result of learning.

4. The unconditioned stimulus is the situation that caused the embarrassing experience. This situation is a combination of being called on, being stared at, and the boys giggling. We can't be sure of the exact combination of the factors. It could be any one of them, two of them, or all three.

5. The unconditioned response was Duranna's stomach clenching and her face turning red. (This is a reflexive response to the situation.)

6. The conditioned stimulus is an environment in which students are being questioned. It has become associated with the initial embarrassing situation.

7. Duranna's uneasiness is the conditioned response. Notice that uneasiness is a response that is similar to the unconditioned response—stomach clenching and face turning red.

Notice that the conditioned and unconditioned stimuli are not necessarily related in any way (just as Pavlov's assistants and the meat powder are not related), but they become associated. The conditioned and unconditioned stimuli are similar or identical (similar in Duranna's case; identical for Pavlov's dogs).

8. Her uneasiness has now generalized to geometry because the environment there is similar to the environment in American history.

9. Duranna discriminates between Spanish, where the questioning is patterned, and American history and geometry, where the process has been anxiety inducing.

10. Mr. Harkness needs to call on Duranna in a situation where he is certain that she is not taken by surprise. After Duranna is called on several times without incident (the conditioned stimulus occurring repeatedly in the absence of the unconditioned stimulus), her uneasiness should begin to disappear. He also needs to make and enforce a rule that forbids students from laughing at each other's embarrassment.

Exercise 6.2

1. Miguel is being punished for speaking out in class, which is evidenced by the decreasing incidence of question-asking behavior. This is a form of presentation punishment, since an undesired consequence is being given, rather than something desirable being taken away.

2. Mr. Orr's behavior is being negatively reinforced. Miguel's questions make him uncomfortable since he can't always answer them. His sarcasm stops Miguel's behavior which removes an aversive stimulus (being asked questions he may not be able to answer). As a result we see his sarcasm increasing.

3. For this statement to be true, the students would have to prefer doing map work rather than longitude and latitude problems. The map work (the preferred activity) could then be used as a reinforcer for the less preferred activity (doing longitude and latitude problems).

Exercise 6.3

1. The concept is *extinction*—the rapid reduction in behavior after a continuous reinforcement schedule. Normally, the door opens every time (continuous reinforcement) as evidenced by Mrs. Thornton's comment, "That's never happened before." The door opening each time is a reinforcer for putting the key in and attempting to open the door. This time when it didn't open, Mrs. Thornton quickly gave up, which is characteristic of behavior when a continuous reinforcement schedule is used and the reinforcers are removed. If the door had been "balky," meaning she had to struggle to get it open (an intermittent schedule) she would have persevered longer.

2. The concept being demonstrated in this example is *discrimination*. Mary is discriminating between the spider and the other animals, which are insects.

3. The example illustrates *punishment* (specifically *presentation punishment*). Ken is receiving something that is reducing his behavior. (To clarify how this answer is different from extinction, look again in your text. In the example in the text, Renita received nothing for her efforts—no reinforcer or punisher. Ken, in contrast, received the low grade.)

4. Mrs. Howe is making an effort to shape her students' behavior by reinforcing behaviors that are successive approximations of the desired behavior.

5. The case study is an example of *satiation*. Mrs. Starke has apparently sent too many positive notes home to the point that they've lost their potency as reinforcers.

6. Mr. Weiss was applying a *fixed interval schedule* of reinforcement to his classroom. While this can have disadvantages, as discussed in the text of the chapter, his giving a problem every day kept the interval short, so student effort remained high. This is not an example of continuous reinforcement, because not every studying behavior is reinforced. The students are reinforced on the interval of one day.

Exercise 6.4

1. The story is a form of *symbolic modeling*. When the two lazy little pigs get eaten, the readers are vicariously punished; the readers observe the consequences of the little pigs' actions, and perhaps adjust their own behavior accordingly. When the conscientious little pig outwits the wolf, the readers are vicariously reinforced. The effect on behavior that this is intended to have is to facilitate existing behaviors. The students know how to be conscientious, and the combination of the symbolic modeling of the conscientious little pig and vicarious reinforcement is intended to increase conscientiousness.

2. Readers are caught in a dilemma between vicarious reinforcement and vicarious punishment. They are vicariously reinforced through Sidney Carton's noble act, but they are vicariously punished through the fact that he gave his life under the guillotine. It is a form of symbolic modeling.

Exercise 6.5

1. *Attention* is illustrated in the case study when Juanita pulled down a map, referred the students to it and had them find themselves on it. She then asked for another city.

2. She promoted *retention* by modeling the process of finding the location of longitude and latitude. She continued the process until she found Mexico City's longitude and latitude.

3. The process of *reproduction* began when she asked Joanie to locate the longitude of Chicago. This continued through the locations of each city.

4. Motivation was illustrated in several places. She began the lesson by explaining that the skill was an important one, used throughout the course. During the course of the lesson she reinforced with comments like, "Good", and "Excellent." Finally, students received points for completing their homework.

Exercise 6.6

1. Modeling occurred when Joe saw his colleagues sitting and working and then sat back down and began scoring some more tests.

2. Joe is being negatively reinforced for coming late. His "going later" behavior is increasing—he is going later and later, so it is an example of reinforcement. Under "normal" conditions he would go to the meeting at 2:00 p.m. By going later and later he is avoiding the meeting, so he is being negatively reinforced for going later and later.

Self-Help Quiz_____

TRUE/FALSE QUESTIONS. Write T in the blank if the statement is true, and write F if the statement is false.

_____ 1. For operantly conditioned behaviors the influence of the environment (stimulus) precedes the behavior, but for classically conditioned behaviors it follows the behavior.

_____ 2. Operantly conditioned behaviors must be reinforced to prevent extinction, but classically conditioned behaviors do not become extinct.

_____ 3. Generalization occurs with operantly conditioned behaviors but not with classically conditioned behaviors.

_____ 4. While positive reinforcement is an increase in behavior, negative reinforcement is a decrease in behavior.

_____ 5. When classically conditioned learning takes place, the unconditioned and the conditioned stimuli will be similar to each other.

MULTIPLE-CHOICE ITEMS. Circle the best response in each case.

6. You're anticipating taking a test from an instructor with a reputation for being "tough." As you wait for the test, you feel jittery and your mouth is dry. Your jitters and dry mouth are best described as:
    a. unconditioned stimuli.
    b. conditioned stimuli.
    c. unconditioned responses.
    d. conditioned responses.

7. Mr. Powell's students are getting a bit rowdy as the end of the day nears. He comments, "If the trash around your desks isn't picked up, and if you're not quiet in one minute, we'll be spending 10 minutes after school." The students immediately pick up the papers around their desk and are sitting quietly as the bell rings. Mr. Powell's technique would be best described as:
    a. negative reinforcement.
    b. presentation punishment.
    c. removal punishment.
    d. discrimination.
    e. satiation.

8. Mr. Allen tries to be judicious in praising his students. He wants to praise them enough but not too much. To implement this process, he praises his students when he feels like they give an insightful response or a response reflecting considerable effort. His schedule would be best described as:
    a. continuous.
    b. fixed ratio.
    c. variable ratio.
    d. fixed interval.
    e. variable interval.

9. Mr. Allen's desire (in item 8) to give "enough praise" but not "too much" indicates that he's aware of two concepts. The two concepts are best described as:
    a. potency and satiation.
    b. potency and extinction.
    c. generalization and discrimination.
    d. extinction and satiation.
    e. generalization and extinction.

10. In a lesson on place value, Kim sees the numbers 42 and 24 and says, "In the first number the four is in the tens column, and in the second it's in the ones column." Kim's comment best illustrates which of the following?
    a. Classical conditioning
    b. Discrimination
    c. Generalization
    d. Vicarious conditioning

11. In item 10, Kim's learning would be best classified in which of the following categories?
    a. Contiguity
    b. Classical conditioning
    c. Operant conditioning
    d. Symbolic modeling

12. Joanne is being disruptive in Mrs. Henderson's class. Exasperated, Mrs. Henderson tells Joanne to pull her desk out into the hall and sit there until she is told otherwise. Mrs. Henderson's technique is best describe as an attempt to administer:
    a. negative reinforcement.
    b. presentation punishment.
    c. removal punishment.
    d. vicarious punishment.

13. Two of your students are whispering instead of doing their assigned seatwork. You go to them and tell them to stop whispering. They comply. This incident best illustrates:
    a. negative reinforcement.
    b. presentation punishment.
    c. removal punishment.
    d. satiation.

14. Mr. Parker comments to his second graders as they are beginning a seat work assignment, "I'm very pleased to see that Debbie is already working and has finished the first two problems." Mr. Parker's comment is best described as an attempt to implement which of the following with his class?
    a. Positive reinforcement
    b. Negative reinforcement
    c. Vicarious reinforcement
    d. The Premack Principle

15. Which of the following most accurately describes Mr. Parker's behavior in Item 14?
    a. He is attempting to be a model for both Debbie and the rest of the students.
    b. He is attempting to be a model for Debbie but not necessarily be a model for the rest of the students.
    c. He is attempting to be a model for the rest of the students but not necessarily be a model for Debbie.
    d. He is attempting to use Debbie as a model for the rest of the students.

Use the following example for items 16 and 17.

Tim is in kindergarten. His mother takes him to school. Tim is happy when his mother is there but is upset when she leaves. Mr. Soo begins to talk and joke with Tim while his mother is there, and now Tim is satisfied when his mother leaves.

Consider this situation to be a case of classical conditioning.

16. The unconditioned stimulus would be:
   a. the school.
   b. Mr. Soo talking and joking with Tim.
   c. Tim's mother.
   d. happiness.
   e. upset.

17. The unconditioned response would be:
   a. the school.
   b. happiness.
   c. upset.
   d. satisfaction.
   e. Tim's mother.

Use the following example for items 18 and 19.

Martina is very uneasy in anticipating the beginning of her junior high school experience. Sensing her uneasiness, her dad drove her to school the first morning. They have a close relationship, and Martina feels very warm when she's with him. Martina's dad dropped her off at school, and she walked uncertainly into her home room. As she came through the door, Mrs. Hafner smiled broadly, put her arm around Martina and said, "Welcome to our school. Your records tell us that you're new here. I know you're going to like it." Martina felt instant relief. Mrs. Hafner proved to be consistent in her manner. Now, as she goes into the school each day, Martina is quite at ease.

18. The best illustration of the conditioned stimulus would be:
   a. the school.
   b. Mrs. Hafner's warmth.
   c. feeling at ease.
   d. feeling instant relief.

19. The conditioned response would be:
   a. the warm feeling she has with her father.
   b. relief.
   c. Mrs. Hafner's manner.
   d. feeling at ease.

Use the following example for items 20 and 21.

"This test was impossible. They're always so tricky," Mr. Tuff's students complain as he finishes his discussion of a test he had just handed back. "And they're so long," they continue.

Mr. Tuff then consciously makes his next test easier and shorter, hoping his students won't complain so much. He gives the test, scores it, and returns it.

"Not again," some students comment about half way through the discussion of the test. "Yes, you must love to write tricky items," some others add.

Again, in preparing his next test, he reduces the application level of the items and makes the test still shorter.

20. In its impact on Mr. Tuff's behavior, the case study best illustrates:
    a. positive reinforcement.
    b. negative reinforcement.
    c. presentation punishment.
    d. removal punishment.
    e. a conditioned response.

21. In its impact on the students' behavior, the case study best illustrates:
    a. positive reinforcement.
    b. negative reinforcement.
    c. presentation punishment.
    d. removal punishment.
    e. a conditioned response.

22. Mrs. Batton gets up from her reading group every few minutes to go and circulate among the students who are doing seatwork to offer encouragement. In its influence on the behavior of the students doing seatwork, her actions best illustrate an application of:
    a. fixed-interval reinforcement.
    b. variable-interval reinforcement.
    c. variable-ratio reinforcement.
    d. vicarious reinforcement.

23. Your instructor assigns a written project to be turned in and says that it will be graded. You work conscientiously on the project, but your friend does a haphazard job the night before it is due. The instructor simply puts a check mark on the project, indicating that it has been turned in, and you and your friend each receive 5 points for having done the project. Based on social cognitive theory, which of the following best explains the outcome of yours and your friend's behaviors?
    a. You are both reinforced since you both received credit for having completed the project.
    b. You are both punished, since the instructor gave you points instead of a letter grade.
    c. You are being directly reinforced because you worked hard on the project, whereas your friend is being vicariously reinforced since he or she worked less hard.
    d. You are being punished, whereas your friend is being reinforced, since you got the same number of points on the project.

24. In a question and answer session, Mr. Hanson says, "Now what is the first step in the problem, Jimmy?"

". . . I'm not sure," Jimmy responds after sitting and looking at the problem for several seconds.

"Help him out, Kelly," Mr. Hanson smiles.

"We first must find the common denominator," Kelly answers. Later in the lesson, Mr. Hanson is examining another problem.

"OK, now what do we do? Jimmy?"

"I don't know," Jimmy says after glancing at the problem.

"Help him out once more, Kelly," Mr. Hanson says supportively.

   a) Explain Jimmy's behavior, identifying the specific concept or concepts from behaviorism that best apply. (Support your statements with evidence from the example.)
   b) What is Jimmy likely to do the next time he is called on?
   c) Describe what Mr. Hanson might have done differently that would have been more effective.

25. A middle-aged man who has become a little rotund would like to get in shape but is very uneasy about going to a fitness center, since he has long ago lost his "athletic appearance." At the urging of friend, he finally goes to a fitness club near where he lives just to take a look.

Upon arriving at the club he is surprised to see several people about his age and build laboring over the machines and free weights. The man is now consistently working out.

Using social cognitive theory, provide a detailed and complete explanation for the man's behavior (the fact that he is now working out). Include in your explanation:
   1) the form of modeling—direct, symbolic, or synthesized
   2) the effect of modeling on behavior—learning a new behavior, facilitating an existing behavior, changing an inhibition, or arousing an emotion.
   3) an explanation for why the models were effective.

Self-Help Quiz Answers_____

1. f
2. f
3. f
4. f
5. f
6. d   You are displaying a conditioned response. (Remember, an unconditioned response is unlearned. We don't respond reflexively or instinctively to tests.)
7. a   The students displayed the desired behavior (picking up the trash and sitting quietly). Notice also that while Mr. Powell threatened the students with punishment, he didn't actually punish them.
8. c   The students are praised based on their responses, and they are praised on an unpredictable basis.
9. a   Mr. Allen is trying to maintain his praise as potent reinforcers. Too much praise could lead to satiation, which means that the praise could lose its potency.
10. b   Kim is discriminating between the 10's place and the units place.
11. c   Kim had been reinforced for discriminating between the two. The behavior is more complex than simple contiguity, it is a voluntary response, so it can't be classical conditioning, and while we don't have evidence that no modeling took place, it is unlikely that the modeling would be on film or in cartoons.
12. c   Joanne is being removed from the classroom, and she is put in a situation where presumably she is unable to get positive reinforcement.
13. b   The students were given something (your reprimand), which decreased their behavior.
14 c   Mr. Parker is attempting to vicariously reinforce the class by directly reinforcing Debbie, and using her as a model for the rest of the class.
15. d   (See the feedback for item 14.)

16. c   Tim is already happy with his mother. (This analysis is based on the assumption that children's love for their parents is innate.)

17. b   (See the feedback for item 16.)

18. a   Mrs. Hafner's warmth is an unconditioned stimulus which resulted in the unconditioned response—relief. The school becomes associated with Mrs. Hafner's warmth, so it is the conditioned stimulus. (Martina's father merely drops her off. As a result, neither Mrs. Hafner nor the school have become associated with him, so he is not the unconditioned stimulus. Notice how this situation is different from the one with Tim, his mother, and Mr. Soo. In that case Mr. Soo became associated with Tim's mother, because they all stood together and talked. In that problem, Mr. Soo becomes the conditioned stimulus and satisfaction is the conditioned response.)

19. d   Martina feels at ease when she enters the school, so this feeling is the conditioned response. Notice that this is a response to the school. As we saw in item 18, the school is the conditioned stimulus.

20. c   His behavior is being reduced—he reduces the length and difficulty of the test, so it is punishment. The students are presenting him with their complaints. (The behavior is voluntary, so it is not a conditioned response.)

21. b   An aversive stimulus—the length and difficulty of the test—is being reduced, so the students' complaints are being negatively reinforced. (Their complaints occur sooner, so their complaining behavior is increasing.)

22. b   Her encouragement is a form of reinforcement, and "every few minutes" is a variable interval.

23. d   This situation is best explained through "nonoccurrence of expected consequences." You expect to receive more credit for your hard work than your friend should receive, since you worked harder. This doesn't occur, so the nonoccurrence serves as a punisher for you. The exact opposite occurs for your friend.

24. a)   Since Jimmy's behavior is increasing—he says "I don't know," sooner the second time than he did the first time, he is being reinforced. The reinforcer is Mr. Hanson "removing" the question from him (taking him off the "hook"), so it is an example of negative reinforcement.

     b)   Jimmy is likely to say, "I don't know," even sooner than he did before.

     c)   Mr. Hanson should give Jimmy some prompts or cues that will allow him to answer instead of turning the question to another student.

25.   *Direct modeling* is illustrated—the man directly observes others working out. The situation illustrates the effectiveness of *perceived similarity*—the other people he observes are similar in age and build, and the effect on behavior is *facilitating an existing behavior*. (Changing inhibitions refers to socially unacceptable behavior, so we wouldn't conclude that his inhibitions about working out have been reduced.)

CHAPTER 7: COGNITIVE VIEWS OF LEARNING

Chapter Outline_____

I. Cognitive perspectives on Learning
   A. Principles of cognitive learning theory
     1. Learners are mentally active
     2. Learning and development depend on learners' experiences
     3. Learners construct knowledge
     4. Knowledge that is constructed depends on learners' prior knowledge
     5. Learning is enhanced in a social environment
     6. Learning requires practice and feedback
   B. A definition of learning
II. Memory stores in our information processing system
   A. Sensory Memory
   B. Working Memory
     1. Limitations of working memory
     2. Reducing cognitive load: Overcoming the limitations of working memory
       a. Chunking
       b. Automaticity
       c. Dual processing
   C. Long-Term Memory
     1. Representing declarative knowledge in memory: Schemas
       a. Meaningfulness: Reducing cognitive load on working memory
       b. Meaningfulness and cognitive load: Implications for learning and teaching
       c. Schemas as scripts
     2. Representing procedural knowledge in memory: Conditions and actions
       a. Developing procedural knowledge
       b. Developing procedural knowledge: Implications for learning and teaching
III. Cognitive processes in our information processing system
   A. Attention: The beginning of information processing
     1. Attracting and maintaining attention
   B. Perception: Finding meaning in stimuli
   C. Rehearsal: Retaining information through repetition
   D. Meaningful encoding: Making connections in long-term memory
     1. Organization: Representing relationships in content
     2. Imagery: Applying dual-coding theory
     3. Elaboration: Extending understanding
     4. Activity: Capitalizing on a learning principle
   E. Forgetting
     1. Forgetting as interference
     2. Forgetting as retrieval failure
IV. Metacognition: Knowledge and control of cognitive processes
   A. The development of metacognition
V. Information processing in the classroom: Instructional principles
   A. The impact of diversity on information processing
     1. Diversity and perception
     2. Diversity, encoding, and retrieval
     3. Instructional adaptations for background diversity
   B. Putting information processing into perspective

Chapter Objectives_____

- Describe the principles on which cognitive learning theories are based, and identify illustrations of the principles.

- Use the characteristics of the memory stores in our information processing system to explain events in and outside the classroom.

- Describe the cognitive processes in our information processing system, and identify examples of the processes in classroom events.

- Define metacognition, and identify examples of metacognition in classroom events.

- Describe the principles for applying information processing theory in classrooms, and identify examples of the principles in learning activities.

Chapter Overview_____

In Chapter 6 we saw that behaviorists focus on observable behaviors that are influenced by experience. We also analyzed learning from a social cognitive perspective, focusing on mental processes such as beliefs and expectations that learners use as they observe others' actions. Now, we continue our focus on cognitive views of learning, and we begin with information processing, a theory that stresses information stores "in people's heads" together with cognitive processes, such as *attention, perception,* and *encoding,* that move information from one store to another. We can't directly observe these information stores and cognitive processes so we create a model to help us visualize how information moves through the system, much in the same way as we create models to help us visualize the structure of atoms and molecules.

Our information processing system is composed of information stores–in which knowledge is housed; cognitive processes–which move information from one store to another; and metacognition–which is knowledge of and control over our cognitive processes.

Metacognition is developmental; for example, older learners are better than younger ones at directing their attention toward important information (a form of meta-attention) and using strategies to encode information into long-term memory (a form of metamemory). Metacognition is very important in learning; learners who are aware of the way they learn and make an effort to capitalize on the ways that they learn best achieve more than learners who aren't as metacognitive.

Meaningfulness can be increased, and encoding made more efficient, if information is carefully organized, if new learning is consciously attached to old through elaboration in the form of reviews, comparisons, and the use of examples, and if learners are put in active roles during learning activities.

Effective teachers present information in small pieces, question students to check their comprehension, and help them integrate new understanding and existing background knowledge with additional questioning and interaction. They also provide students with many opportunities to practice, so that as much of their procedural knowledge as possible becomes automatic.

Application Exercises_____

We encourage you to first write your responses to each of the exercises below, and then check your answers with the feedback that immediately follows the exercises.

Exercise 7.1

1. Identify at least two characteristics that behaviorism and cognitive learning theory have in common and at least two others that they do not.

2. A pre-algebra teacher has written the following on the chalkboard:

    4 + 5(7 - 3) - 9/3

    She then asks, "What are we going to do first to simplify this expression? What is important to remember whenever we simplify something like this?" Criticize her questioning based on your understanding of sensory memory.

3. Describe a simple alternative to improve the teacher's questioning illustrated in Item 2.

4. You are introducing a unit on the Far East in your world history class. You present information outlining the impact of religion on life in Japan in the early 20th century, exploitation by the British and other Western nations, the indignation Japan felt after World War I, Japan's overpopulation and scarce natural resources in the 1920s and 1930s, and how all these factors led to Japan's decision to attack the United States. The students seem interested, watching you attentively as you present the information.

    However, the next day when you begin your review of the previous day's information, it's as if they hadn't listened after all. Using your understanding of working memory as a basis, explain why this might have happened.

5. Based on what we know about working memory, why is a textbook an important supplement to teacher lectures?

6. Two high school teachers were discussing their classes. The physics teacher commented, "I'm having a terrible time. The kids seem to understand the problems when I explain them, but they get wrapped up in their algebra when they try to do the problems on their own, so they wind up confused."

    Relate the physics teacher's description to our discussion of working memory, and explain why her students are having difficulty. Include the concept of automaticity in your explanation.

7. Students with good vocabularies have two important advantages in listening to lectures over those whose vocabularies are limited. What are these advantages? Explain.

8. When students perform each of the following, which type of knowledge–declarative or procedural–is primarily being demonstrated? Explain.
    a. State that Abraham Lincoln was the president of the United States during the Civil War.
    b. Ride a bicycle.
    c. State that isosceles triangles have two equal sides.
    d. Identify isosceles triangles in a group of plane figures.
    e. Calculate the areas of a right triangle and an isosceles triangle.

9.   Consider these definitions:
     a.   Common nouns are parts of speech that name persons, places, and things.
     b.   Proper nouns name specific persons, places, and things.

     Create a schema that would incorporate the two definitions.

Exercise 7.2

Look at the topics and describe lesson beginnings that could be used to attract the students' attention and pull them into the lesson. (A variety of lesson beginnings are possible. Suggest at least two different ways of beginning each.)

1.   You are beginning a unit on longitude and latitude in your geography class.

2.   You want your students to understand the rule for punctuating possessive nouns–a singular possessive uses an apostrophe-*s*, and a plural possessive uses only an apostrophe if the plural noun ends in *s* and an apostrophe-*s* if the plural noun does not end in *s*.

3.   You are beginning a lesson on the skeletal system with your science students.

Exercise 7.3

1.   You have taught your students about direct and indirect objects and you begin a review by writing the following sentence on the chalkboard:

     Kathy handed Tim the papers.

     What question could you now ask that would be an effective way of diagnosing the students' perceptions? (Be specific. Either write down or say to yourself the exact question you would ask.)

2.   Explain why teachers are discouraged from sitting down or standing behind a podium when they teach, based on the characteristics of our information processing system.

3.   What is the simplest and most effective way a teacher can check the accuracy of student perceptions?

4.   Read the following case study and explain the difference in the two teachers' reactions based on your understanding of factors that influence perception in processing information.

     Two young teachers were interviewed by a principal for jobs at the same school. (There were two openings, so they each hoped to get a job.) They were very excited about the prospect of working together, so they went to lunch and discussed their respective interviews.
     "How was it?" Marianne asked.
     "Awful," Katarina responded. "He grilled me and made me feel like I was the dumbest thing in the world. How about you?"
     "I thought mine went really well," Marianne said tentatively, with a puzzled look on her face. "He asked me a lot of questions, but it seemed to me that he was just trying to see if I knew what I wanted from teaching."
     "I should never have applied for this job," Katarina continued disconsolately. "Donna (a friend of hers who teaches at the school) warned me about this guy. After today, I don't think I could ever work for him."
     "Gosh, I'm really looking forward to it," Marianne responded. "I went to a workshop last week on what to do in an interview. They said we'd be asked a lot of questions, and it's the interviewer's way of finding out how we think, so I guess I was sort of ready for it."

5. Suppose we look up a telephone number, follow it by looking up several others, and find that we cannot remember the first one. Offer two different explanations for why we cannot remember the first number.

6. Think again about the rule, "A singular possessive uses an apostrophe-*s*, and a plural possessive uses only an apostrophe if the plural noun ends in *s* and an apostrophe-*s* if the plural noun does not end in *s*." Describe a context in which the rule could be taught that would aid meaningfulness and retrieval.

7. Think about Juan and Randy in David Shelton's lesson at the beginning of the chapter. We would predict that Juan would be able to retrieve information about the solar system more readily than would Randy. Explain why we would make this prediction based on the information in this section.

Exercise 7.4

1. A first- and a sixth-grade student are each asked to give directions about some building blocks to one of their classmates whose vision is blocked by a screen. Each student has a round red block, a square red block, and a blue block. The first grader is directed to tell her counterpart to put the round red block on the blue block. She responds, "Pick up the red one and put it on the blue one." Her classmate scans his display of blocks, sees two red ones, and picks one up. The sixth grader, in contrast, says, "Pick up the round red block, and put it on the blue block."

   Explain the difference in the first-grader's and the sixth-grader's directions based on developmental difference in metacognition.

2. Look at the following examples and explain what they have in common.
   a. Mrs. Jensen was giving directions for the social studies test on Friday. Marissa raised her hand and asked, "I'm sorry, but I'm not sure what you said about the second part of the test. Will it be multiple choice or essay?"

   b. Steve was doing his homework while listening to the radio. He noticed that he was periodically listening to the radio instead of focusing on his work, so he got up and turned off the radio.

   c. Claudia was studying her notes for her science test. "Why can't I remember the difference between spring tide and neap tide?" she mumbles to herself. "I'll read it once more." She then went back to her text and highlighted the description of each.

   d. A high school sophomore was up late baby-sitting on a school night and knew that she was going to have a rough time staying awake at school the next day. As she walked into her English class, she said to herself, "I'll sit in the most uncomfortable position I can, and that will keep me awake."

3. We begin the Application Exercises sections in each of the chapters with the statement, "We encourage you to first write your responses to each of the exercises below, and then check your answers with the feedback that immediately follows the exercises." Based on the factors that influence meaningful encoding, why would we so strongly emphasize that you first write your answers before checking the feedback?

4. Each of the chapters in this Study Guide begins with a detailed outline of the chapter content. With respect to meaningful encoding, what function are these outlines intended to serve?

5. Suppose you're trying to understand the concept *metacognition*. What is the most effective way to elaborate on your understanding of the concept?

Feedback for Application Exercises_____

Exercise 7.1

1. Cognitive and behavioral theories both focus on learning and they both focus on stimuli and responses. (To see how stimuli and responses exist in information processing look at the Information Processing Model first illustrated in Figure 7.2 of your text. You see "stimuli" entering sensory memory on the left side of the model, and you see "response" emerging from working memory.) Behaviorism and cognitive learning theories differ in their definition of learning–behaviorism describing learning as a change in observable behavior and cognitive theories defining learning as a change in learners' internal mental capacities, which in turn can produce a change in behavior.

2. The teacher posed the question, "What are we going to do first to simplify this expression?" and before the students had a chance to answer, she posed a second question, "What is important to remember whenever we simplify something like this?" Because information is quickly lost from sensory memory if processing doesn't begin (through attention), one of two things is likely to happen: (1) the students will attend to the first question and lose the second one from sensory memory, or (2) their attention to the first question will be disrupted by the second question, so their attention to the first one will be incomplete. Either situation decreases learning.

3. She should ask the first question, wait for a response from a student, and then ask the second question.

4. Working memory has only limited capacity. You have introduced a great deal of information in the lesson–religion, exploitation, indignation, overpopulation, scarce natural resources–and how all the details of these factors led to the Japanese attack on the United States. Since the students seemed attentive, it is likely that their working memories were overloaded, and rather than being able to encode the information into long-term memory, it was lost from their working memories.

5. Because of working memory's limited capacity and the rate at which information is transferred into long-term memory, it is likely that students "miss" some of the presentation, i.e., their working memory capacities are exceeded, and some information is lost. A textbook is then used to "fill in the gaps."

6. Too much working memory space is taken up by the algebraic manipulations involved in the problems, as evidenced by the teacher's comment, "They get wrapped up in the algebra," leaving inadequate space for the actual physics involved. To overcome the difficulty, the algebra skills should be automatic, so the amount of working memory space they occupy is reduced, leaving more working memory that can be devoted to the physics in the problems.

7. First, for students who have good vocabularies, more of the content of the lectures will be meaningful, since they will be able to attach the content of the lectures to their already existing schemas. Second, many of the word meanings will be automatic for students with good vocabularies, which frees working memory space that can be focused on processing the information in the lecture.

8. Choices a, c, and d require declarative knowledge, since the tasks require "knowledge of facts, definitions, generalizations, and rules." Choices b and e require procedural knowledge, since they involve "knowledge of how to perform activities." Remember, procedural knowledge involves conditions and actions, and riding a bicycle and solving for the areas of the triangles involves taking an action based on the conditions.

9. A schema could appear as follows:

We must keep in mind, however, that schemas are individual and idiosyncratic, meaning the schema for one learner can be different from that of another. An improperly constructed schema is a source of learner misconceptions.

Two other points are important. First, what you see technically isn't the schema; it is a model. A model helps us visualize what we can't observe directly. A schema is the way knowledge is organized and stored in our memories. Since we can't directly observe schemas, we use models to help us visualize the schemas. Second, when we see the model of the schema presented in visual form, we capitalize on dual-processing theory to help us better understand the model.

Exercise 7.2

1. You could begin the lesson by asking the students what they would do if they met a new friend and they wanted to tell the friend exactly where they lived. How might they describe their location for their friend?
   A second option could be to bring in a globe, have the students describe its characteristics, and then ask the students how they might describe a location on it.

2. Present the students with a paragraph in which the rules are embedded. Then ask the students why words such as boy's, girls', and children's are punctuated the way they are.
   A second option would be to have the students describe some things that belong to one or more of them. Write their descriptions on the board properly punctuating the possessives. Then ask them why different words are punctuated the way they are.

3. Bring in a model skeleton and have the students describe it. Then tell them that the class needs to explain why the skeleton exists the way it does, e.g., closed skull, curved ribs, large upper leg bone, etc.
   A second option would be to have the students feel their own skeletons and describe them. Then ask them to explain why their skeletons exist the way they do.

Exercise 7.3

1. An ideal question would be, "Describe what you see in this sentence." The students' answers would give you insight into the meaning they attach to the sentence, and perception is the meaning learners attach to stimuli.

2. Students tend to pay attention to teachers who move around and are animated in their presentations and explanations, which means that teacher animation and movement are attention getters. Standing behind a podium and sitting are not effective attention getters.

3. The simplest way of checking student perceptions is by asking an open-ended question such as, "What do you see?" "What do you notice?" or "Describe the information for us." The question ensures that the students will be successful, and the responses will give you indicators of their perceptions.

4. The case study illustrates the impact that experience has on the perception of an event. Because of their experiences the two teachers went into the interviews with very different expectations, and as a result they interpreted their interviews very differently.

5. One theory would suggest that the other numbers interfered with remembering the first one. A second theory would suggest that you were unable to retrieve the first one primarily because it had not been encoded effectively enough to allow the retrieval.

6. Embedding examples of rules in a paragraph would the best way to capitalize on context. Isolated sentences are not an appropriate context.

7. Juan's schema for the solar system was more complete and interconnected than was Randy's. Because there were more links in his schema, retrieval would be easier for him. (Look again at Figure 7.4 of your text for a visual comparison of the two students' schemas.)

Exercise 7.4

1. Young children don't have well-developed metacognitive abilities. The first-grader is unlikely to realize that her message isn't clear. (She is not aware of the clarity of her communication, and she doesn't demonstrate control over it.) The sixth-graders' metacognition (metacommunication in this case) is more developed.

2. The students are all demonstrating metacognition. The specific types vary, but each is an example of metacognition. We might describe each example as follows:
   a. Marissa is demonstrating metacommunication. She realizes that she may not have understood what Mrs. Jensen was saying, and she demonstrated control over her communication (listening) by asking Mrs. Jensen to repeat the question.
   b. Steve is demonstrating meta-attention. He is aware that he is attending to the radio instead of his homework, and he controls his behavior by turning off the radio.
   c. Claudia is demonstrating metamemory. She realizes that she doesn't remember the difference between neap and spring tide, and she adopts a strategy to help her remember.
   d. The student is demonstrating meta-attention–awareness that she would have difficulty attending and demonstrating control over her attention.

3. We encourage you to first write your responses before checking the feedback because doing so puts you in an active role. Merely reading the exercises and then reading the feedback is a passive process.

4. An outline is a form of organization. Organizing information promotes meaningfulness and encoding by illustrating links (relationships) among the topics.

5. The most effective way to elaborate on your understanding of the concept metacognition (or to elaboration on any concept) is to find or create an example of the concept.

Self-Help Quiz_____

TRUE/FALSE QUESTIONS. Mark T in the blank if the statement is true, and mark F if the statement is false.

_____ 1. While information in working memory is in the form of perceived reality, information in long-term memory is in the form of objective, or true, reality.
_____ 2. Since working memory is what we call consciousness, its capacity is larger than that of long-term memory, which is unconscious.
_____ 3. Information that is not accurately perceived is lost from working memory.
_____ 4. Information is normally quickly lost from sensory memory, but it can be retained there with rehearsal.
_____ 5. Much of the information from sensory memory enters working memory even though we're not consciously aware of it.

MULTIPLE-CHOICE ITEMS. Circle the best response in each case.

6. Which of the following is the best definition of learning from a cognitive point of view?
   a. A change in individuals' mental structures that provides the capacity to demonstrate changes in behavior.
   b. A change in behavior that occurs as a result of experience. behaviorism
   c. A change in the way we visualize and perceive information as a result of experience.
   d. A change in mental structures that occurs as a result of retrieving previously unconscious information.

7. A teacher is giving a lecture on the differences in the way the Spanish interacted with the natives in the Americas compared to the way the English and French interacted with them, and she included some graphic pictures depicting various forms of mistreatment from all parties. In an effort to cover all the factors in a class period, she lectures quite rapidly. Based on the case study, of the following, which is the most likely result?
   a. The information she is presenting won't enter sensory memory.
   b. The students' attention won't be attracted.
   c. The information is likely to be misperceived.
   d. Some of the information will be lost from working memory.

8. You are showing a film about bats to your third graders. Afterward one of the students comments, "I didn't know that birds have teeth." Of the following, the process most closely related to the third grader's comment is:
   a. attention.
   b. perception.   perceived as bird
   c. rehearsal.
   d. encoding.

9. A teacher wants his students to know the most common prepositions, so he gives them a list and tells them that they have to know all the prepositions by the following week. The process the students will most likely use to learn the prepositions is:
   a. perception.
   b. rehearsal.
   c. elaboration.
   d. organization.

Use the following information for items 10 and 11.

A third grade teacher in continuing her work with place value is introducing the concept of the 100's column. She begins the lesson by having them make several numbers, such as 24, with interlocking cubes. She then uses the cubes to demonstrate 124 for them and asks them to compare it to the other numbers they made.

10. Of the following, the process she is most trying to capitalize on to make the information meaningful is:
    a.   attention.
    b.   perception.
    c.   organization.
    d.   elaboration.

11. In conducting the lesson the way she did, she is also attempting to capitalize on another process used to make the information meaningful. Of the following, her efforts best illustrate attempts to capitalize on:
    a.   attention.
    b.   perception.
    c.   rehearsal.
    d.   activity. – active role

12. You find that your algebra students are having problems solving equations, because they get mixed up on simplifying simple arithmetic expressions. You decide to give them some additional practice. Of the following, which is the most desirable schedule?
    a.   25 minutes every Monday to kick off the week.
    b.   10 minutes on Tuesday and 15 minutes on Thursday.
    c.   15 minutes on Monday and 10 minutes on Friday.
    d.   5 minutes every day.

13. Consider the concept of interference. For which of the following pairs of ideas is interference most likely?
    a.   Nouns and verbs
    b.   Nouns and adverbs
    c.   Verbs and direct objects
    d.   Direct objects and indirect objects   most closely related

14. Research indicates that teachers who move around the room, make eye contact with the students, gesture, and display other related behaviors have students who learn more than teachers who don't demonstrate these behaviors. Of the following, the cognitive process in information processing that most closely relates to these behaviors is:
    a.   attention.
    b.   perception.
    c.   rehearsal.
    d.   encoding.

15. Mr. Hunt always follows his presentations in his algebra I class with an assignment where the students practice the skills and ideas he has presented. Research supports the technique of following presentations with student practice. Of the following, the aspect of promoting meaningful learning that most closely relates to Mr. Hunt's approach is:
    a.   activity.
    b.   attention.
    c.   perception.
    d.   organization.

16. Ben Johnson has had his analytic geometry students working on finding the formulas for parabolas and is now moving to formulas for ellipses. He starts by reviewing the features of parabolas, such as the focal point, and he then moves to the similar features in ellipses, such as having the students note that they have two focal points. Of the following, the concept related to making information meaningful that most closely relates to Ben's technique is:
    a. discrepant events as attention getters, since two focal points compared to one is discrepant.
    b. expectations influencing perception. The students don't expect to see two focal points.
    c. mnemonic devices to make information meaningful.
    d. elaboration to make information meaningful.
    e. activity to make information meaningful.

17. The research says that in order to learn concepts most effectively students should be provided with both a definition of the concept and examples of the concept. This research is most closely related to:
    a. attention getters in information processing.
    b. rehearsal in information processing.
    c. perception in information processing.
    d. forming an association to make information meaningful.

You are using information processing theory as a basis for guiding your instruction and you are teaching your students about direct and indirect objects. Use this idea for Items 18 and 19.

18. Based on information processing, which of the following would be the best way to begin your lesson?
    a. Take a ball out from behind your desk and throw it to one of the students.
    b. Ask the students to describe what direct and indirect objects mean to them.
    c. Write a sentence on the board and underline the direct and indirect object in it.
    d. Tell the students that the topic for the day is direct and indirect objects, and that they will use these parts of speech in their writing.

19. Based on information processing theory, which of the following should you do as the second step in your lesson?
    a. Ask students questions that will check their understanding of your examples.
    b. Have the students rehearse the information you first give them to help retain it in working memory
    c. Devise a means of getting the information into sensory memory.
    d. Have the students practice the information so it will be encoded into long-term memory.

Luis Garcia is teaching his 5th graders about the Northern and Southern states prior to the Civil War. He assigns teams of two to gather information about the colonies and, with his help, they create the following matrix.

	People	Land and Climate	Economy
Northern States	Small towns Religious Valued Education Cooperated with each other	Many trees Remains of glaciers Poor soil Short growing season Cold winters Mountains	Syrup Rum Lumber Shipbuilding Fishing Small farms
Southern States	Aristocratic Social class distinction	Good soil Hot weather Large rivers Long growing season Coastal plain	Large farms Tobacco Cotton Unskilled workers Servants and slaves

20. Luis's use of the matrix/chart in his lesson best illustrates which of the following as an attempt to help the students encode the information into long-term memory by making it more meaningful?
     a. Activity
     b. Organization
     c. Elaboration
     d. Perception
     e. Mnemonics

21. Luis had the students—with his help—gather and organize the information to be put in the matrix. On which of the following was Luis most attempting to capitalize by having the students do as much of the work as possible?
     a. Activity
     b. Imagery
     c. Organization
     d. Rehearsal

22. A teacher complains, "I stood there for 15 minutes and explained the procedure for solving the problems until I was blue in the face. I know the procedure was a little hard, but this morning they came in and it was if they had only heard half of what I said. I don't get it." Of the following, the component of our information processing system that most closely relates to this problem is:
     a. perception.
     b. sensory memory.
     c. working memory.
     d. rehearsal.
     e. long-term memory.

23. The primary purpose in preparing practice exercises such as the ones you're now analyzing is to:
     a. attract and maintain your attention.
     b. be certain that you're perceiving the exercises properly.
     c. be sure that your working memory isn't overloaded when you take a quiz or test.
     d. help you encode this information by putting you in an active role.
     e. give you practice in rehearsing the information we're now studying.

24. Brandon and Giselle are studying for a test. "What are you doing?" Brandon asks.
     "I always write out the answers, rather than simply read the answer given in the book," Giselle responds. "I remember the information way better if I do that."
     Of the following, Giselle is most demonstrating:
     a. elaboration.
     b. meta-attention.
     c. proactive facilitation.
     d. metamemory.

25. Molly Ryan wants her students to be able to solve percent mixture problems. She begins by showing the students a graduated cylinder with the alcohol solution in it and asks the students to identify cases where they might want to increase or decrease the strength of solutions.
     She then says, "As you see have 50 milliliters of solution in the graduated cylinder. It is a 25% alcohol solution. How much water must you add to make a 10% solution?" She continues by saying, "We've been studying percents, so let's see what we remember."
     After several questions, she then models solutions to several problems, carefully demonstrating and describing each step in the process as she wrote the solutions on the board, and as she models, she makes comments like, "The first thing I think about is, am I making the solution stronger or weaker. That will help me see if my answer makes sense." She then leads a discussion of several problems, strongly emphasizing that the students' think about each step and put their understanding into words as they discuss the problems.
     Finally, she gives them 10 problems to solve as seatwork, and tells them to finish as homework any that they don't complete in class.

Assess the extent to which Molly applied the principles of instruction for applying information processing in classrooms. Address each of the principles in your assessment.

Self-Help Quiz Answers_____

1. f
2. f
3. f
4. f
5. f
6. a   Choice b is the definition of learning according to behaviorism. Choice c is related, since changes in our mental structures can change the way we perceive information, but it is an incomplete description. Choice d is also related, but it focuses on retrieval, which is only one aspect of cognitive learning.
7. d   Lecturing rapidly is likely to result in the amount of information exceeding the capacity of working memory. Information enters sensory memory, whether or not we're aware of it, and the graphic pictures would be likely to attract the students' attention. We don't have evidence one way or the other to conclude whether or not the information will be misperceived.
8. b   The child perceives the bat as a bird, which results in his comment. This child has encoded flying animals as birds (choice d), so encoding is involved as well. However, the information in the item focuses on perception. We see no evidence of the encoding process presently taking place, so the best answer is b.
9. b   Since the students are merely given a list, they will likely memorize it, which employs rehearsal.
10. d   She is attempting to have the children "elaborate" from two-digit numbers to three-digit numbers.
11. d   By having the students make the numbers with their cubes, she is attempting to put them in an "active" role. (Rehearsal is a process used for memorized information, such as math facts.)
12. d   Spaced practice is more effective than massed practice. Five minutes a day provides the most spaced practice.
13. d   Direct and indirect objects are most closely related to each other, and closely related ideas are more likely to interfere with each other than are ideas that are not closely related. (Teaching the two ideas at the same time is one way to try to prevent interference.)
14. a   Moving around the room, making eye contact, gesturing, and displaying other energetic behaviors are attention getters.
15. a   Practice puts the students in an active role. Attention and perception are not regarded as "techniques" to promote meaningfulness, and we have no evidence one way or the other about organization.
16. d   Elaboration, organization, and activity are the strategies that help make information meaningful. Mnemonics are forms of elaboration, but we have no evidence of either mnemonics or activity in this example.
17. d   Having a definition and examples allows the students to form associations–between the examples and the definition, and the examples with each other. Forming associations promotes meaningfulness. We have no evidence one way or the other about attention, perception, or rehearsal, based on the information in the item.
18. a   Based on information processing, learning begins with attention, and of the choices given, throwing a ball is the best attention getter.
19. a   Asking students questions that check their understanding of the examples you've provided is the most effective way to check their perceptions, and perception is the second process that occurs in the information processing model.
20. b   The matrix serves as an organizer.
21. a   The students are in active roles when they gather and organize the information.
22. c   Students behaving as if they only heard half of what the teacher said, particularly since she stood there and "explained the procedure for solving the problems until I was blue in the face," suggests that the learners' working memories had become overloaded.

23. d While attention is involved (choice a), this isn't the primary purpose. Perception is also involved (choice b), but another technique would be used if accurate perception was the goal. Your working memory isn't being overload (choice c), because you can take as much time as you need to process the information, and you're doing much more than rehearsing (choice e) when you practice the exercises.

24. d Giselle is demonstrating knowledge of, and control over, her memory. Metamemory is a form of metacognition.

25. Molly applied the first principle: "Begin lessons with an activity that attracts attention," by showing the students a graduated cylinder with the alcohol solution in it and asking the students to identify cases where they might want to increase or decrease the strength of solutions.

   She applied the second, "Conduct frequent reviews to activate students' prior knowledge and check their perceptions," when she said, "We've been studying percents, so let's see what we remember."

   By modeling the solutions to several problems, carefully describing each step in the process, and writing the solutions on the board, she applied the third principle, "Proceed in short steps and represent content both visually and verbally to reduce cognitive load."

   She applied the fourth principle, "Help students make information meaningful, and aid encoding through organization, imagery, elaboration, and activity," by having the students put their understanding into words, which put them in cognitively active roles. They were also in active roles when they solved their own problems. (We don't have evidence to determine whether or not she capitalized on organization, imagery or elaboration.)

   Finally, she applied the last principle, "Model and encourage metacognition," when she made comments such as, "The first thing I think about is, am I making the solution stronger or weaker. That will help me see if my answer makes sense," and emphasizing that the students think about each step as they solve the problems.

CHAPTER 8: CONSTRUCTING KNOWLEDGE

Chapter Outline_____

I.   What is constructivism?
      A.   Cognitive constructivism
      B.   Social constructivism
           1.   Sociocultural learning theory
           2.   The classroom as a community of learners
           3.   Cognitive apprenticeship
           4.   Situated cognition
II.   Characteristics of constructivism
      A.   Learners construct understanding that makes sense to them
      B.   New learning depends on current understanding
      C.   Social interaction facilitates learning
      D.   Meaningful learning occurs within real-world tasks
III. Outcomes of knowledge construction
      A.   Concepts
           1.   Theories of concept learning
           2.   Examples: The key to learning and teaching concepts
           3.   Concept mapping: A learning strategy
      B.   Schemas
      C.   Misconceptions and conceptual change
           1.   Misconceptions' resistance to change
           2.   Teaching for conceptual change
IV.   Implications of constructivism for teaching
      A.   The teacher's role in constructivist classrooms
      B.   Suggestions for classroom practice
           1.   Provide a variety of examples and representations of content
           2.   Connect content to the real world
           3.   Treat verbal explanations skeptically
           4.   Promote high levels of quality interactions
      C.   Assessment and learning: The role of assessment in constructivist classrooms
      D.   Putting constructivism into perspective
V.   Constructivism in classrooms: Instructional principles
      A.   Learning contexts: Knowledge construction in urban environments
           1.   The need for examples
           2.   Real-world connections
           3.   Interaction

Chapter Objectives_____

- Describe the difference between cognitive and social constructivism, and identify examples of each in descriptions of learning activities.

- Identify characteristics and applications of constructivism in events in and outside of classrooms.

- Analyze applications of concept learning including teaching for conceptual change.

- Identify examples of suggestions for classroom practice in descriptions of learning activities.

- Analyze applications of constructivist learning theory in classroom activities.

Chapter Overview_____

Constructivism is a cognitive view of learning theory grounded in the thinking of Piaget and Vygotsky, whose works you studied in Chapter 2. Constructivism includes four essential characteristics. First, people construct their own understanding of information and events. We don't behave like tape recorders, creating exact copies of what we see or hear. Rather we cognitively organize our experiences in ways that make sense to us. The fact that we all construct understanding is the essential principle of constructivism. Second, we construct understanding based on what we already know. Third, since understanding is constructed, individuals' constructions will vary, so social interaction facilitates learning. Social interaction provides people with feedback about their existing understanding and allows them to reconstruct understanding when necessary. Finally, real-world tasks promote learning more effectively than tasks that are less authentic.

Teachers help their students construct understanding by providing a variety of high-quality, real-world examples which provide the background knowledge students need for knowledge construction. Then, they carefully guide discussions of the examples to promote valid constructions and assess learners' evolving understanding. As teachers implement constructivism in their classrooms they must have clear goals in mind and keep their instruction and assessments aligned with their goals.

Application Exercises_____

We encourage you to first write your responses to each of the exercises below, and then check your answers with the feedback that immediately follows the exercises.

Exercise 8.1

Read the following case study and answer the questions that follow. The paragraphs are numbered for your reference.

1.   Javier Lopez's students are struggling to understand the concept *work*, which is movement resulting from a force (any push or pull). He has defined force, given several examples of pushes and pulls, and he also defined the concept work and has given the students several examples, such as pushing a book across the table, and pulling one of the students across the floor in a chair. He also pushed on the chalkboard to illustrate a force that doesn't result in any work.
2.   Let's look at some of the interaction that takes place in the lesson.
3.   Javier holds up a chair in front of the class, and, as he's standing still with the chair, asks, "Am I doing any work?"
4.   "Yes," Anya says assertively.
5.   "Explain why you think I'm doing work," Javier continues.
6.   "You'll get tired if you keep doing that."
7.   "Is anything moving?" Javier asks.
8.   "No," Anya responds.
9.   "Am I doing any work?" Javier repeats.
10.   "Yes," Anya repeats. "My mom was holding something for my dad, and she said, 'Please hurry, this is hard work.'"
11.   Javier then puts the chair back down on the floor and slowly lifts it up, so the students can see it moving.
12.   "What am I doing now?" he asks.
13.   "Lifting the chair," Leroy answers.
14.   "Am I doing any work? . . . Tamika?"
15.   "Yes."
16.   "Explain how you know."
17.   "You're pulling on the chair, . . . which is a force, and it moved . . . up."
18.   "Now, am I doing any work?" Javier asks as he is holding the chair, but not moving. "Devon?"
19.   ". . . No."
20.   "Why not?"
21.   ". . . The chair isn't moving."
22.   "So, can I get tired without doing any work? . . . Anya?"
23.   ". . . I . . . guess so."
24.   Javier then has Damien stand up and they grasp hands as if they are going to be in a tug-of-war. He has Damien pull, but doesn't allow any movement.
25.   "Is either of us doing any work? . . . Anya?"
26.   ". . . No," she responds hesitantly.
27.   "How do you know?"
28.   ". . . Neither . . . one . . . moved."

1.   Look at the interaction between Javier and Anya in paragraphs 3-10 and consider the "Characteristics of constructivism" that appear in the outline at the beginning of this chapter of the Student Study Guide and were discussed in the chapter in your text. Which characteristic of constructivism is best illustrated by Anya's insistence that Javier was doing work, in spite of the fact that no movement occurred? Explain.

2.   Look at paragraphs 1, 3, 11, 18, and 24, and consider the "Suggestions for classroom practice" that also appear in the outline at the beginning of this chapter. Which "Suggestion for classroom practice" is best illustrated in these paragraphs? Explain.

3.   Which of the "Characteristics of constructivism" do paragraphs 1, 3, 11, 18, and 24 best illustrate? Explain.

4.   Look at the interaction that occurred in the sequence from paragraphs 11 through 28. Explain how this interaction facilitated Anya's knowledge construction using a cognitive constructivist (Piagetian) point of view, and then explain how this interaction facilitated Anya's knowledge construction from a social constructivist (Vygotskian) point of view.

Exercise 8.2

Read the following case study, which you saw presented in the chapter as an classroom application of constructivist learning theory, and answer the questions that follow. The paragraphs are numbered for your reference.

1.   Judy Nelson was beginning a study of longitude and latitude in social studies with her sixth graders. In preparation, she bought a beach ball, found an old tennis ball, and checked her wall maps and globes.
2.   She began by having students identify where they live on the wall map and then said, "Suppose you were hiking in the wilderness and got lost and injured. You have a cell phone, but you need to describe exactly where you are. How might you do that? You have a map of the area with you, but it's a topographic map showing rivers and mountains."
3.   As students discussed the problem, they realized that typical ways of locating themselves—such as cities and street signs—wouldn't work.
4.   She continued, "It looks as if we have a problem. We want to be able to tell rescuers exactly where we are, but we don't have a way of doing it. Let's see if we can figure this out."
5.   She then held up the beach ball and globe and asked her students to compare the two. They identified north, south, east, and west on the beach ball, and she drew a circle around its center, which they identified as the equator. They did the same with the tennis ball, which she then cut in half, so they could see the two hemispheres.
6.   Judy continued by drawing lines parallel to the "equator" on the beach ball and saying, "Now, compare the lines with each other."
7.   " ... They're all even," Kathy volunteered.
8.   "Go ahead, Kathy. What do you mean by even?" Judy encouraged.
9.   " ... They don't cross each other," Kathy explained, motioning with her hands.
10.   "Okay," Judy smiled.
11.   She then asked for and got additional comparisons, such as, "The lines all run east and west," and, "They get shorter as they move away from the equator," which she wrote on the chalkboard.
12.   Judy then introduced the term latitude to refer to the lines they'd been discussing.
13.   She continued by drawing vertical lines of longitude on the beach ball and identified them as shown in the case study in your text.
14.   The following is some dialogue that then took place:
15.   Judy: How do these lines compare with the lines of latitude?
16.   Tricia: ... They go all around the ball.
17.   Judy: Good. And what else? . . . Elliot?
18.   Elliot: .   .. Length, ... they're all the same length.
19.   Thomas: Lengths of what?
20.   Elliot: The up-and-down lines and the cross ones.
21.   Judy: What did we call the cross ones?
22.   Elliot: ... Latitude.
23.   Jime: We said that they got shorter.... So how can they be the same length?
24.   Tabatha: I think those are longer (pointing to the longitude lines).
25.   Judy: How might we check the lengths?
26.   Jime: ... Measure them, the lines, like with a tape or string or something.
27.   Judy: What do you think of Jime's idea?
28.   The students agreed that it seemed to be a good idea, so Judy helped hold pieces of string in place while Jime wrapped them around the ball at different points, and the class compared the lengths.

29. Chris: They're the same (holding up two "longitude" strings).
30. Nicole: Not these (holding two "latitude" strings).
31. After comparing the strings, Judy then asked students to work in pairs to summarize what they found. They made several conclusions, which Judy helped them rephrase. They were:

Longitude lines are farthest apart at the equator; latitude lines are the same distance apart everywhere.

Lines of longitude are the same length; latitude lines get shorter north and south of the equator.

Lines of longitude intersect each other at the poles; lines of latitude and longitude intersect each other all over the globe.

32. Judy continued, asking, "Now, how does this help us solve our problem of identifying an exact location?" With some guidance, the class concluded that location can be pinpointed by where the lines cross. She noted that this is what they'll focus on the next day

Think about the suggestions for classroom practice that were presented in the chapter. Identify each of the suggestions in the case study, and document your responses by citing the paragraphs to which you're referring in each case.

Exercise 8.3

Read the following case study and answer the questions that follow it.

Jan Schwartz's fifth-grade music class was learning a ballad about cowboys. As they turned to the page in the music book, a hand went up.

"What's a dogie?"

"Actually, Kim, it's pronounced dögee, long 'e'. It does kind of look like the word doggy, doesn't it? Who knows what a dögee is? . . . Anyone? . . . Well, let's look at the sentence and see if we can find out. It says, 'Get along, little dögee.' What are the cowboys doing? . . . Jed?"

". . . They're herding cattle."

"Good, and so a little cow would be a . . . Tanya?"

". . . Calf."

"Very good! A dögee is a calf, but a special kind of calf–one that's lost its mother. Why would that be important to a cowboy? . . . Shannon?"

". . . Because they wouldn't know who to follow or where to go."

"Excellent, Shannon! Class, look at the picture of the cattle drive on the front of the album. Can you see any potential dögies?" she asked, holding the picture up for them.

1. What concept was Jan teaching?

2. Identify a characteristic of the concept

3. Identify an example of the concept.

4. How "easy" was this concept to learn? Explain why.

5. Which theory of concept learning–rule-driven, prototype, or exemplar–best explains how we learn a concept such as the one illustrated in Jan's lesson? Explain why this theory provides the best explanation.

Feedback for Application Exercises_____

Exercise 8.1

1. *New learning depends on current understanding* is the characteristic of constructivism best illustrated in these paragraphs. The most concrete example is Anya's comment in paragraph 10 when she said, "My mom was holding something for my dad, and she said, 'Please hurry, this is hard work.'" Anya's

understanding of the concept *work* was influenced by her background experiences and current understanding.

2. Of the "Suggestions for classroom practice" presented in the outline, "Provide a variety of examples and representations of content" is best illustrated in these paragraphs. For instance, he provided several examples in paragraph 1, and another in paragraph 11, and he presented non-examples in paragraphs 3, 18, and 24. In teaching a concept such as work, non-examples are very important, because, as you saw with Anya's thinking in the vignette, learners tend to equate work with effort, ignoring the fact that work requires movement.

3. *New learning depends on current understanding* is the characteristic of constructivism best illustrated by the paragraphs. Examples and representations are what students use to construct their understanding. They provide the background knowledge needed to construct understanding.

4. From a cognitive constructivist (Piagetian) point of view, we would explain Anya's change in thinking by saying that she had a scheme for the concept *work*, which she then, individually, modified because of her additional physical and social experience.

From a social constructivist point of view (grounded in Vygotsky's work), we would explain Anya's change in thinking by saying that she "appropriated" understanding from the social environment (Javier's classroom and the social interaction that took place in it), and she then internalized that understanding.

Exercise 8.2

The first suggestion for classroom practice is, "Provide a variety of examples and representations of content." In Paragraph 5 Judy provided a concrete example of hemispheres by cutting the tennis ball in half, and in Paragraphs 5 and 6 she provided examples of lines of latitude by drawing parallel lines around the beach ball. Then, in Paragraph 13 she provided examples of longitude by drawing lines through the "poles" on her beach ball.

The second suggestion for classroom practice says, "Connect content to the real world." In Paragraphs 2-4 Judy presented the problem of finding their exact location that provided context for the rest of her lesson.

The third and fourth suggestions for classroom practice are, "Be skeptical of explanations" and "Promote high levels of interaction." Judy developed the entire lesson with questioning, so high levels of interaction existed throughout the lesson. She guided the students' developing understanding with her questioning instead of trying to promote understanding using explanation.

Exercise 8.3

1. Jan is teaching the concept dögee. (Notice how Jan helped her students use context clues to teach the concept. This is a helpful and widely applicable concept learning strategy for use with printed material.)

2. The essential characteristic of dögee is "motherless." From the student responses we can conclude that other characteristics such as "four-legged" and "nurses from mother" were part of the students' schemas for calf, but these aren't essential characteristics.

3. The teacher used the picture of a cattle drive to present an example of the concept. This is an essential component of concept learning, but one that is often by-passed because examples for some concepts are hard to find or create.

4. This concept is easy to learn, because it only has one essential characteristic–motherless, and the characteristic is concrete.

5. Rule-driven theories of concept learning best explain how a concept like dögee is learned. Dögee is determined by a well-defined rule–it is a motherless calf. Other concepts, such as adverb in language arts, work in science, prime number in math, and longitude in social studies, are well-defined, and can also be better explained by rule-driven than either prototype or exemplar theories.

Self-Help Quiz_____

TRUE/FALSE QUESTIONS. Mark T in the blank if the statement is true, and mark F if the statement is false.

_____ 1. Social interaction is essential for social constructivism, but it doesn't play a role in cognitive constructivism.
_____ 2. Social constructivist views of learning provide for a more significant teacher role than do cognitive constructivist views of learning.
_____ 3. When basing instruction on constructivist views of learning, teachers have less important roles than they do when basing instruction on behaviorist or social cognitive views of learning.
_____ 4. When instruction is based on constructivist views of learning, students must set their own learning goals.
_____ 5. The most important factor in teaching concepts is to provide students with a clear and precise definition.

Use the following vignette for items 6-9.

Mrs. Laureano is teaching the concept *insect* to her third graders. She shows the students detailed, colored pictures of *ants* in a line moving toward an ant hill, a *beetle* crawling through some grass, a *butterfly* flying between two trees, and a *mosquito* sitting on a person's arm. She has the students observe and describe the pictures and then guides them to the conclusion that "Insects are cold-blooded animals with an exoskeleton, three body parts, and six legs." She then presents the students with pictures of a crab, a grasshopper, and a spider and asks them to identify which is or are insects based on their definition. They then discuss their results, concluding that the grasshopper is an insect, since it is the only one of the three examples with three body parts, an exoskeleton, and six legs.

6. As an application of the principles of instruction for applying constructivism in classrooms, which of the of the following is the best assessment of the implementation of her lesson?
   a. It is consistent with the principles of instruction, since she provided examples of insects, social interaction was evident, and assessment was an integral part of the lesson.
   b. It is inconsistent with principles of instruction, since she provided the examples instead of having the students find the examples for themselves.
   c. It is inconsistent with the principles of instruction, since understanding the concept insect isn't an authentic (real world) task and therefore shouldn't be taught.
   d. It is inconsistent with instruction based on constructivism, since she established the learning objective for the lesson instead of having the students establish the objective.

7. Based on the information in the vignette, of the following, which is the best description of the concept's characteristics?
   a. Ant, beetle, butterfly, mosquito
   b. Cold-blooded animal
   c. Three body parts, six legs
   d. The statement, "Insects are cold-blooded animals with an exoskeleton, three body parts, and six legs."

8. Based on the description, which theory of concept learning best explains how the concept is learned?
   a. *Rule-driven* theory best explains how the concept is learned in this case, since students classified the grasshopper as an insect based on a rule saying that insects must have an exoskeleton, three body parts, and six legs.
   b. *Prototype* theory best explains how the concept is learned in this case, since Mrs. Laureano presented the butterfly as a prototype.
   c. *Prototype* theory best explains how the concept is learned in this case, since Mrs. Laureano provided a definition into which prototypes could be placed.
   d. *Exemplar* theory best explains how the concept is learned in this case, since Mrs. Laureano presented the ant, beetle, butterfly, and mosquito as exemplars.

9. As we saw in the vignette, Mrs. Laureano didn't merely show pictures of ants, but rather showed them in a line moving toward an ant hill, and also showed the *beetle* crawling through some grass, the *butterfly* flying between two trees, and the *mosquito* sitting on a person's arm. The fact that she attempted to present the insects in this way best illustrates which of the following principles of instruction for applying constructivism in classrooms.

    a.   Provide a variety of examples and other representations of content.

    b.   Connect content to the real world.

    c.   Treat explanations skeptically.

    d.   Promote high levels of interaction.

    e.   Make assessment an integral part of the teaching-learning process.

Use the following vignette to answer items 10 and 11.

Phenix Davis, a science teacher, wants her students to understand the characteristics of the solar system. She prepares a model showing the planets in their relative distances from the sun. She explains the model, pointing out that the first four planets are called the inner planets and the other five are called the outer planets.

Loretta Wilson, a social studies teacher, wants her students to understand how geography, economy, and recreational patterns are interrelated. She shows the students a map that illustrates different geographic regions, such as mountains and plains, a matrix comparing the economies of the areas, and pictures illustrating the recreational patterns in these areas.

Jonah Washington, a math teacher, wants his students to be able to simplify arithmetic expressions and has his students simplify a series of expression such as 3 + 5(8 - 2) - 7.

Ruben Askew, a 4th grade teacher, wants his students to identify the correct verb in sentences, such as "Andrea and Jose (is, are) the fastest runners on the girls' and boys' track teams." He has the students complete a series of exercises in which they have to identify the correct verb.

Provide a variety of examples and representations of content is one of the principles of instruction for applyng constructivism in classroom.

10. The teacher who *most effectively* applied this principle was:

    a.   Phenix

    b.   Loretta

    c.   Jonah

    d.   Ruben

11. The teacher who *least effectively* applied the principle was:

    a.   Phenix

    b.   Loretta

    c.   Jonah

    d.   Ruben

12. As part of a unit on percents and decimals, Tamika Edwards gave her students ads from three different newspapers, each advertising the same products. Students worked in pairs to determine the cost per ounce for products such as orange juice and canned vegetables. After the students completed their calculations, Tamika led a whole-class discussion in which the students explained their thinking and decided which products actually were the least expensive per ounce. Tamika periodically made comments, such as "Excellent thinking," and "Very good analysis," when students demonstrated a clear understanding of the topic.

Based on instruction grounded in constructivist views of learning, which of the following statements is the best assessment of Tamika's lesson?
   a. It was an effective activity, because students were reinforced for clear thinking and deep understanding.
   b. It was an ineffective activity, because Tamika gave the students the newspaper ads instead of having the students find the ads themselves.
   c. It was an ineffective activity, because whole-group discussions are not appropriate when basing instruction on constructivist views of learning.
   d. It was an effective activity, because it provided an authentic task and capitalized on student-student interaction.

13. Of the following, which is the most important problem with using explanations as the primary way of developing student understanding?
   a. Explanations tend to put students in passive roles instead of encouraging their active involvement in the learning activity.
   b. Explanations tend to be inaccurate, so students develop misconceptions about the topics they study.
   c. Teachers rarely use examples when they provide explanations, so students are unable to construct understanding.
   d. Explanations rarely include information about the real world, so students aren't involved in authentic tasks.

14. Students periodically make surprising conclusions, such as, "Mushrooms always grow in damp places, which is why they look like umbrellas." Based on the characteristics of constructivism, which of the following is the most likely reason students make these conclusions?
   a. Teachers fail to clearly explain the topics they teach, so students don't develop clear understandings.
   b. Students create and develop these conclusions based on the experiences they have.
   c. Students aren't adequately reinforced for valid conclusions, so they develop invalid ones.
   d. Teachers don't adequately model the thinking that is required to form valid conclusions.

Use the following vignette for items 15-21.

Four teachers are attempting to help their students understand the concepts *adjective* and *adverb*.

Mr. Anderson displays several sentences–some of which contain adjectives and others of which that contain adverbs–on the overhead. He points out the adjectives, underlines them, and points to the noun they modify. He uses a similar process with the sentences containing the adverbs, identifying the adverb and pointing out the verb, adjective, or other adverb that they modify. He then gives the students several sentences for practice, directing them to underline the adjective and adverb, and circle the word it modifies.

Mrs. Ortega presents a paragraph which contains three underlined adjectives and three italicized adverbs in the sentences that make up the paragraph. The class discusses the common features of the underlined and italicized words and what they modify, and, with Mrs. Ortega's guidance they arrive at a definition of adjectives and adverbs. The students then write a paragraph containing at least three adjectives and three adverbs.

Mr. Weiss presents several sentences which contain underlined adjectives and adverbs. He asks the students to look for the word that each modifies and identify it as a noun or a verb. He then asks them what the words that modify nouns must be, and when no one answers he asks them what modifies nouns. They respond, "Adjectives," and he points out that these are adjectives. He does the same thing with adverbs, and he then has them work several exercises identifying the part of the sentence each adjective and adverb modifies in each case.

Mrs. Sanderson presents a passage in which several examples of adjectives and adverbs are embedded. She asks the students to describe the passage, and after they have made several observations, she underlines the adjectives, pointing out that they modify a noun in each case. She circles the noun they modify to be sure that the students focus on the relationship between the noun and the adjective. She then repeats the process with the adverbs.

15. Mrs. Ortega presented her examples in a paragraph, and Mrs. Sanderson presented hers in a passage.
     Of the following, which principle of instruction for applying constructivism in classrooms is best illustrated by their attempts?
     a.   Provide a variety of examples and other representations of content.
     b.   Connect content to the real world.
     c.   Treat explanations skeptically.
     d.   Promote high levels of interaction.
     e.   Make assessment an integral part of the teaching-learning process.

16. Near the end of their lessons, Mr. Anderson gave the students several sentences for practice, directing them to underline the adjective and adverb, and circle the word it modifies; Mrs. Ortega had the students write a paragraph containing at least three adjectives and three adverbs; and Mr. Weiss had them work several exercises identifying the part of the sentence each adjective and adverb modifies in each case.
     Of the following, which principle of instruction for applying constructivism in classrooms is best illustrated by their attempts?
     a.   Provide a variety of examples and other representations of content.
     b.   Connect content to the real world.
     c.   Treat explanations skeptically.
     d.   Promote high levels of interaction.
     e.   Make assessment an integral part of the teaching-learning process.

17. Mrs. Ortega had the class discuss the common features of the underlined and italicized words and words they modified in the paragraph she presented, and Mrs. Sanderson had the students describe the passage she presented.
     Of the following, which principle of instruction for applying constructivism in classrooms is best illustrated by their attempts?
     a.   Provide a variety of examples and other representations of content.
     b.   Connect content to the real world.
     c.   Promote high levels of interaction.
     d.   Make assessment an integral part of the teaching-learning process.

18. In his lesson, Mr. Anderson displayed several sentences–some of which contain adjectives and others of which that contain adverbs–on the overhead, pointed out the adjectives, underlined them, pointed to the noun they modified, and using a similar process with the sentences containing adverbs. Using the principles of instruction for applying constructivism in classrooms, which of the following is the best assessment of him pointing out the adjectives, the nouns they modified, and using a similar process for the sentences containing adverbs?
     a.   It is inconsistent with the principle: *Provide a variety of examples and other representations of content*, since he presented the students with sentences containing adjectives instead of having them generate their own examples.
     b.   It is inconsistent with the principle: *Treat explanations skeptically*, since he developed the lesson using explaining as the primary way of helping the students understand the content.
     c.   It is consistent with the principle: *Promote high levels of interaction*, since interaction isn't necessary to teach well-defined concepts like *adjective* and *adverb*.
     d.   It is consistent with the principle: *Connect content to the real world*, since concepts like *adjective* and *adverb* don't have real world applications.

19. Which of the principles of instruction for applying constructivism in classrooms was evident in each teachers' lesson?
     a.   Provide a variety of examples and other representations of content.
     b.   Connect content to the real world.
     c.   Treat explanations skeptically.
     d.   Promote high levels of interaction.
     e.   Make assessment an integral part of the teaching-learning process.

20. The teacher who was most consistent with constructivist views of learning in his or her instruction was:
    a. Mr. Anderson.
    b. Mrs. Ortega.
    c. Mr. Weiss.
    d. Mrs. Sanderson.

21. The teacher who was least consistent with constructivist views of learning in his or her instruction was:
    a. Mr. Anderson.
    b. Mrs. Ortega.
    c. Mr. Weiss.
    d. Mrs. Sanderson.

22. Of the following, which is the best example of an authentic task?
    a. Students rewrite sentences to correctly indicate the possessive form of nouns.
    b. Students write a paragraph in which the rules for spelling and grammar are applied correctly.
    c. Students write an editorial for the school newspaper.
    d. Students write a one-paragraph summary of a section in their geography book.

23. In the chapter you saw in Jenny Newhall's lesson with the beam balances that Suzanne concluded that the number of tiles was all that was necessary to make the beam balance; she ignored the distance from the fulcrum as contributing to making the beam balance. Using the factors that contribute to misconceptions as a basis, explain why Suzanne acquired this misconception.

24. Kevin, a fifth-grader, is doing a homework assignment involving reducing fractions to lowest terms. He correctly reduces 5/25 to 1/5. However, when faced with the problem of reducing 12/30, Kevin gets ½ as an answer.

    Using the suggestions from the section of the chapter titled "Assessment and Learning: The Role of Assessment in Constructivist Classrooms," describe what your first step should be in responding to Kevin's answer of ½. Based on his thinking in reducing $^5/_{25}$ to $^1/_5$, how might Kevin have arrived at ½ when reducing $^{12}/_{30}$ to lowest terms. (This is a real-world example, i.e., Kevin really did get ½ as an answer. The feedback to this item summarizes his thinking.)

25. Mrs. Carlsen wants her students to understand that when we exert a force on an object, it goes faster and faster, i.e, it accelerates. She explains acceleration, such as objects speeding up as they fall to the earth, but she is uneasy about the extent to which the students understand the concept acceleration. So, she demonstrates force and acceleration by pulling a small cart across the front of the classroom using a spring scale that exerts a constant force. She also holds a tennis ball above her head and drops it and then shows a computer simulation that illustrates the acceleration of the dropped ball in slow motion. The students work in groups to discuss what they've seen, and Mrs. Carlsen guides them with questioning until they understand that when they see the distance between the images of the ball get greater and greater, the ball is accelerating. Gradually, they begin to understand the idea of acceleration.

    Identify in Mrs. Carlsen's lesson each of the principles for applying constructivism in classroom that were discussed in the chapter.

Self-Help Quiz Answers_____

1. f
2. t
3. f
4. f
5. f

6.   a   Mrs. Laureano provided examples of insects, and social interaction was evident. Both are principles of instruction for applying constructivism in teaching. Instruction based on constructivism doesn't require that students find their own examples (choice b), and understanding the concept *insect* is an appropriate learning objective (choice c). (As you saw in the chapter, "Authentic activities foster the kinds of thinking and problem-solving skills that are important in out-of-school settings, whether or not the activities themselves mirror what practitioners do" (Putnam & Borko, 2000, pp. 4-5). So, teaching the concept *insect* is an authentic task if it promotes the kind of thinking that is important in out-of-school settings. Principles of instruction for applying constructivism in teaching don't suggest that students establish the learning objectives (choice d).

7.   c   Three body parts and six legs are the concept's defining elements. Ant, beetle, butterfly, and mosquito (choice a) are *examples*, not *characteristics*. Cold-blooded animal (choice b) is a larger category—another, larger concept—of which insect is a subcategory, and the statement "Insects are cold-blooded animals with an exoskeleton, three body parts, and six legs" (choice d) is a definition.

8.   a   The students classified the grasshopper as an insect based on a rule stating that in order to be an insect an animal must have an exoskeleton, three body parts, and six legs.

9.   b   By presenting the examples in the context of natural habitats Mrs. Laureano was attempting to connect the topic to the real world.

10.   b   Loretta's map, matrix, and pictures are three different ways of representing aspects of the topic. In each of the other cases, the forms of the representations remained the same.

11.   a   Phenix showed only the model of the solar system, and she then verbally explained the inner and outer planets. While the form of the examples is the same for Jonah and Ruben, at least they had a series of examples.

12.   d   Determining cost per ounce, which is a form of informed consumer thinking, is a real-world (authentic) task. And, a great deal of social interaction took place in the lesson. Authentic tasks and social interaction are characteristics of constructivism. Reinforcement for correct responses is more a part of behaviorism than of constructivism (choice a). Whether or not Tamika provided the ads wasn't important with respect to constructivism (choice b). Whole-group discussions are an important part of social interaction (choice c).

13.   a   Putting learners in passive roles is an important weakness of explaining. None of the other choices is necessarily true. Explanations, in general, *are* accurate (choice b). Teachers often use examples in their explanations (choice c), and explanations often contain information about the real world (choice d).

14.   b   Constructing new understanding based on existing understanding is a characteristic of constructivism. None of the other choices is a characteristic of constructivism. In addition, if we try to "see where kids are coming from," we can see how they might construct their conclusion. Mushrooms do indeed grow in damp places, and umbrellas are also used in damp weather. So, putting the two together to conclude that mushrooms look like umbrellas because they live in damp places isn't as "off the wall" as it originally appears.

15.   b   By putting the examples into the context of a paragraph or passage, the teachers are attempting to connect the content to the real world. In the real world we read books, news magazines, newspapers, and other written materials. All the information in them is in the form of passages, not isolated sentences.

16.   e   Each of the exercises the teachers had their students complete was a form of assessment.

17.   c   The discussions in which the teachers' students were involved were forms of social interaction.

18.   b   Mr. Anderson simply explained the information for the students. He did provide examples (choice a); he did not use social interaction (choice c), and *adjective* and *adverb* do indeed have real world applications (choice d).

19.   a   All the teachers provided the students with examples.

20.   b   First, working with a written paragraph and writing their own paragraphs are more "real world" than any of the other tasks. Also, more social interaction took place in the lesson than in the other three lessons, and Mrs. Ortega having the students write a paragraph in which examples of adjectives and adverbs were embedded was a form of assessment.

21.   a   Sentences are less "real world" than working with paragraphs and other written passages. Also, Mr. Anderson "points out the adjectives, underlines them, and points to the noun they modify.

He does the same thing with the sentences containing the adverbs," so little evidence of social interaction exists in the lesson.

22.   c   Writing an editorial for the school newspaper is the most real-world of the choices given.

23.   A variety of factors can contribute to misconceptions. One is learners' basic attempts to make sense of their experiences, and Suzanne was attempting to make sense of the balance beam problem. She also inferred that it was the number of tiles that *caused* the beam to balance, because having the same number on each side and the beam balancing occurred together in this case. As a result, having the same number of tiles on each side of the fulcrum *appeared* to be a correct solution.

24.   As it says in the chapter, "Students' thinking is the essential feature," so your first step should be to ask Kevin how he arrived at the answer of ½. This question would give you insight into his thinking, and then, based on his thinking, you could ask a series of questions that would guide him to valid understanding.

Constructivism helps us understand how Kevin might have arrived at ½ as an answer. Since he reduced $^5/_{25}$ to $^1/_5$, by dividing the numerator and denominator by 5, he used the same reasoning to reduce $^{12}/_{30}$. He divided 12 by 12 and got 1, and he divided 30 by 12 and got 2. He then simply ignored the remainder of 6.

25.   Each of the principles of instruction for applying constructivism in classrooms was illustrated in Mrs. Carlsen's lesson. She realized that her explanation, alone, didn't produce understanding, so she adapted her lesson. She used a series of examples–pulling the cart across the front of the room, dropping the tennis ball, and using the computer simulation–to illustrate acceleration, and she capitalized on social interaction in both the small groups and whole class. And, the concept *acceleration* is very much a part of the real world.

CHAPTER 9: COMPLEX COGNITIVE PROCESSES

Chapter Outline_____

I.   Problem solving
   A.   Well-defined and ill-defined problems
   B.   A problem solving model
      1.   Identifying the problem
      2.   Representing the problem
      3.   Selecting a strategy
         a.   Algorithms
         b.   Heuristics
      4.   Implementing the strategy
      5.   Evaluating the results
   C.   Expert-novice differences in problem-solving ability
      1.   Developing expertise: The role of deliberate practice
   D.   Helping learners become better problem solvers: Instructional principles
      1.   Present problems in real-world contexts and take students' prior knowledge into account
      2.   Capitalize on social interaction
      3.   Provide scaffolding for novice problem solvers
         b.   Analyzing worked examples
      4.   Teach general problem-solving strategies
   E.   Problem-based learning
II. The strategic learner
   A.   Metacognition: The foundation of strategic learning
      1.   Prior knowledge
      2.   A repertoire of strategies
   B.   Study strategies
      1.   Note taking
      2.   Using text signals
      3.   Summarizing
      4.   Elaborative questioning
      5.   SQ3R
   C.   Developing strategic learning in students: Instructional principles
III. Critical thinking
   A.   The challenge of critical thinking
   B.   Elements of critical thinking
      1.   Component skills
      2.   Domain-specific knowledge
      3.   Metacognition
      4.   Motivation
   C.   Developing critical thinking: Instructional principles
IV. Transfer of learning
   A.   General and specific transfer
   B.   Factors affecting the transfer of learning
      1.   Similarity between learning situations
      2.   Depth of original understanding
      3.   Learning context
      4.   Quality and variety of examples and learning experiences
      5.   Emphasis on metacognition

Chapter Objectives

- Identify examples of ill-defined and well-defined problems and describe the role of deliberate practice in solving them.

- Explain differences between effective and ineffective strategies in studying behaviors.

- Define critical thinking and identify its characteristics in classroom activities.

- Identify factors that influence transfer in examples of classroom activities.

Chapter Overview

In Chapter 7 we examined information processing. In Chapter 8 we discussed the processes involved in constructing knowledge in detail. As part of our study we learned that the contents of long-term memory as well as the processes used to construct understanding and encode information into long-term memory influence how effectively learners retain and retrieve information.

In this chapter we examine complex cognitive processes, such as problem solving, the use of learning strategies, and transfer of learning. As the term *complex cognitive processes* implies, each requires higher-level thinking and sophisticated use of processes such as organization, elaboration, activity, and metacognitive monitoring.

Problem solving begins with identifying a problem, and proceeds to representing the problem, selecting and implementing a strategy, and evaluating the results. Strategies for solving problems include trial and error, means-end analysis, and drawing analogies. Expert problem solvers are better at representing problems, solve them more holistically and strategically, and monitor their progress more effectively than do novices. Specific approaches to teaching problem solving capitalize on social interaction, present problems in meaningful contexts, include practice in problem finding, and provide instructional scaffolding.

Cognitive strategies are plans for accomplishing learning goals. Metacognition is the foundation of effective strategy use and, in addition, effective strategy users have a repertoire of strategies and a broad base of background knowledge.

Critical thinking is the ability to accurately and efficiently gather, interpret, and evaluate information. It incorporates component skills, such as comparing, hypothesizing, and generalizing, together with domain-specific knowledge, metacognition, and motivation.

Transfer occurs when learners are able to take information or skills they've learned in one situation and apply them in a new context. Factors affecting transfer include the similarity between two learning situations, the variety, context, and quality of learners' experiences, depth of understanding and practice, and the metacognitive dispositions to look for opportunities to use information. The key to all forms of transfer is a variety of high quality examples presented in realistic contexts.

Application Exercises_____

We encourage you to first write your responses to each of the exercises below, and then check your answers with the feedback that immediately follows the exercises.

Exercise 9.1

Read the following descriptions of a class involved in problem solving and answer the questions that follow:

Jack Watson's algebra class was working on applications of problem solving. To begin the class, Jack put the following problem on an overhead:

A goat is tied to the corner of a 40-ft-square barn with a 30-ft rope. If it can graze everywhere outside of the barn that its rope allows it to reach, what is the size of its grazing area?

"What do we need to do first?" he began. "Taffy?"
" . . . Figure out what we know and need to find out."
"Good, Taffy. Let's start with givens. What do we know? Betty?"
"Well, we know how big the sides of the barn are . . . 40 ft, and . . . we know that the rope is 30 ft long."
"Okay. Now would anyone like to come up and draw us a picture to help us see what we are trying to figure out?. . . Shanda?"
". . . Well, I think the problem looks like this. We have a circle with a radius of 30 ft. But the barn is here. It cuts out part of that circle. We have to find the area of the circle that's not in the barn because no grass grows in the barn, and he couldn't get in to eat it anyway."
"Excellent drawing, Shanda. So how do we translate this into a formula? Kerry?"
"The formula for the area of a circle is A equals pi times the radius squared. So we need to find that and subtract 1/4 from it . . . to allow for the barn."
"Who can do that on their calculator and then share with us on the board? Brad?"
"Hmmm . . . Okay. I think the answer is 2,826."
"It's 2,826 what, Brad?"
"Oh, right! Square feet. Does that sound about right?"
"Is that what everyone else got? Kim?"
". . . I don't think so. I think . . . he forgot to subtract the quarter of a circle in the barn. So it should be 2,119.5 square ft, I think," Kim responded hesitantly.
"How about anyone else?" Jack queried. "Check it out."
Several other students rechecked and confirmed Kim's results.
Jack then continued, "Good, everyone. . . . Now, two things we can learn from this problem. First, always go back to the notes you took when you set up the problem. If Brad had checked with the diagram we drew, he would have caught his mistake. Second, make sure you have the right units. If it's area, it needs to be square something."

1. Identify steps from the general problem solving model that are illustrated in the description. Make direct reference to the information in the description in identifying the steps.

2. Are any of the steps from the general problem solving model missing? If so, identify those steps.

3. Is the problem well-defined or ill-defined? Explain.

4. Did the students use an algorithm to solve the problem or did they use a heuristic? Explain.

5. How effectively did Jack implement the suggestions for helping students become better problem solvers in his activity? Explain.

Exercise 9.2

Read the following example and answer the questions that follow it.

> Kendra Phillips is working with her class on the development of their study strategies. She begins the activity by saying, "Today we're going to learn a new way to check whether we understand what we're reading. There are several steps in the process. After every paragraph that we read, we need to make a statement that summarizes the main ideas in it. Then we'll make a question about the material in that paragraph. Our passage for today is about snakes. I'll read the first paragraph out loud and then try to summarize.
>
> "'The snake's skeleton and parts of its body are very flexible–almost like a rubber hose with bones. A snake's backbone can have almost 300 vertebrae, almost 10 times as many as a human's. These vertebrae are connected by cartilage that allows easy movement. Because of this bendable, twistable spinal construction, a snake can turn its body in almost any direction at almost any point'," Kendra read.
>
> "Hmm, let's see," she continued. "What would be a sentence that summarizes this paragraph? How about, Snakes have lots of bones? That's okay, but it doesn't tell why it's important. How about, Snakes have lots of bones in their backbones, and that allows them to move and bend? . . . Yes, that's better. Now I need a good question. How, why, and when words are often helpful. How about this one: Why do snakes have so many bones in their backbones? That's a good one because it aims at the main idea in the paragraph.
>
> "Now, let's see. Are there any ideas in the paragraph that aren't clear? . . . What is cartilage? . . . Oh, yes. It's the flexible material between bones, like the cartilage in our knees between the bones in our upper leg and our lower leg.
>
> "What will the next paragraph be about? . . . I wonder if it will explain how snakes' flexible spines help them to survive and hunt. . . . Now let's try another paragraph, and I want one of you to try these four steps."

(adapted from Brown & Palinscar, 1985).

1. Was Kendra's focus on basic study strategies or on comprehension monitoring? Explain how you know based on information taken directly from the case study.

2. Based on the information in the chapter, how effectively did Kendra implement the suggestions for "Helping students become effective strategy users"?

Look at the following statements:
>   "Japanese-made cars are better than American-made cars,"
>   "Candidate Smith has a better position on tax reform than candidate Jones,"
>   "A square is a kind of rectangle."

3.   If an individual "spontaneously" asks, "How do you know?" in response to any one or more of the three statements, which of the Elements of Thinking is best illustrated by this behavior? (Spontaneously asking the question.)

4.   If a person answers the question ("How do you know?") which basic process and which subprocess are being best illustrated? Explain.

Exercise 9.3

The following descriptions show how three teachers taught their students about reptiles. Analyze the three episodes in terms of the discussion of transfer in the chapter and decide which teacher's students would have the highest likelihood of transfer and which would be least likely to transfer. Explain your reasoning in the analysis.

Mrs. Jung carefully explained what reptiles are, where they live, and what they eat. She then told her students that animals such as alligators, crocodiles, turtles, and snakes are reptiles.

Mrs. McManus brought her son's pet snake to class. She also showed the students colored pictures of an alligator, a turtle, and a horned toad. She had the students observe the snake and the pictures and discuss the characteristics they all had in common.

Mr. Hume explained what reptiles are and told the students that snakes, lizards, alligators, and turtles are reptiles. He also showed the students a picture of a sea turtle, so they knew that some reptiles live in water.

Feedback for Application Exercises_____

Exercise 9.1

1. The different problem solving stages occurred as follows:

Identifying and representing the problem: The following part of the dialogue illustrates these first two phases of the process:
    "What do we need to do first?" he began. "Taffy?"
    " . . . Figure out what we know and need to find out."
    "Good, Taffy. Let's start with givens. What do we know? Betty?"
    "Well, we know how big the sides of the barn are–40 ft–and we know that the rope is 30 ft long."
    "Okay. Now would anyone like to come up and draw us a picture to help us see what we are trying to figure out? Shanda?"
    "Well, I think the problem looks like this. We have a circle with a radius of 30 ft. But the barn is here. It cuts out part of that circle. We have to find the area of the circle that's not in the barn because no grass grows in the barn, and he couldn't get in to eat it anyway."

Selecting and implementing a strategy: Selecting and implementing a strategy were illustrated in the following part of the dialogue:
    "Excellent drawing, Shanda. So how do we translate this into a formula? Kerry?"
    "The formula for the area of a circle is A equals pi times the radius squared. So we need to find that and subtract 1/4 from it . . . to allow for the barn."
    "Who can do that on their calculator and then share with us on the board? Brad?"
    "Hmmm . . . Okay. I think the answer is 2,826."
    "It's 2,826 what, Brad?"
    "Oh, right! Square feet. Does that sound about right?"

Evaluating the results: Evaluating the results occurred in the following part of the dialogue:
    "Is that what everyone else got? Kim?"
    ". . . I don't think so. I think . . . he forgot to subtract the quarter of a circle in the barn. So it should be 2,119.5 square ft, I think," Kim responded hesitantly.
    "How about anyone else?" Jack queried. "Check it out."
    Several other students rechecked and confirmed Kim's results.

2. All the steps in the general problem solving model were present. The students didn't get much practice in "problem finding," but this is typical of instruction in problem solving.

3. This was a well-defined problem. The problem asked for the area of the grazing area, which is a clear goal state, and clear solution paths existed for reaching the goal state.

4. The students used an algorithm. The formula for finding the area of a circle involves an algorithm.

5. Jack presented a fairly traditional approach to problem solving. The problem was in context, but it could have been personalized to make it more meaningful for the students. Finding the area of a portion of the room, or the students' desks, for example, would have been a more meaningful context.
    There was a moderate amount of social interaction involved in the lesson, and the students were given adequate scaffolding. For example, Brad received immediate feedback about his solution.

Jack made some effort at teaching general problem solving strategies when he commented, "Good, everyone. . . . Now, two things we can learn from this problem. First, always go back to the notes you took when you set up the problem. If Brad had checked with the diagram we drew, he would have caught his mistake. Second, make sure you have the right units. If it's area, it needs to be square something."

Exercise 9.2

1. Kendra's focus was primarily on comprehension monitoring. For example, she said, "After every paragraph that we read, we need to make a statement that summarizes the main ideas in it. Then we'll make a question about the material in that paragraph." This comment relates to summarizing and self-questioning, both comprehension monitoring strategies.

2. Kendra was quite effective in implementing the suggestions for helping students become effective strategy users. She modeled the process, thinking aloud throughout the modeling. She then planned to have the students practice the strategy.

3. "Spontaneously" asking the question suggests an attitude or a disposition. This suggests the disposition to ask for evidence for conclusions.

4. The process being illustrated in answering the question is, "Assessing conclusions based on observation," and the subprocess is "Confirming conclusions with facts."

Exercise 9.3

Three criteria for effective transfer are quality, variety, and context. We have little evidence about the context in any of the three episodes. The quality of Mrs. Jung's examples wasn't good, since she only used verbal descriptions. The quality of Mr. Hume's examples was a bit better, since he used a picture of a sea turtle. Mrs. McManus clearly had the best quality examples, and even though Mr. Hume had the added variety of the sea turtle, Mrs. McManus's quality would more than make up for this deficit, so the likelihood of transfer would be the greatest in her case. The poor quality examples in Mrs. Jung's case would make transfer least likely for her students.

Self-Help Quiz

TRUE/FALSE QUESTIONS. Mark T in the blank if the statement is true, and mark F if the statement is false.

_____ 1. Most problem-solving experiences students have in schools involve ill-defined problems.
_____ 2. A well-defined problem for one learner may be an ill-defined problem for a different learner.
_____ 3. Research indicates that students learn most of the study skills that they are able to use without formal instruction from a teacher.
_____ 4. Dispositions are one element of the critical thinking process that transfer in a general sense, as opposed to domain-specific knowledge which transfers poorly to new situations.
_____ 5. In general, transfer tends to be very specific.

MULTIPLE CHOICE QUESTIONS: Circle the best response in each case.

6. Of the following the best example of a problem is:
    a. you don't know the meaning of the word demagogue, so you look it up in the dictionary.
    b. you don't know the product of 445 x 722, so you take out your calculator and find the answer.
    c. you don't know how to get to your friend's house, so you call him and get directions.
    d. you don't know the phone number of the restaurant, from which you want to order a pizza, but your roommate has taken the phone book to her room.

Use the following vignette for items 7-12.

Steve Fraser displays a drawing of an island on the overhead projector. The drawing includes landforms, ocean currents, and the prevailing wind direction.
    "Now," he says after the students have looked at the drawing, "How do you suppose we could determine what the best location for a city would be on this island?"
    "I think that we should first decide what factors to consider in what makes a location effective," Tanya suggests.
    "Good idea," Steve nods. "So, how might we do that?
    "We've studied some of the major cities in the United States, like New York, San Francisco, Seattle, and Chicago," Gabe offers. "We could see what they have in common."
    Steve has the students work in pairs to gather information about each of the cities and they finally decide that being near a good harbor, being a major transportation hub, and having a relatively good climate are three important characteristics that they have in common.
    After analyzing the cities, the class discusses the location for their city on the island. They finally decide on a location, and Steve then says, "Okay everyone, let's think about what we've done. Talk with your partner for two minutes and determine whether or not we've picked the best location."
    Steve then brings the groups together to discuss their analyses.

7. In thinking about well-defined and ill-defined problems, which of the following is the best analysis of the problem Steve presented?
    a. It is well defined, since Steve asked a specific question: "How do you suppose we could determine what the best location for a city would be on this island?"
    b. It is well defined, since Steve asked the students to determine the "best" location for the city.
    c. It is ill defined, since Steve didn't model a process for solving the problem.
    d. It is ill defined, more than one location for a city might have been possible, and a certain method for solving the problem didn't exist.

8. Steve's question, "How do you suppose we could determine what the best location for a city would be on this island? . . ." best illustrates his attempt to help his students with which step in the problem solving process?
    a. Identifying the problem
    b. Representing the problem
    c. Selecting a strategy
    d. Implementing a strategy
    e. Evaluating the results

9. Gabe suggested, "We've studied some of the major cities in the United States, like New York, San Francisco, Seattle, and Chicago. . . . We could see what they have in common." Of the following, his suggestion best illustrates which step in the problem solving process?
    a. Identifying the problem
    b. Representing the problem
    c. Selecting a strategy
    d. Implementing a strategy
    e. Evaluating the results

10. Steve having the students work in pairs to gather information about each of the cities best illustrates which step in the problem-solving process?
    a. Identifying the problem
    b. Representing the problem
    c. Selecting a strategy
    d. Implementing a strategy
    e. Evaluating the results

11. During the lesson Steve said, "Okay everyone, let's think about what we've done. Talk with your partner for two minutes and determine whether or not we've picked the best location." This statement encouraged the students to complete which step in the problem-solving process?
    a. Identifying the problem
    b. Representing the problem
    c. Selecting a strategy
    d. Implementing a strategy
    e. Evaluating the results

12. Of the following, on which instructional principle for helping students become better problem solvers did Steve most effectively capitalize?
    a. Capitalize on social interaction
    b. Provide scaffolding for novice problem solvers by analyzing worked examples
    c. Teach general problem solving strategies
    d. Teach problem solving through problem-based learning

13. Four people see a drawing showing the path of the cue ball (the ball driven into the other balls in pool) before striking the object ball, and the paths of both the cue ball and the object ball after the object ball has been struck.
    Jerome says, "The cue ball went off to the left and the other ball went off to the right."
    Sharon says, "It's a conservation of momentum problem."
    Steve says, "The cue ball must have hit the other ball at an angle."
    Linda says, "The harder you hit the cue ball, the faster the other ball will go. This cue ball must have been struck fairly hard."

If the students demonstrate the characteristics of expertise identified by research, the one whose comments indicate the most expertise is:
   a. Jerome
   b. Sharon
   c. Steve
   d. Linda

14. Which of the following best illustrates strategic learning?
   a. Reading an assigned passage in history
   b. Finding the lowest common denominator when adding fractions
   c. Identifying an example of an inference in a written paragraph
   d. Writing notes in the margins of your textbook

15. Three students are discussing their approaches to understanding the information being taught in their economics class.

   "I always read economics before I go to class," Kim comments. "Mrs. Hernandez sometimes blasts through the stuff. If I've already read it, I don't get lost."

   "I always read my economics before I do English," Albert shrugs. "That gets it out of the way, and then I can enjoy myself. I like English."

   "I never miss a homework assignment in that class," Sandra adds. "You know how Mrs. Hernandez is about homework. I'd never go to that class without doing it."

The student that is illustrating the most "strategic" behavior is:
   a. Kim
   b. Albert
   c. Sandra

16. You want to teach your students about prepositions. Of the following, which is most effective for promoting transfer?
   a. Present a list of prepositions and explain how they're used.
   b. Present a list of sentences that have prepositions in them and guide the students to identifying the prepositions in each case.
   c. Present a paragraph that includes several prepositions and guide the students to identifying the prepositions in each case.
   d. Explain to the students that prepositions are always in phrases, and all they have to do is identify the phrase. Then show them several prepositional phrases.

17. The aspect of transfer that is the focus of Item 15 is:
   a. variety of examples.
   b. quality of examples.
   c. context for examples.
   d. both variety and quality of examples.

18. Maurice has learned to add fractions in math. When he encounters a word problem in science he is able to use fractions to solve it. This situation most closely relates to:
   a. concept learning.
   b. a study skill.
   c. discovery learning.
   d. specific transfer.

19. You have taught your students the concept *rhombus* (figures with four equal sides and opposite angles equal). Of the following, which is the best way to determine if transfer has occurred?
    a. Show them a parallelogram, square, trapezoid, and hexagon, and ask them to point to any examples of rhombuses.
    b. Show them a square and ask if it is a rhombus.
    c. Ask them to write a definition of rhombus on a sheet of paper.
    d. Show them a regular hexagon (six equal sides and six equal angles) and ask if it is a rhombus.

Three teachers were teaching their students about adverbs.

Mrs. Evans told the students that adverbs modify verbs, adjectives, and other adverbs, and went on to say words such as *quickly, openly, very,* and *rapidly* were adverbs and wrote the words on the board.

Mrs. D'Armas showed the students the sentences:
"Joe quickly jumped into the straight lunch line when Mrs. Smith reminded him."
"Ronnie very openly described his strong feelings about the incident."
"Jim has extra large biceps."
She pointed out that the underlined words were adverbs, and the class determined what they modified. They then formed a definition of adverbs and she wrote it on the board.

Mrs. Voltaire wrote the statement, "Adverbs are parts of speech that modify verbs, adjectives, and other adverbs," on the board and showed the students the following sentence:
"Jo powerfully made her argument by stating the facts in the matter."
She then had Susan walk across the floor, and prompted the students to state, "Susan walked quickly across the floor." She then wrote the sentence on the board, and she underlined the word *quickly*. She then pointed out that the underlined word in the sentence was an adverb.

20. The next day, Mrs. D'Armas showed the students the sentence:

Steve is rapidly improving in his work in advanced math,

and asked Julio, one of her students, to identify the part of speech represented by the word *rapidly* in the sentence. Julio responded, "It's an adverb." The type of learning represented by their answer is best described as:
    a. problem solving.
    b. strategic learning.
    c. critical thinking.
    d. specific transfer.
    e. general transfer.

21. Suppose Mrs. D'Armas wants to emphasize critical thinking in her students. As a followup question to the question she asked Julio in item 20, which of the following is most effective for promoting critical thinking?
    a. What would be another example of an adverb?
    b. What is the definition of an adverb?
    c. What is another part of speech that is closely related to adverbs?
    d. How do we know that *rapidly* is an adverb?

22. Think about the three teachers. The one whose students are most likely to transfer the information is:
    a. Mrs. Evans
    b. Mrs. D'Armas
    c. Mrs. Voltaire

23. The one whose students are least likely to transfer the information is:
    a. Mrs. Evans
    b. Mrs. D'Armas
    c. Mrs. Voltaire

24. In order to promote transfer, of the following, which is the best example for teaching the principle, "Objects expand when they're heated"?
    a. Ask the students why they suppose bridges have expansion joints in them.
    b. Ask the students to think about a sidewalk. Prompt them to notice that a sidewalk is not a solid piece of concrete; rather it is in sections. Ask them why they think the sections exist.
    c. Fill two identical balloons with similar amounts of air. Put one in hot water and put the other in ice.
    d. Write the statement, "Objects expand when they're heated," on the board. Ask the students if they can think of cases where they've seen heated objects expand.

25. Explain why your choice in Item 24 is the best example using the factors that affect the transfer of learning as a basis for your explanation.

Self-Help Quiz Answers_____

1. f
2. t
3. f
4. t
5. t
6. d   A problem exists when a person has a goal but lacks an obvious way of achieving the goal. In each of the first three choices, an obvious way of reaching the goal exists, but in choice d the way of reaching the goal is less obvious.
7. d   Steve's problem is consistent with the definition of an ill-defined problem. Asking a specific question doesn't make a problem well defined (choice a), nor does asking the students to find the "best" location for a city (choice b). Failing to model a process for solving a problem doesn't make the problem ill defined (choice c).
8. a   Asking the students to determine the best location for a city identifies the problem.
9. c   Gabe was offering a strategy for determining the best location for a city by examining the characteristics of major cities.
10. d   When the students gathered information about the major cities, they were implementing their strategy.
11. e   By encouraging the students to think about whether or not they selected the best location, they were evaluating their results.
12. a   Evidence of social interaction exists in the lesson. We see no evidence of using worked examples (choice b), or teaching general problem-solving strategies (choice c). While Laura used a problem-based learning approach, using problem-based learning is not one of the instructional principles.
13. b   Sharon's comment indicates that she sees the illustration as an interconnected relationship. Experts see patterns and relationships to a greater extent than do novices.
14. d   Writing notes in the margin of your book is a "technique to enhance performance on a learning task." Each of the other choices simply involves the task itself; they don't involve techniques to enhance performance on the task.
15. a   Kim is demonstrating the most "strategic" behavior. Reading the information ahead of time is a "technique to enhance performance on a learning task."
16. c   Presenting the prepositions in the paragraph provides the most effective context, and guiding the students to identify the prepositions in the paragraph provides practice and results in the deepest understanding. (Based on information from Chapter 7, it also puts the students in the most active role.)

17.　c　Based on the information in the description, we have little information about either the variety of examples or the quality of the examples. We do know, however, that the prepositions have been embedded in the context of a written paragraph.

18.　d　He is performing the task in a slightly different context.

19.　a　The ability to identify examples is a good measure of transfer of concept learning. Having them draw a rhombus would also be a good way of indicating that their understanding of the concept has transferred.

20.　d　The ability to identify *rapidly* as an example of an adverb indicates specific transfer.

21.　d　By asking, "How do we know. . ." she is asking the students to provide evidence for the conclusion that *rapidly* is a adverb. The ability to make conclusions based on evidence illustrates critical thinking.

22.　b　Mrs. D'Armas provided a definition, an example of each of the forms of adverbs, and the adverbs were in the context of sentences. Mrs. Evans provided only words, and Mrs. Voltaire only illustrated adverbs that modify verbs, both with her sentence and having Susan walk across the floor.

23.　a　Mrs. Evans had poor quality examples, and they were not in context.

24.　c　This choice is the *only actual example*. Choice a isn't an example, and it requires prior knowledge that the students may not have. The same is true for choice b. Choice d is a definition, and it also requires prior knowledge that the learners may not possess. (The need for providing high quality examples is essential when considering the diversity in our students, since their background knowledge may vary a great deal.)

　　　　Another simple way of explaining why choice c is the best is to point out that all the information the students need to understand the idea is in the example. They will be able to see that the balloon in the hot water expands, and they'll be able to see that the balloon in the cold water contracts.

25.　　　The feedback for item 24 is an explanation for why choice c is the most effective.

CHAPTER 10: THEORIES OF MOTIVATION

Chapter Outline_____

I.   What is motivation?
    A.   Extrinsic and intrinsic motivation
    B.   Motivation to learn
II.   Behavioral views of motivation
    A.   Using rewards in classrooms
    B.   Criticisms of behavioral approaches to motivation
    C.   Using rewards in classrooms: Instructional principles
III. Humanistic views of motivation
    A.   Development of the whole person
        1.   Maslow's hierarchy of needs
            a.   Deficiency and growth needs
            b.   Putting Maslow's work into perspective
        2.   The need for positive regard: The work of Carl Rogers
    B.   Humanistic views of motivation: Instructional principles
IV.   Cognitive theories of motivation
    A.   Expectancy x value theory
        1.   Expectancy for success
        2.   Factors influencing task value
            a.   Intrinsic interest
            b.   Importance
            c.   Utility value
            d.   Cost
    B.   Self-efficacy: Beliefs about capability
        1.   Factors influencing self-efficacy
        2.   The influence of self-efficacy on motivation
        3.   Developmental differences in self-efficacy
    C.   Goals and goal orientation
        1.   Learning and performance goals
        2.   Goals and theories about the nature of intelligence
        3.   Social goals
        4.   Work-avoidance goals
        5.   Goals, motivation, and achievement
        6.   Using goals effectively
            a.   Effective goal setting
            b.   Goal monitoring
            c.   Strategy use
            d.   Metacognition
    D.   Attribution theory
        1.   Impact of attributions on learners
        2.   Learned helplessness
        3.   Attribution training
    E.   Beliefs, goals, and attributions: Instructional principles
    F.   Self-determination theory
        1.   The need for competence
            a.   Attributional statements
            b.   Praise and criticism
            c.   Emotional displays
            d.   Offers of help
        2.   The need for control
        3.   The need for relatedness
    G.   Assessment and learning: The role of assessment in self-determination
    H.   Diversity in motivation to learn

Chapter Objectives_____

- Identify differences between extrinsic motivation, intrinsic motivation, and motivation to learn in classroom activities.

- Describe criticisms of behavioral views of motivation, and explain how rewards can be used to increase motivation to learn.

- Explain the basic premise of humanistic views of motivation and identify applications of humanistic motivation theory in classrooms.

- Describe the basic assumption on which cognitive motivation theories are based, and analyze applications of these theories in events in and outside of classrooms.

- Analyze applications of self-determination theory in classroom learning activities.

- Use self-worth theory and studies of arousal and anxiety to explain learner behavior.

Chapter Overview_____

Learning and what teachers can do to increase it is the core concept in your text. To promote learning we must understand the characteristics of the learners we're teaching, which was the content of Chapters 2-5. In Chapters 6-9 we examined the learning process itself, from behaviorist, social cognitive, information processing, and constructivist points of view. Now we turn to motivation. In this chapter we're trying to answer the question: "What is learner motivation and what can we as teachers do to increase it?"

Theories of motivation explain both extrinsic motivation—motivation to engage in an activity as a means to an end; and intrinsic motivation—motivation to engage in an activity for its own sake. Challenge, curiosity, control, and fantasy are sources of intrinsic motivation.

Behaviorism describes motivation using the effective application of rewards. Teachers apply behaviorist views of motivation when they base rewards on the quality of the work and use rewards to involve students in activities that are not initially intrinsically interesting. Rewards that communicate increasing competence can be intrinsically motivating.

Humanistic views of motivation assume that people have an innate need for personal growth and development. The humanistic view focuses on the whole person, and personal growth is fundamental. The "whole person" is reflected in Maslow's hierarchy of needs. Teachers apply humanistic approaches to motivation when they afford students unconditional positive regard, create safe and orderly classrooms, and consider the learning-teaching process from students' points of view.

Cognitive theories examine people's beliefs and expectations and suggest that people are instinctively motivated by a need to understand the way the world works. Expectancy x value theory, self-efficacy theory, goal theory, attribution theory, and self-determination theory all consider learners' beliefs, expectations, and needs to understand the world. Teachers apply cognitive theories of motivation and enhance learners' sense of self-worth when they provide learners with evidence of accomplishment, emphasize the utility value of increased skills, promote interest through modeling, personalizing content, providing concrete examples, and involving students. They also emphasize learning and social responsibility goals.

Application Exercises_____

We encourage you to first write your responses to each of the exercises below, and then check your answers with the feedback that immediately follows the exercises.

Exercise 10.1

For each of the following items, be sure to carefully defend your answer based on the information you've studied in the chapter.

1. In the chapter's opening case study, Jim's comment, "It's actually interesting the way she's always telling us about the way we are because of something that happened a zillion years ago. . . . I never thought about this stuff in that way before," indicates that his motivation has increased as a result of Kathy's teaching. Which theory of motivation—behaviorist behaviorist, humanistic, or cognitive—best explains Jim's motivation?

2. Suppose the following encounter had taken place in Kathy's lesson:

    Nikki: I believe the Crusades were a failure. They . . .
    Joe: Wait a minute! (interrupting) How about the new fighting techniques they learned?
    Kathy: Joe. (stated firmly) What is one of the principles we operate on in here?
    Joe: We don't have to agree with someone else's point, but we do have to listen. . . . Sorry.

    Which theory of motivation best explains the importance of the principle, "We don't have to agree, but we have to listen?"

3. Toward the end of the case study Kathy commented, "Now isn't that interesting! . . . See, here's another case where we see ourselves in the 20th century finding a relationship to people who lived a thousand years ago. That's what history is all about." Explain the motivating effects of this comment from a cognitive point of view.

4. Explain the motivating effects of Kathy's comment in Item 3 from a humanistic point of view.

5. In the case study, David whispered to Kelly, "Brewster loves this stuff." Which theory of motivation best explains the motivating effects of Kathy's behavior that led to David's comment?

6. In their encounter before class, Kathy said to Harvey, "Yes, but look how good you're getting at writing," as she smiled and pointed her finger at him. "I think you hit a personal best on your last paper. You're becoming a very good writer."

    Is this comment likely to increase or decrease Harvey's intrinsic motivation? Explain on the basis of research examining the effects of reinforcers on intrinsic motivation.

Exercise 10.2

The following is a synthesis of Kathy Brewster's work with her students. Read the case study and answer the questions that follow. (The paragraphs are numbered for your reference.)

1. "We'd better get moving," Susan urged Jim as they approached the door of Kathy Brewster's classroom. "The bell is gonna ring, and you know how Brewster is about this class. She thinks it's SO important."
2. "Did you finish your homework?" Jim asked and then stopped himself. "What am I talking about? You've done your homework in every class since I've known you."
3. "Sure, I don't mind it that much.... It bothers me when I don't get something, and sometimes it's even fun. My dad helps me. He says he wants to keep up with the world," Susan laughed.

4. "In some classes, I just do enough to get a decent grade, but not in here," Jim responded. "I used to hate history, but I sometimes I even read ahead a little, because Brewster really makes you think. It's actually interesting the way she's always telling us about the way we are because of something that happened a zillion years ago.... I never thought about this stuff in that way before."

5. "Gee, Mrs. Brewster, that assignment was impossible," Harvey grumbled as he walked in.

6. "That's good for you," Kathy smiled. "I know it was a tough assignment, but you need to be challenged. It's hard for me too when I'm studying and trying to put together new ideas, but if I hang in, I always feel like I can get it."

7. "Aw, c'mon, Mrs. Brewster. I thought you knew everything."

8. "I wish. I have to study every night to keep up with you people, and the harder I study, the smarter I get," Kathy nodded. "And, ... I feel good about myself when I do."

9. "But you make us work so hard," Harvey continued in feigned complaint.

10. "Yes, but look how good you're getting at writing," Kathy smiled again, pointing her finger at him. "I think you hit a personal best on your last paper. You're becoming a very good writer."

11. "Yeah, yeah, I know," Harvey smiled on his way to his desk, ". . . and being good writers will help us in everything we do in life," repeating a rationale the students continually hear from Kathy.

12. "Stop by and see me after class," Kathy quietly said to Jenny as Jenny came in. "I'd like to talk to you for a minute."

13. Kathy finished her beginning-of-class routines and then pulled down a map in the front of the room. "Let's review for a moment to see where we are. We began our discussion of the Crusades yesterday. How did we start?"

14. ". . . We imagined that we all left Lincoln High School and that it was taken over by people who believed that extracurricular activities should be eliminated," Carnisha volunteered.

15. "Good," Kathy smiled. "Then what?"

16. "We decided we'd talk to them ... We'd be on a 'crusade' to change their minds."

17. "Very good. . . . Now, what were the actual Crusades all about? ... Selena?"

18. ". . . The Christians wanted to get the Holy Land back from the Muslims."

19. "And why? ... Becky?"

20. "The Holy Lands were important for the Christians. I suppose they just wanted them because of that."

21. "Also, the map shows how much territory the Muslims were getting, and the people in Europe were like afraid the Muslims would take over their land," Cindy added.

22. "Good thought, Cindy. . . . They certainly were a military threat. In fact, the conflict that occurred in Kosovo is a present day reminder of the clash between Christians and Muslims. How else might they have been threatening?"

23. "Maybe ... economically," Brad added. "You're always telling us how economics rules the world."

24. "Excellent, Brad," Kathy laughed. "Indeed, economics was a factor. In fact, we'll see that the military and economic threats of the Muslims, together with the religious issue, were factors that led to Columbus's voyage to the New World.... Think about that. The Muslims in 1000 A.D. have had an influence on us here today.

25. "Now, for today's assignment," Kathy continued, "you were asked to write a paragraph answering the question, 'Were the Crusades a success or a failure?' You could take either position. The quality of your paragraph depends on how you defended your position, not on the position itself. Remember, your writing and the ability to make and defend an argument is a skill that goes way beyond a specific topic like the Crusades. This applies in everything we do.

26. "So, let's see how we made out. Go ahead.... Nikki?"

27. "I said they were a failure. . . . The Europeans didn't accomplish what they were after ... to get the Holy Land back for Christianity," Nikki said. "There were several Crusades, and after only one did they get sort of a foothold, and it only lasted . . . like about 50 years, I think."

28. "How about you, Joe?"

29. "I said they were a success because the Europeans learned new military strategies that they later used ... here, in the Americas. If it hadn't been for the Crusades, they wouldn't have learned the techniques, ... at least not for a long time. It even changed our ideas about guerrilla fighting."

30. "Also good, Joe," Kathy nodded. "This is exactly what we're after. Nikki and Joe took opposite positions in their paragraphs, but they each provided several details in support.

31. "Let's look at another one. . . . What was your position, Anita?"

32.   "I said they ... were a success. Western Europe took a lot from their culture . . . in the Middle East. Like, some of the spices we eat today first came to Europe then."

33.   "Now isn't that interesting!" Kathy waved energetically. "See, here's another case where we see ourselves today finding a relationship to people who lived 1,000 or more years ago. That's what history is all about."

34.   "Brewster loves this stuff," David whispered to Kelly, smiling slightly.

35.   "Yeah," she replied. "History has never been my favorite subject, but some of this stuff is actually kind of neat."

36.   "Okay. One more," Kathy continued, "and we'll move on."

37.   The class reviewed another example, and then Kathy told the students to revise their paragraphs based on what they had discussed and turn in a product for peer review the next day.

38.   "Remember, think about what you're doing when you make your revisions," she emphasized. "Read your paragraph after you write it, and ask yourself, 'Do I actually have evidence here, or is it simply an opinion?' ... The more aware you are when you write, the better your work will be. And, remember we made a commitment to ourselves at the beginning of the year that we were going to help each other as much as we could when we give each other feedback on our writing. . . . So, I know that you'll come through.

39.   "One more reminder," Kathy said as the period was nearly over, "group presentations on the Renaissance are Wednesday and Thursday. You decide what groups will be on each day. For those who chose to write the paper on the Middle Ages, remember we agreed that they're due next Friday."

40.   As the students were leaving the room, Jenny stopped at her desk. "You wanted to see me, Mrs. Brewster? . . . What's up?"

41.   "I've been watching you for a few days, and you don't seem to be yourself. You're somewhere else. . . . Is everything okay?"

42.   "I . . . yes, . . . no, not really," Jenny said, her eyes starting to fill with tears. "My mom and dad are having trouble, and I'm really, really scared. I'm afraid they're going to break up."

43.   "Do you want to talk?"

44.   ". . . No . . . not right now."

45.   Kathy reached over, touched Jenny on the shoulder, and said, "I realize that there isn't anything that I can do directly, but I'm here if you want to talk about it, . . . or anything else . . . anytime."

46.   "Thanks, . . . I will," Jenny smiled weakly as she turned to go.

47.   As Kathy was working after school, Harvey poked his head into the room.

48.   "Come in," she smiled. "How's the writer?"

49.   "I just came by to say I hope I didn't offend you this morning, complaining so much about all the work."

50.   "Not at all. . . . I haven't given it a second thought.

51.   "I guess you already know how much you've done for me," Harvey continued. "You believed in me when the rest of the world wrote me off. . . . My drug conviction is off my record now, and I haven't 'used' in over a year. I couldn't have made it without you. You made me work and put in all kinds of extra time with me. You pushed me and wouldn't let me give up on myself. I was headed for trouble, and now . . . I'm headed for college."

52.   "We all need a nudge now and then," Kathy smiled. "That's what I'm here for. I appreciate it, but no need to thank me. I didn't do it; you did . . . . Now, scoot. I'm thinking up a rough assignment for you tomorrow."

53.   "Mrs. Brewster, you're relentless," Harvey waved as he headed out the door.

Consider the following cognitive theories of motivation:
- Expectancy x Value Theory
- Self-efficacy Theory
- Goal Theory
- Attribution Theory
- Self-Determination Theory

Identify which of these theories is best illustrated in the sets of paragraphs taken from Kathy Brewster's lesson above. A theory may be illustrated once, more than once, or not at all. Carefully explain in each case. (Remember, the theory best illustrated must accommodate the information in all the paragraphs, not just one or a few.)

1.   Paragraphs 8-10.

2.   Paragraphs 11, 14-16, 24-25.

3.   Paragraphs 9-10, 30, 39, 47-51.

4.   Paragraph 38 .

Exercise 10.3

Look at the following exchange between Kathy Brewster and Harvey:

Harvey: Gee, Mrs. Brewster, that assignment was impossible (as he walks in the door).
Kathy: That's good for you (smiling). I know it was a tough assignment, but you need to be challenged. It's hard for me too when I'm studying and trying to put together new ideas, but if I hang in, I always feel like I can get it.
Harvey: Aw, c'mon, Mrs. Brewster. I thought you knew everything.
Kathy: I wish. I have to study every night to keep up with you people, and the harder I study, the smarter I get. And, ... I feel good about myself when I do.
Harvey: But you make us work so hard.
Kathy: Yes, but look how good you're getting at writing. I think you hit a personal best on your last paper. You're becoming a very good writer.

1.   What view of intelligence was Kathy modeling when she said, "The harder I study, the smarter I get."

2.   Using Self-Worth Theory as a basis for your conclusion, assess the effectiveness of Kathy's comment: "Yes, but look how good you're getting at writing. I think you hit a personal best on your last paper. You're becoming a very good writer." Was this comment more or less effective than the comment, "Yes, but look how good you're getting at writing. I think you hit a personal best on your last paper. Your hard work is paying off isn't it," would have been? Explain.

Exercise 10.4

For Items 1 through 4, decide if self-determination theory would recommend (R) or would not recommend (NR) the teacher statement. Explain why in each case.

1.   In handing out a test to her class, a teacher says, "Work hard on this test now. It's kind of a tough one."

2.   In handing back a test, the teacher notices that Tommy has gotten an A on it. With a smile, he says, "Well done, Tommy. That was easy, wasn't it?"

3.   Sympathetically, a teacher says to a student who has just received a D on a math quiz, "Try not to feel too bad about this, Billy. I know math is hard for you."

4.   To a girl of average ability who has just received a B on a test, a teacher says, "Very well done, Susan. You're getting good at this stuff."

For items 5, 6, and 7, decide on the basis of attribution theory whether or not the students would be likely to make the statements that appear in each case. Explain your reasoning.

5. "I'm generally pretty good in science, but I don't think I'll do well on this next test. I have a funny feeling about it."

6. "I'll never be able to get it. I have a mental block against Spanish. I've never been able to get it straight."

7. "I'm scared of this test. I guessed on four questions last time and got three right. I don't know if I can pull that off again."

Feedback for Application Exercises_____

Exercise 10.1

1. The increase in Jim's motivation can best be explained on the basis of cognitive theories of motivation. His comment best indicates a response to a need to understand the way the world works, which is the foundation of cognitive motivation theory.

2. The importance of the principle is best explained on the basis of humanistic views of motivation. Knowing that they will be allowed to respond without fear of interruption (or ridicule) increases a student's sense of safety, which is part of Maslow's Hierarchy of needs. Maslow's work best fits humanistic views of motivation.

3. Cognitive theorists would suggest that Kathy's statement describing a relationship between a thousand years ago and the present appeals to learners' instinctive need for order, predictability, and how the world works.

Kathy is also modeling genuine interest in the content she is teaching, which is related to cognitive theory (specifically social cognitive theory).

4. Humanistic theorists would suggest that the description of the relationship appeals to Maslow's level of "Intellectual Achievement."

5. David's comment to Kelly was a response to Kathy's enthusiasm. The motivating effects of enthusiasm are best explained through modeling, which is consistent with cognitive views of motivation.

6. This comment is likely to increase Harvey's intrinsic motivation. Kathy's praise was a positive reinforcer for Harvey, and research indicates that reinforcers that communicate increasing competence can increase intrinsic motivation. (In contrast, reinforcers given for simple participation in an activity, or reinforcers used to control behavior, decrease intrinsic motivation.)

Exercise 10.2

1. The motivating effects of this exchange are best explained with self-efficacy theory. Hearing that he is "becoming a very good writer" can increase Harvey's belief in his capability of writing effective papers. This belief is the definition of self-efficacy.

2. The motivating effects of the information in this set of paragraphs is best explained with expectancy x value theory. In paragraph 11, Harvey commented, "Yeah, yeah, I know. . . . Being good writers will help us in everything we do in life." This comment illustrates the utility value of being a good writer. Utility value is one of the factors that increases task value in expectancy x value theory.

Paragraphs 14-16 illustrate the personalization of the topic Kathy was teaching. Personalizing content increases the intrinsic interest in the topic, and intrinsic interest is another factor that increases task value.

Kathy further personalized the content in paragraph 24 by demonstrating how events of long ago influence our present lives, and she further emphasized the utility value of their work by saying, "Remember, your writing and the ability to make and defend an argument is a skill that goes way beyond a specific topic like the Crusades. This applies in everything we do."

3. The motivating effects of the information in this set of paragraphs is best explained with self-determination theory. In paragraphs 9 and 10 Kathy gives Harvey feedback about his increasing competence, and the need for competence is basic and innate according to self-determination theory.

In paragraphs 30 and 39 Kathy helped the students develop perceptions of control by saying that they could take either position in their essays if they could provide support (30), and in 39 she gave them the choice of making a presentation or writing a paper. Being given choices also increases perceptions of control.

In paragraphs 47-51 Kathy helped meet Harvey's need for relatedness by taking a personal interest in him. The need for relatedness is also basic and innate according to self-determination theory.

4. Paragraph 38 is best explained with goal theory. When Kathy said, "Ask yourself, 'Do I actually have evidence here, or is it simply an opinion?'. . . The more aware you are when you write, the better your work will be," she was emphasizing metacognition, which is part of using goals effectively.

Then, when she said, "And, remember we made a commitment to ourselves at the beginning of the year that we were going to help each other as much as we could when we give each other feedback on our writing," she was emphasizing a social responsibility goal. As you saw in the chapter, social responsibility goals lead to increased motivation and achievement.

Exercise 10.3

1. In saying, "The harder I study, the smarter I get," Kathy was modeling an incremental view of intelligence. This view holds that intelligence can be increased with effort. (In contrast, an entity view holds that intelligence is fixed.)

2. Using self-worth theory as a basis for the assessment, Kathy's statement was more effective than saying to Harvey, "Your hard work is paying off isn't it." According to self-worth theory, being perceived as having high ability is important to people, because self-worth and ability are interdependent. By saying, "You're becoming a very good writer," Kathy was implying to Harvey that his writing ability was high. For some people, having to work hard is an indicator of low ability, so telling Harvey that his hard work was paying off could imply that he had low ability, which could detract from his sense of self worth.

Exercise 10.4

1. Self-determination theory would recommend the statement. The teacher's statement puts students in a "win win" situation. If they do well, they have evidence of increasing competence, since competence is required to accomplish difficult tasks.

2. This statement would not be recommended. Accomplishment on an easy task does not indicate that competence is increasing, so this doesn't help meet learners' need for competence.

3. This is not a recommended statement. The teacher is unwittingly suggesting that Billy is incompetent.

4. This statement is recommended. The teacher is suggesting to Susan that her competence is increasing.

5. According to attribution theorists, this is an unlikely statement. The student attributes past success to ability which is a stable cause, leading to the expectation of similar results in the future.

6. The theory would suggest that this is a likely statement. The student attributes failure to a stable cause (ability), which, as in Item 5, leads to the expectation of similar results.

7. This is a likely statement. Success on the last test was attributed to luck, which is unstable, leading to the expectation of different results in the future.

Chapter 10: Theories of Motivation

Self-Help Quiz_____

TRUE/FALSE QUESTIONS. Write T in the blank if the statement is true and write F if the statement is false.

_____ 1. Your students are finding out what kinds of materials are attracted to magnets and are very involved in the activity. According to research, offering them a reward for their participation is likely to detract from their intrinsic motivation.
_____ 2. According to Maslow, people can become self-actualized after they've met their needs for intellectual achievement and aesthetic appreciation.
_____ 3. According to Maslow, belonging to a family or social group will not be a need for people until their need for safety is met.
_____ 4. According to research, people with an incremental view of ability are likely to set more challenging goals than people with an entity view of ability.
_____ 5. According to Bandura, people achieve a sense of self-efficacy based primarily on the extent to which they're successful.

MULTIPLE-CHOICE ITEMS. Circle the best response in each case.

For Items 6-11, mark A if the example best fits a humanistic view of motivation, mark B if it fits a behaviorist view, and C for a cognitive view.

6. "I try to give my kids' tests back to them the next day. They try harder when they know how they're doing."

7. "Kenny is always seeking attention. I think he has a bad home life, so the attention makes him feel like he's 'in with the guys'."

8. "I needed that grade. When I do well, I try harder; when I do poorly, I don't try so hard."

9. "Steve is always acting up. He wouldn't do it except he gets the attention of the other kids in the class."

10. "I try get the kids to think they're learning something important and challenging. Then, I fix it so they can 'get it', so they feel 'smart'."

11. "I always try to start my lessons with a problem or something they don't quite expect. It helps keep the kids interested."

12. Janet enjoys living in a large city, because "It gives me a chance to go to a play now and then, a concert, and maybe even the opera." Based on Maslow's work, we would conclude from this information that:
    a. Janet's intellectual achievement need has been satisfied.
    b. Janet is a self-actualized person.
    c. Janet has reasonably high self-esteem.
    d. Janet often feels uneasy when she's alone.

13. Of the following, the concept most closely related to self-determination theory is:
    a. reinforcement.
    b. competence.
    c. safety.
    d. intrinsic interest.

14. Susan is improving her ability in algebra, and she now is able to solve simultaneous equations with considerable skill. According to cognitive theories of motivation, what is the most likely outcome of this experience?
   a. Susan feels reinforced each time she correctly solves a problem.
   b. Susan will develop a sense of self-efficacy.
   c. Susan's self-esteem will improve.
   d. Susan's need for intellectual achievement will be met.

15. Leah seems to be very interested in aesthetic activities. She very much enjoys the symphony, ballet, and art openings. She is also taking a course in art history, and is working hard in it. Leah's motivation in her art history course is best explained by which of the following?
   a. Self-efficacy theory
   b. Expectancy x value theory
   c. Attribution theory
   d. Self-determination theory.

Use the following example for items 16-20.

Their teacher has returned a test, and the students are commenting on the results.
   "I just can't do it," Kathy moaned, slapping her test down on her desk after seeing a D on it. "I guess I just can't do French."
   Billy nonchalantly shrugged, seeing a C-, "Not bad, considering how much I studied. I would have done fine, but I just couldn't get into studying for this one. I never opened my book."
   "Weird," Jeff added. "I got a B and I really didn't understand this stuff. I must have been good at guessing or something. I don't know how I did it."
   Seeing a C, Sandra said shaking her head, "I knew this test was going to really rough, and I just wasn't ready. I will be next time though."

16. The theory used to explain each of the students' comments is based on which of the following premises?
   a. People have an innate desire to understand why they perform the way that they do.
   b. People have an innate need to be competent in their fields of study.
   c. People achieve higher if they think about the way they study an learn.
   d. Past performance on a task increases people's beliefs about their capabilities of accomplishing similar tasks.

17. The student who is in the greatest danger of developing "learned helplessness" is:
   a. Kathy.
   b. Billy.
   c. Jeff.
   d. Sandra.

18. The student who is most likely to have an incremental view of ability is:
   a. Kathy.
   b. Billy.
   c. Jeff.
   d. Sandra.

19. The student whose comment is best explained by self-worth theory is probably:
   a. Kathy.
   b. Billy.
   c. Jeff.
   d. Sandra.

20. The student with the most desirable attribution is:
    a.   Kathy.
    b.   Billy.
    c.   Jeff.
    d.   Sandra.

21. You have a student who has an incremental view of ability. He scores poorly on one of your tests. Based on this information, which of the following is most likely?
    a.   He will avoid challenging tasks in the future to protect his self-esteem.
    b.   He will develop a sense of learned helplessness.
    c.   He will consciously avoid trying, so he can attribute lack of success to lack of effort rather than lack of ability.
    d.   He will view his lack of success as lack of effort and will try harder in the future.

22. Tamika Jenkins, a seventh-grade math teacher, has students offer input into the classroom rules and procedures that they will follow for the year. The class discusses the input, and Tamika develops her rules and procedures based on the discussions. Of the following, the theory of motivation that best explains the value of Tamika's efforts is:
    a.   Self-efficacy theory.
    b.   Goal theory.
    c.   Expectancy x value theory.
    d.   Self-determination theory.

23. In her interaction with Harvey in the chapter Kathy Brewster said, "I have to work every night to keep up with you people, and the harder I study, the smarter I get ... and I feel good about myself when I do." Which of the following theories best explains Kathy's efforts?
    a.   Self-efficacy theory. Kathy was trying to increase beliefs about Harvey's capability of doing the work in her class.
    b.   Self-determination theory. Kathy was trying to increase Harvey's perception of his competence.
    c.   Self-worth theory. Kathy was consciously attempting to link self-worth to effort and improvement.
    d.   Expectancy x value theory. Kathy was attempting to increase Harvey's expectancy for success.

24. The motivating effects of increased understanding and background knowledge can be explained with both expectancy x value theory and self-determination theory. Write a two-line explanation for the value of increased understanding on the basis of each theory.

25. Darren was a low achiever in Laura Cossey's seventh grade math class. As Laura monitored the students during seat work, she saw that Darren had made little progress on the word problems.
    "Come on, Darren. I know you can do this work," Laura whispered. "When I see a problem like this, I first think, 'How can I break the problem into parts?' and they I try to draw a picture of each part. I'll be back here in a few minutes to see how you're doing."
    In a few minutes, Laura returned, leaned over Darren, and said, "What do we have?"
    Darren was still somewhat uncertain, but he obviously had gone over the problem and tried to get started. He pointed to the problem and said, "They want to know the percent decrease in the cost."
    "Good," Laura smiled. "Now, what else do you know?"
    As Darren began explaining his understanding of the problem, Laura asked only as many questions as necessary to keep him on the right track. Finally, as he arrived at a solution, she said, "That's excellent thinking, Darren. . . . Now, look at the problem again to see whether it all makes sense. I'll be back in a minute to see your final solution. You be ready to explain to me exactly how you did it. Okay?" She smiled and moved on to another student.

Which theory of motivation best explains Laura's efforts? Explain in detail.

Self-Help Quiz Answers

1. t
2. f
3. t
4. t
5. f
6. c Knowing "how they're doing" relates to the "need to understand," which is a fundamental idea on which cognitive theories of motivation are based.
7. a A need to be "in with the guys" implies a belonging need, and the consideration of needs such as belonging most closely relates to humanistic views of motivation.
8. b The example only describes a relationship between the grade and how hard the student tries. There is no implication of any internal needs or processes that are operating. The grade serves as a reinforcer.
9. b There isn't an implication of the attention meeting a need, such as a need for belonging. The attention serves instead as a reinforcer.
10. c The teacher in this case is trying to develop high self-efficacy in the students. The teacher's efforts can also be explained with self-determination theory. The teacher is trying to make the students feel competent. The need for competence is basic and innate according to self-determination theory, which is a cognitive theory of motivation.
11. c The teacher is trying to capitalize on curiosity motivation, which is best explained with cognitive theories. Something that arouses curiosity relates to the "need to understand," which is fundamental to cognitive theories of motivation.
12. c According to Maslow, in order to be at the level of growth needs, deficiency needs must have been met, and the example implies that Janet is at the level of aesthetic appreciation. Further, Maslow says that growth needs are never "met." Therefore Janet's intellectual achievement need cannot have been met (choice a). We don't have enough information to determine whether or not she is a self-actualized person (choice b), and feeling uneasy is a form of not feeling safe. To be at aesthetic appreciation, she would have to have her safety needs met (choice d).
13. b According to self-determination theory, the need for competence is basic and innate. Reinforcement is a behaviorist concept (choice a), safety is most closely related to humanistic views of motivation (choice c), and intrinsic interest is a component of expectancy x value theory.
14. b Self-efficacy is a concept related to cognitive views of motivation. Tangible evidence of improvement tends to increase self-efficacy. Reinforcement is a behaviorist concept and self-esteem and intellectual achievement are most closely related to humanistic views of motivation.
15. b Leah appears to be intrinsically interested in the arts. Her hard work results from this interest. Intrinsic interest is a factor that increases the task value component of expectancy x value theory.
16. a. The students are each offering an explanation for their performance. The need to explain to understand why they perform the way that they do is the basic premise of attribution theory. The need to be competent is a premise of self-determination theory (choice b). Achieving higher if people think about the way they study and learn illustrates metacognition, and metacognition is most closely related to goal theory (choice c). People's beliefs about their capabilities of accomplishing tasks describes self-efficacy (choice d).
17. a Kathy suggesting that she just can't do French attributes her performance to lack of ability. In extreme cases attributions of lack of ability can lead to learned helplessness.
18. d Sandra says, "I knew this test was going to really rough, and I just wasn't ready. I will be next time though." She is making an attribution of effort (or lack of effort). Of the students in the example, she is most likely to believe that she can change her own ability through hard work.
19. b Billy makes a point of saying that he didn't study. This is his effort to create the perception that he has high ability, since he must have high ability in order to get a C- minus without exerting any effort. (Kathy makes no effort to look "smart." She admits that she has problems in French.)
20. d Sandra believes that she's in control and that she can improve her grade with effort. This belief can lead to sustained motivation.

21. d   Learners with an incremental view of ability tend to believe that they can improve with effort.

22. d   Tamika's efforts are best explained by self-determination theory. She is helping increase the students' sense of control over their environment. The need for control (autonomy) is basic and innate according to self-determination theory.

23. c   Kathy's comment, "I feel good about myself when I do," is a statement about self-worth, and in in saying, "The harder I study, the smarter I get ... and I feel good about myself when I do," she was attempting to link self-worth to effort and perseverance. This effort was an attempt to dispel the notion that effort and ability are inversely related, which some students believe.

24.   According to expectancy x value theory, learners' intrinsic interest in a topic increases as their understanding of the topic increases. Intrinsic interest is a factor that increases task value.

          According to self-determination theory, the need for competence is basic and innate. Increased understanding and background knowledge helps meet the need for competence.

25.   Laura's efforts can best be explained with self-efficacy theory. First, she encouraged Darren to try working the problem. This was a form of verbal persuasion, and verbal persuasion is one of the factors influencing self-efficacy. Second, she modeled her thinking when she said, "When I see a problem like this, I first think . . . ." Modeling is a second factor that influences self-efficacy. Finally, Laura provided only enough guidance to be sure that he made genuine progress toward the solution on his own. Having evidence of his capability of accomplishing the task is the most important factor influencing self-efficacy.

CHAPTER 11: MOTIVATION IN THE CLASSROOM

Chapter Outline_____

I. Class structure: Creating a learning-focused environment
II. Self-regulated learners: Developing student responsibility
    A. Developing self-regulation: Applying self-determination theory
    B. Helping students develop self-regulation: Instructional principles
III. Teacher characteristics: Personal qualities that increase student motivation to learn
    A. Personal teaching efficacy: Beliefs about teaching and learning
    B. Modeling and enthusiasm: Communicating genuine interest
    C. Caring: Meeting the need for belonging and relatedness
        1. Communicating caring
    D. Teacher expectations: Increasing perceptions of competence
    E. Demonstrating personal qualities that increase motivation: Instructional principles
IV. Climate variables: Creating a motivating environment
    A. Order and safety: Classrooms as secure places to learn
    B. Success: Developing learner self-efficacy
    C. Challenge: Increasing perceptions of competence and self-determination
    D. Task comprehension: Increasing perceptions of autonomy and value
    E. The TARGET Program: Applying goal theory in classrooms
V. Instructional variables: Developing interest in learning activities
    A. Introductory focus: Attracting students' attention
    B. Personalization: Links to students' lives
    C. Involvement: Increasing intrinsic motivation
        1. Using open-ended questioning to increase involvement
        2. Using hands-on activities to promote involvement
    D. Feedback: Meeting the need to understand
    E. Applying the climate and instructional variables in your classroom: Instructional principles
    F. Assessment and learning: Using feedback to increase interest and self-efficacy
    G. Learning contexts: Motivation to learn in the urban classroom
        1. The impact of teachers
            a. Caring
            b. Order and safety
            c. Involvement
            d. Challenge

Chapter Objectives_____

- Explain the differences between a learning-focused and a performance-focused classroom.

- Describe strategies that can be used to develop learner self-regulation and explain different levels of student self-regulation.

- Identify the personal characteristics of teachers who increase students' motivation to learn, and analyze these characteristics in classroom activities.

- Analyze teachers' behaviors using the climate variables as a basis, and describe the relationships between the climate variables and the categories in the TARGET model.

- Identify examples of teachers implementing the instructional variables in learning activities.

Chapter Overview_____

In Chapter 10 you studied theories and research that help us understand why certain teacher actions, such as praising students for their increasing competence, creating a positive classroom environment, using concrete and personalized examples, promoting high levels of involvement, and providing detailed feedback about performance on assessments, increases students' motivation to learn. In this chapter these theories and research are synthesized into a Model for Promoting Student Motivation that can be applied in all classrooms and at all grade levels.

The model is composed of four components. The first, self-regulated learners, emphasizes the development of students' inclination and ability to accept responsibility and control their own learning. Teacher characteristics, the second component, describes the importance of variables such as personal teaching efficacy, modeling and enthusiasm, caring, and positive teacher expectations in promoting learner motivation. The third component, climate variables, emphasizes the contribution of classroom environments that emphasize safety and order, promote learner success and perceptions of challenge, and make tasks clear and comprehensible to learner motivation. Finally, instructional variables describe the role of factors such as the way lessons are introduced, student involvement, personalized experiences, and feedback in promoting intrinsic interest in the topics students study.

It is important to remember that the variables in the model are interdependent; a single variable cannot be effectively applied if the others are lacking.

Application Exercises_____

Use the following case study to answer application exercises 11.1-11.3.

The following is the same synthesis of Kathy Brewster's work that you saw in Chapter 10 of this study guide. In Chapter 10 you related the case study to the theories of motivation described in Chapter 10 of your text. In this chapter you will relate the case study to the variables in the Model for Promoting Student Motivation. Read the case study and answer the questions that follow. (The paragraphs are numbered for your reference.)

1.   "We'd better get moving," Susan urged Jim as they approached the door of Kathy Brewster's classroom. "The bell is gonna ring, and you know how Brewster is about this class. She thinks it's SO important."
2.   "Did you finish your homework?" Jim asked and then stopped himself. "What am I talking about? You've done your homework in every class since I've known you."
3.   "Sure, I don't mind it that much.... It bothers me when I don't get something, and sometimes it's even fun. My dad helps me. He says he wants to keep up with the world," Susan laughed.
4.   "In some classes, I just do enough to get a decent grade, but not in here," Jim responded. "I used to hate history, but I sometimes I even read ahead a little, because Brewster really makes you think. It's actually interesting the way she's always telling us about the way we are because of something that happened a zillion years ago.... I never thought about this stuff in that way before."
5.   "Gee, Mrs. Brewster, that assignment was impossible," Harvey grumbled as he walked in.
6.   "That's good for you," Kathy smiled. "I know it was a tough assignment, but you need to be challenged. It's hard for me too when I'm studying and trying to put together new ideas, but if I hang in, I always feel like I can get it."
7.   "Aw, c'mon, Mrs. Brewster. I thought you knew everything."
8.   "I wish. I have to study every night to keep up with you people, and the harder I study, the smarter I get," Kathy nodded. "And, ... I feel good about myself when I do."
9.   "But you make us work so hard," Harvey continued in feigned complaint.
10.   "Yes, but look how good you're getting at writing," Kathy smiled again, pointing her finger at him. "I think you hit a personal best on your last paper. You're becoming a very good writer."
11.   "Yeah, yeah, I know," Harvey smiled on his way to his desk, ". . . and being good writers will help us in everything we do in life," repeating a rationale the students continually hear from Kathy.
12.   "Stop by and see me after class," Kathy quietly said to Jenny as Jenny came in. "I'd like to talk to you for a minute."
13.   Kathy finished her beginning-of-class routines and then pulled down a map in the front of the room. "Let's review for a moment to see where we are. We began our discussion of the Crusades yesterday. How did we start?"
14.   ". . . We imagined that we all left Lincoln High School and that it was taken over by people who believed that extracurricular activities should be eliminated," Carnisha volunteered.
15.   "Good," Kathy smiled. "Then what?"
16.   "We decided we'd talk to them ... We'd be on a 'crusade' to change their minds.
17.   "Very good. . . . Now, what were the actual Crusades all about? ... Selena?"
18.   ". . . The Christians wanted to get the Holy Land back from the Muslims."
19.   "And why? ... Becky?"
20.   "The Holy Lands were important for the Christians. I suppose they just wanted them because of that."
21.   "Also, the map shows how much territory the Muslims were getting, and the people in Europe were afraid the Muslims would take over their land," Cindy added.
22.   "Good thought, Cindy. . . . They certainly were a military threat. In fact, the conflict that occurred in Kosovo is a present day reminder of the clash between Christians and Muslims. How else might they have been threatening?"
23.   "Maybe ... economically," Brad added. "You're always telling us how economics rules the world."
24.   "Excellent, Brad," Kathy laughed. "Indeed, economics was a factor. In fact, we'll see that the military and economic threats of the Muslims, together with the religious issue, were factors that led to

Columbus's voyage to the New World.... Think about that. The Muslims in 1000 A.D. have had an influence on us here today.

25.   "Now, for today's assignment," Kathy continued, "you were asked to write a paragraph answering the question, 'Were the Crusades a success or a failure?' You could take either position. The quality of your paragraph depends on how you defended your position, not on the position itself. Remember, your writing and the ability to make and defend an argument is a skill that goes way beyond a specific topic like the Crusades. This applies in everything we do.

26.   "So, let's see how we made out. Go ahead.... Nikki?"

27.   "I said they were a failure. . . . The Europeans didn't accomplish what they were after ... to get the Holy Land back for Christianity," Nikki said. "There were several Crusades, and after only one did they get sort of a foothold, and it only lasted . . . like about 50 years, I think."

28.   "How about you, Joe?"

29.   "I said they were a success because the Europeans learned new military strategies that they later used ... here, in the Americas. If it hadn't been for the Crusades, they wouldn't have learned the techniques, ... at least not for a long time. It even changed our ideas about guerrilla fighting."

30.   "Also good, Joe," Kathy nodded. "This is exactly what we're after. Nikki and Joe took opposite positions in their paragraphs, but they each provided several details in support.

31.   "Let's look at another one. . . . What was your position, Anita?"

32.   "I said they ... were a success. Western Europe took a lot from their culture . . . in the Middle East. Like, some of the spices we eat today first came to Europe then."

33.   "Now isn't that interesting!" Kathy waved energetically. "See, here's another case where we see ourselves today finding a relationship to people who lived 1,000 or more years ago. That's what history is all about."

34.   "Brewster loves this stuff," David whispered to Kelly, smiling slightly.

35.   "Yeah," she replied. "History has never been my favorite subject, but some of this stuff is actually kind of neat."

36.   "Okay. One more," Kathy continued, "and we'll move on."

37.   The class reviewed another example, and then Kathy told the students to revise their paragraphs based on what they had discussed and turn in a product for peer review the next day.

38.   "Remember, think about what you're doing when you make your revisions," she emphasized. "Read your paragraph after you write it, and ask yourself, 'Do I actually have evidence here, or is it simply an opinion?' ... The more aware you are when you write, the better your work will be. And, remember we made a commitment to ourselves at the beginning of the year that we were going to help each other as much as we could when we give each other feedback on our writing. . . . So, I know that you'll come through.

39.   "One more reminder," Kathy said as the period was nearly over, "group presentations on the Renaissance are Wednesday and Thursday. You decide what groups will be on each day. For those who chose to write the paper on the Middle Ages, remember we agreed that they're due next Friday."

40.   As the students were leaving the room, Jenny stopped at her desk. "You wanted to see me, Mrs. Brewster? . . . What's up?"

41.   "I've been watching you for a few days, and you don't seem to be yourself. You're somewhere else. . . . Is everything okay?"

42.   "I. . . yes, . . . no, not really," Jenny said, her eyes starting to fill with tears. "My mom and dad are having trouble, and I'm really, really scared. I'm afraid they're going to break up."

43.   "Do you want to talk?"

44.   ". . . No . . . not right now."

45.   Kathy reached over, touched Jenny on the shoulder, and said, "I realize that there isn't anything that I can do directly but I'm here you want to talk about it, . . . or anything else . . . anytime."

46.   "Thanks, . . . I will," Jenny smiled weakly as she turned to go.

47.   As Kathy was working after school, Harvey poked his head into the room.

48.   "Come in," she smiled. "How's the writer?"

49.   "I just came by to say I hope I didn't offend you this morning, complaining so much about all the work."

50.   "Not at all. . . . I haven't given it a second thought.

51.   "I guess you already know how much you've done for me," Harvey continued. "You believed in me when the rest of the world wrote me off. . . . My drug conviction is off my record now, and I haven't 'used'

in over a year. I couldn't have made it without you. You made me work and put in all kinds of extra time with me. You pushed me and wouldn't let me give up on myself. I was headed for trouble, and now . . . I'm headed for college."

52.   "We all need a nudge now and then," Kathy smiled. "That's what I'm here for. I appreciate it, but no need to thank me. I didn't do it; you did . . . . Now, scoot. I'm thinking up a rough assignment for you tomorrow."

53.   "Mrs. Brewster, you're relentless," Harvey waved as he headed out the door.

Exercise 11.1

1.   Identify the variable in the Model for Promoting Student Motivation best illustrated by paragraphs 8 and 34 of the case study. Explain.

2.   Identify the two variables in the Model for Promoting Student Motivation best illustrated by paragraphs 13-16 of the case study. Explain.

3.   Kathy demonstrated caring in two places in the case study. Identify the places and explain how caring was demonstrated.

Exercise 11.2

1.   Look at paragraphs 37-39 of the case study. To which component of the Model for Promoting Student Motivation do these paragraphs most closely relate? Explain.

2.   To which variable in the Model for Promoting Student Motivation does paragraph 38 of the case study most closely relate? Explain.

Exercise 11.3

1.   You are a language arts teacher and you're planning a lesson on direct and indirect objects. Offer a specific suggestion for what you might do to apply the instructional variable introductory focus at the beginning of your lesson.

2.   You are the same language arts teacher planning a lesson on direct and indirect objects. Describe a simple way of capitalizing on the motivating effects of personalization in your lesson.

3.   Students are talking, and one says to the other, "Wait. I'm checking over my homework. You know what it's like. . . . You don't do a good job on your homework in this class, and you're dead." To which variable in the Model for Promoting Student Motivation does the comment most closely relate? Explain.

4.   A teacher has a rule, "Listen politely when someone in the class is talking." She enforces the rule consistently, and she particularly emphasizes that students may say nothing that hurts their classmates' feelings. To which variable in the Model for Promoting Student Motivation does the comment most closely relate? Explain.

Feedback for Application Exercises_____

Exercise 11.1

1. Paragraphs 8 and 34 best illustrate modeling. In paragraph 8, Kathy describes her own efforts, and in paragraph 34 David whispers, "Brewster loves this stuff." His conclusion was a result of Kathy modeling her enthusiasm for history.

2. Paragraphs 13-16 illustrate both introductory focus and personalization. In these paragraphs Kathy attempted to attract the students' attention and provide an umbrella for the lesson. And, the class's "crusade" to prevent the elimination of extracurricular activities was a form of personalization.

3. Kathy demonstrated caring in her dealings with both Jenny and Harvey. She was sensitive enough to recognize that Jenny wasn't herself, and she inquired about it, and she worked with Harvey and provided the unconditional positive regard that Carl Rogers believed was essential for personal growth. Also, in both cases, she willingly spent time after class with both students.

Exercise 11.2

1. Paragraphs 37-39 most closely relate to the self-regulated learners component of the model. (Teacher characteristics, climate variables, and instructional variables are the other components.) Accepting responsibility and making decisions are essential characteristics of self-regulation, and Kathy's students had to decide which position they were going to take, and they also had to decide whether they were going to write a paper or make a group presentation. In addition, in paragraph 38 Kathy emphasized metacognition, which is an important characteristic of self-regulation.

2. As you saw in the feedback for Item 1, Kathy emphasized metacognition—one of the variables in the self-regulated learners component of the model—in paragraph 38.

Exercise 11.3

1. One way to apply the variable introductory focus would be to begin a lesson with a question or problem. For example, the teacher might write a pair of sentences on the board, such as the following:

Steve sketched Conchita a picture of his new house.
Mom gave Sen a football for his birthday.

She could then ask the question, "What do Conchita and Sen have in common in the two sentences?" and "What do picture and football have in common in the two sentences? . . . Examining these common features is what we're going to be doing today." The questions and the statement about the day's lesson act as an attention getter and provide an umbrella for the lesson.

Many other possibilities exist. Anything the teacher does to attract students' attention and provide an umbrella for the lesson is an application of introductory focus.

2. The simplest way to capitalize on personalization is to put students' names, the school, or their teachers into the examples. This is what Kathy did in her lesson.

3. The comment most closely relates to teacher expectations. It communicates that the teacher expects the students to complete all homework to a high standard. (Research indicates that teacher expectations are one of the most important factors that influence learner motivation and achievement.)

4. This practice most closely relates to order and safety. By consistently enforcing a rule that prevents students from saying or doing anything to hurt their classmates' feelings, the teacher creates a classroom environment in which the students feel comfortable in answering questions and expressing opinions without fear of ridicule or embarrassment.

Self-Help Quiz_____

TRUE/FALSE QUESTIONS. Write T in the blank if the statement is true and write F if the statement is false.

_____ 1. Metacognition is an important part of learning, but it isn't essential for motivation.

_____ 2. Of the cognitive theories of motivation, self-regulation is most strongly grounded in self-determination theory.

_____ 3. Teachers most effectively communicate their own interest in the topics they teach through modeling.

_____ 4. Learners believe that teachers who hold them to high standards of performance care about them more than teachers whose standards of performance are lower.

_____ 5. Teachers should primarily call on students who raise their hands, because calling on students who don't raise their hands "puts them on the spot."

MULTIPLE-CHOICE ITEMS. Circle the best response in each case.

6. In an effort to protect students' self-esteem teachers will sometimes lower their expectations and accept low-standard work from students. According to research, this practice indicates a lack of which of the following?
   a. Modeling and enthusiasm
   b. Strategy use
   c. Personalization
   d. Caring

7. "There isn't much we can do with these kids," Sara Hindman, a fifth-grade teacher sighs. "They get no support from home, they won't do their homework, and they have terrible attitudes."

   "I'm not sure," Valencia Brown, responds. "I think we should force them to learn whether they act like they want to or not. I believe we can do it. Down in their hearts they actually want to learn. They're afraid they can't so, they act like it isn't important."

   Valencia's comments best illustrate which of the following variables from the Model for Promoting Student Motivation?
   a. Modeling and enthusiasm
   b. Personal teaching efficacy
   c. Positive expectations
   d. Order and safety

8. A learning-focused environment is important for motivation. Which one of the following statements made by teachers best promotes a learning-focused environment?
   a. "Let's try hard now. I want to see as many A's as possible on the quiz."
   b. "Very good, everyone. Two-thirds of the class got a B or better on the assignment."
   c. "Very well done. Most of you are improving on each quiz."
   d. "C'mon now. Jared, Naomi, Nikki, and Hector got the only scores over 90 on the last quiz. Let's see a few more up there next time."

9. "Darren," Mr. Fuller admonishes after Darren has interrupted Teresa's answer. "We listen politely when someone else is talking."

   The variable in the Model for Promoting Student Motivation to which Mr. Fuller's admonishment most closely relates is:
   a. metacognition.
   b. personal teaching efficacy.
   c. task comprehension.
   d. order and safety.

Use the following vignette for items 10-12.

"As you're studying a new concept, what is one of the first things you should be asking yourself?" Crystal Emery asks her students.

After thinking for several seconds, Mike responds, "You're always after us to remember to try and think of an example."

"Good," Crystal smiles. "That's exactly it. We want to be continually thinking as we study, and keeping the need for examples in mind is one of the best things we can do."

10. The *component* of the Model for Promoting Student Motivation to which Crystal's encouragement most closely relates is:
   a. Self-regulated learners: Developing student responsibility.
   b. Teacher characteristics: Personal qualities that increase student motivation.
   c. Climate variables: Creating a motivating environment.
   d. Instructional variables: Developing interest in learning activities.

11. The *variable* in the Model for Promoting Student Motivation to which Crystal's encouragement most closely relates is:
   a. modeling.
   b. monitoring goals.
   c. metacognition.
   d. challenge.

12. Of the following, the theory of motivation that best supports Crystal's efforts is:
   a. self-efficacy theory.
   b. self-determination theory.
   c. expectancy x value theory.
   d. attribution theory.

Use the following vignette for Items 13-16.

On Monday after the Jackson High football team's 21-20 Saturday night victory over arch-rival Fullerwood High, Rodney Leist writes the following sentence on the board:

The game was incredibly exciting, and our team pulled out the victory at the very end.

"What is one adjective in the sentence. . . . Darrell?" Rodney asks.
". . ."
"What do we know about the game?" Rodney continues.
" . . . It was exciting," Darrell says hesitantly after several seconds.
"Yes, good," Rodney smiles. "Exciting describes the game, so exciting is an adjective."

13. Of the following, Rodney's second question ("What do we know about the game?") best illustrates his attempt to increase motivation with which of the following variables in the Model for Promoting Student Motivation?
   a. Modeling and enthusiasm
   b. Success
   c. Challenge
   d. Introductory focus

14. Of the following, the variable in the Model for Promoting Student Motivation that Rodney was attempting to implement with his example was:
    a. modeling and enthusiasm.
    b. task comprehension.
    c. introductory focus.
    d. personalization.

15. The theory of motivation that best explains the effectiveness of Rodney's example is:
    a. behaviorism.
    b. expectancy x value theory.
    c. self-efficacy theory.
    d. self-determination theory.

16. Rodney's statement, "Exciting describes the game, so exciting is an adjective," after Darrell's uncertain response best illustrates which of the following variables in the Model for Promoting Student Motivation?
    a. Modeling and enthusiasm.
    b. Task comprehension.
    c. Success.
    d. Feedback.

Use the following vignette for items 17-18.

Tiffany Roundtree displays two plastic drinking cups half full of clear liquid (one is water and the other is alcohol). She drops an ice cube into the cups, and to the students' surprise, the cube floats in the first (the water) and sinks in the second (the alcohol).
"Okay," Tiffany smiles at the students' quizzical looks. "Let's try and figure out what happened here. . . . What do you notice? . . . Kristina?"
"The ice floats in that one (pointing at the first cup), and sank in that one (pointing at the second)."
"Okay, . . . what else?" Tiffany continues. "Kevin?"
"Both the liquids are clear."
"Yes, they are," Tiffany nods.
Tiffany then continues with the lesson.

17. Of the following, Tiffany's use of the cups, water, alcohol, and ice at the beginning of her lesson best illustrates an attempt to capitalize on which of the following variables in the Model for Promoting Student Motivation?
    a. Task comprehension
    b. Challenge
    c. Personalization
    d. Introductory focus

18. Of the following, the variable in the Model for Promoting Student Motivation that Tiffany's questions best illustrate is:
    a. involvement.
    b. challenge.
    c. personalization.
    d. personal teaching efficacy.

Use the following vignette to answer items 19-20.

Mrs. Richards conducts help sessions for her students two nights a week after school. She also works with them before school and even during their lunch hour if they ask for help.

19. The variable of the Model for Promoting Motivation that these behaviors most closely relate to is:
    a. modeling.
    b. caring.
    c. personalization.
    d. feedback.

20. Of the following, the theory of motivation that best explains the importance of Mrs. Richards' actions is:
    a. expectancy x value theory.
    b. self-efficacy theory.
    c. self-worth theory.
    d. self-determination theory.

21. Mr. Moran always returns his quizzes the day after they're given and he goes over frequently missed items carefully. The variable of the Model for Promoting Motivation that this behavior most closely relates to is:
    a. modeling.
    b. expectations.
    c. personal teaching efficacy.
    d. task comprehension.

22. Whenever students fail to respond to her questions, or they give an incorrect answer, Mrs. McDonald asks another, simpler question that the students are able to answer. The variable in the Model for Promoting Motivation that this behavior most closely relates to is:
    a. enthusiasm.
    b. modeling.
    c. expectations.
    d. caring.

23. Mrs. Reynolds attempts to begin each of her lessons with a question or problem that sets the tone for the day. The variable in the Model for Promoting Motivation that best relates to her effort is:
    a. involvement.
    b. introductory focus.
    c. task comprehension.
    d. challenge.
    e. personalization.

24. "We're going to go over numbers 4, 7, and 9 on the quiz," Mr. Betancourt comments, as he returns a quiz the students took the day before. "And remember, we don't just want the right answers. We want information that helps us understand why those answers are the correct ones."
    Which *component* of the Model for Promoting Student Motivation and which *variable* are best illustrated in Mr. Betancourt's comment? Explain.

25. "Geography influences the way we live," Mayte Gonzalez says to her students as they compare the influence of geography on lifestyles in New York compared to Florida. "It impacts the way we make money, how we spend our leisure time, and even the way we dress. This is why we study it, and we'll look for these relationships in all the rest of our units."
    Which variable in the Model for Promoting Student Motivation is best illustrated by Mayte's statements? Explain.

Self-Help Quiz Answers

1. f
2. t
3. t
4. t
5. f
6. d The following quote is presented in the chapter:
One of the best ways to show respect for students is to hold them to high standards—by not accepting sloppy, thoughtless, or incomplete work, by pressing them to clarify vague comments, by encouraging them not to give up, and by not praising work that does not reflect genuine effort. Ironically, reactions that are often intended to protect students' self-esteem—such as accepting low quality work—convey a lack of interest, patience, or caring (Stipek, 2002, p. 157).
7. b Valencia was expressing a belief about teachers' ability to get kids to learn regardless of their backgrounds.
8. c This statement focuses on improvement being the criterion for success. Choice (a) focuses on grades, and (b) and (d) focus on social comparisons.
9. d By requiring students to listen politely when their classmates are talking, Mr. Fuller is trying to create a safe and orderly classroom environment.
10. a When Crystal said, "We want to be continually thinking as we study, and keeping the need for examples in mind is one of the best things we can do," she was encouraging the students to be metacognitive about their study, and metacognition is one of the variables within the component, self-regulated learners: developing student responsibility.
11. c When Crystal said, "We want to be continually thinking as we study, and keeping the need for examples in mind is one of the best things we can do," she was encouraging the students to be metacognitive about their study.
12. b Crystal is attempting to promote metacognition in her students. Being metacognitive is an important characteristic of self-regulation. Self-regulation is best explained by self-determination theory.
13. b By asking an open-ended question, for which virtually any answer is acceptable, Rodney was attempting to help Darrell be successful.
14. d By creating an example that described a school-related, real-world event that occurred two days before, Rodney was attempting to capitalize on the motivating effects of personalization.
15. b Research indicates that personalizing examples increases students' intrinsic interest in an activity. Intrinsic interest is a factor that increases task value, and task value is a component of expectancy x value theory.
16. d Rodney's statement gave Darrell information about the accuracy of his response.
17. d Tiffany attempted to attract the students' attention with her demonstration, and the demonstration provided the umbrella for her lesson.
18. a Tiffany asked open-ended questions, which are effective for involving students. (Open-ended questions are also effective for promoting success.)
19. b Being willing to spend time with students is an important indicator of caring. While she is "personally" involved with her students, "personalization" refers to representing the topics that are being taught in such a way that students can relate to them personally.
20. d By spending her personal time with them, Mrs. Richards demonstrates that she cares about her students. The importance of caring is best explained by the need for relatedness which is basic and innate according to self-determination theory.
21. d Going over quizzes and tests provides students with "knowledge of results," which is characteristic of task comprehension. (Going over tests and quizzes, of course, provides feedback as well.)
22. c Prompting students until they're able to answer communicates that the teacher "expects" all students to be involved. (This also promotes success, another important variable.)
23. b Introductory focus is the variable teachers implement when they want to attract students' attention and provide an umbrella for the rest of the lesson.

24.   Mr. Betancourt says, "We want information that helps us understand why those answers are the correct ones" he was referring to feedback. Feedback is information learners receive about the accuracy or appropriateness of their responses. Feedback is the *variable* and instructional variables is the *component* of the model best illustrated in Mr. Betancourt's comment.

25.   Task comprehension is the variable best illustrated by Mayte Gonzalez's comments. She is explaining why geography is important and why they are studying it.

CHAPTER 12: CREATING PRODUCTIVE LEARNING ENVIRONMENTS: CLASSROOM MANAGEMENT

Chapter Outline_____

I.   The importance of well-managed classrooms
    A.   Public and professional concerns
    B.   The complexities of classrooms
        1.   Classroom events are multidimensional and simultaneous
        2.   Classroom events are immediate
        3.   Classroom events are unpredictable
        4.   Classroom events are public
    C.   Influence on motivation and learning
    D.   Goals of classroom management
        1.   Developing learner responsibility
        2.   Creating a positive classroom climate
        3.   Maximizing time and opportunity for learning
II. Planning for productive classroom environments
    A.   Accommodating student characteristics
    B.   Arranging the physical environment
        1.   Arranging desks
        2.   Personalizing your classroom
    C.   Organizing for instruction
    D.   Creating and teaching rules: Instructional principles
        1.   Teaching rules and procedures
        2.   Beginning the school year
        3.   Monitoring rules
    E.   Learning contexts: Classroom management in urban environments
        1.   Caring and supportive teachers
        2.   Clear standards for acceptable behavior
        3.   High structure
        4.   Effective instruction
III. Communication with parents
    A.   Benefits of communication
    B.   Involving parents: Instructional principles
    C.   Communication with parents: Accommodating learner diversity
        1.   Economic, cultural, and language barriers
        2.   Involving minority parents
IV. Intervening when misbehavior occurs
    A.   Guidelines for successful interventions
        a.   Demonstrate withitness
        b.   Preserve student dignity
        c.   Be consistent
        d.   Follow-through
        e.   Keep interventions brief
        f.   Avoid arguments
    B.   Cognitive interventions
        1.   Verbal-nonverbal congruence
        2.   I-messages
        3.   Logical consequences
    C.   Behavioral interventions
        1.   Designing and maintaining a behavioral management system
    D.   An intervention continuum
        1.   Praising desired behavior
        2.   Ignoring inappropriate behavior
        3.   Using indirect cues

    4. Using desists
    5. Applying consequences
V. Serious management problems: Violence and aggression
  A. School violence and aggression
    1. Responding to aggression against peers
    2. Responding to bullying
    3. Responding to defiant students
  B. Long-term solutions to violence and aggression

Chapter Objectives

- Describe the relationships between classroom management, the complexities of classrooms, and motivation and learning.

- Analyze the planning components for creating productive learning environments in examples of classroom activities.

- Explain how effective communication with parents helps meet classroom management goals and why communication with parents who are members of cultural minorities is particularly important.

- Describe effective interventions in cases of learner misbehavior.

- Describe legal responsibilities and steps involved in responding to acts of violence and aggression.

Chapter Overview

In Chapters 2-5 your study centered on students, how they develop, and the ways they differ. Your efforts shifted in Chapters 6-9 to the nature of the learning process itself, and you then examined learner motivation and what teachers can do to increase it in Chapters 10 and 11. We now turn to the development of productive learning environments.

Productive learning environments are orderly, and they focus on learning. In this chapter we examine teacher practices that help create and maintain orderly, learning-focused classroom environments. Then, in Chapter 13 we discuss principles of instruction that increase learning for all students, regardless of grade level, content area, or topic.

The cornerstone of efficient management is a well-designed system of procedures—the routines that students follow in their daily activities—and rules, which provide the standards for student behavior. To be most effective, teachers prepare a small number of clearly stated rules, they allow the students to provide input into their preparation, and they provide reasons for the rules' existence.

When teachers must intervene to eliminate disruptive behavior, they keep the interventions brief, they follow through to be certain students comply with the rules, and rules are enforced consistently.

Severe management problems, such as defiance or violence, require both immediate, short-term attention and longer-term solutions that deal with the sources of the problem. Teachers should immediately get help in the case of a violent or defiant student, and they should not attempt to solve the problem alone.

Application Exercises_____

Exercise 12.1

Read the following episode, then answer the questions that follow.

Joe, a fifth grade teacher, stopped by to pick up Andrea, his fiancee and an eighth grade science teacher. They fell into a discussion of student discipline and looked at Andrea's rules, which were listed in her classroom:
1. Do not speak without permission.
2. Do not laugh, snicker, make jokes, or in any way react to another student's answer.
3. Do not leave your desk without permission.
4. Be prepared and ready when class begins.
"My list is similar," Joe commented, "except I don't have your second one."
"I knew I would need it," Andrea responded, "so I laid it on them. And we work on it all the time. Every time it happens, I stop the class for a moment and we discuss it, and they have another example to think about. This is a tough one for junior high students.
"I originally told them," she explained, "that part of the reason we were in school was to learn to respect each other and treat each other decently, and this rule would help us learn to do that."

1. How does Andrea's comment, "I knew I would need it," in reference to her second rule, and Joe's lack of a similar comment relate to our discussion of student characteristics?

2. Using one of the guidelines for forming rules as a basis, critique Andrea's first three rules.

3. Using a third guideline, criticize Andrea's second rule in the context of her remark, ". . . so I laid it on them."

4. How does Andrea's comment, "And we work on it all the time," illustrate our discussion about making rules and procedures work?

5. How does Andrea's comment in the last paragraph illustrate one of the guidelines suggested for forming rules?

Exercise 12.2

1. Look again at the examples with Vicki Williams and Donnell Alexander on page 380 of your text. Identify two important characteristics of effective organization present in Donnell's case that were missing in Vicki's.

2. Explain specifically how Vicki's organization is likely to result in her students learning more than will Donnell's students.

Exercise 12.3

1. In the chapter we saw a vignette illustrating Isabel Rodriguez's work with her ninth graders. Here is the vignette again.

> As Isabel was helping Vicki, Ken and Lance began horsing around at the back of the room.
> Isabel quickly excused herself from Vicki, turned, and walked directly to the boys. Looking Lance in the eye, she said pleasantly but firmly, "Lance, we have plenty to do before lunch, and noise disrupts others' work. Begin your homework now," and then looking directly at Ken, she continued, "Ken, you, too. Quickly now. We have only so much time, and we don't want to waste it." She waited until they were working quietly, and then returned to Vicki.

Analyze the effectiveness of her behavior, using the concepts of *withitness* and *overlapping* as the basis for your assessment.

Translate each of the following into "I messages" using the guidelines in the last section.

2. "No assignment? We're never going to learn that way!"

3. "Felicia, be quiet! We can't just blurt out the answers."

Exercise 12.4

Alberto Mancini is an eighth grade math teacher. He has finished an explanation of decimals and percents, and has assigned the students their homework for the next day. He is circulating among the students when Heather gets up, goes to her locker at the back of the room, and noisily shuffles materials in it.

"Heather," Alberto says evenly, "we don't leave our seats without permission."

"I'm just getting some stuff out of my locker," she shoots back.

Alberto walks up to her, looks her in the eye, and says quietly, "I want you to sit down now."

"I need this stuff. You let Karen go to her locker."

"Heather, you know the rules. That's a behavior point lost."

Heather stomps to her desk and loudly slams her books on the floor.

Alberto steps up to her and whispers, "That's a second point, Heather. Please see me after class."

Heather stops after class, and sits down sullenly. Alberto pulls his chair out from behind his desk and sits facing her directly. "Do you have anything you want to say?" he queries.

She sits sullenly, saying nothing.

"If you have anything that you would like to say to me privately, Heather, I'll be happy to listen anytime," he says, leaning toward her. He hesitates a few seconds, then continues, "Now, let me get to the point so we both understand. We must have rules in our classroom, as we discussed at the beginning of the year. I am going to enforce the rules," he continues emphasizing the last sentence and leaning forward again. "It's your choice to break them or not break them, and you know the results.

"I know that you understand what happened today," he continues pleasantly, "but I'll briefly outline it for you to be sure it's clear. . . . Karen asked for permission, and I gave it. She quietly and quickly went to her locker. I believe that you knew you were breaking the rule, and I believe you also know now that you were being disrespectful to your classmates, yourself, and me by slamming your books on the floor. I'll be calling your parents tonight to explain why you'll be serving detention tomorrow. . . . I'll expect to see no more of this in the future," Alberto says pleasantly, getting up. "Here's a tardy slip that will get you into Mrs. Evans's class."

The next morning, Alberto greets the class as he always does and treats Heather as if nothing happened the day before.

1. Using the guidelines and concepts developed in the section on interventions, write an analysis of Alberto's effectiveness in dealing with Heather. Use illustrations taken directly from the example in your description.

2. Identify at least three examples of effective preventive management techniques that Alberto employed in dealing with Heather. Use illustrations taken directly from the example in your description.

Feedback for Application Exercises

Exercise 12.1

1. Andrea is a junior high teacher, and students at this age tend to pick at each other, making remarks and putting their classmates down. By contrast, Joe's fifth graders are less inclined to demonstrate those behaviors, and as a result, a rule such as Andrea's second one is less necessary for his students.

2. Andrea's first three rules are stated negatively: "Do not . . ."

3. "Laying it on them" doesn't allow any student input.

4. "Working on it all the time" is merely another way of indicating that she is carefully monitoring her rules and procedures.

5. This comment indicates that she provided a rationale for the rules that she is using.

Exercise 12.2

1. First, Donnell had her handouts prepared in advance and had them ready to go when her class started. Second, she began immediately after the bell rang. Vicki was still organizing her handouts as the students came into the room, and she didn't get started on time.

2. The difference in the two teachers' organization will be reflected in time for learning. Students quickly adapt to established classroom patterns. For example, Vicki's students will, in general, be in their desks and ready to begin shortly after the bell rings. Donnell will likely have to spend several minutes getting her students settled. In some cases the differences can result in 10-15 minutes more—per day—of time for learning. Over time, the differences in the amount learned can become significant.

Exercise 12.3

1. Isabelle demonstrated both withitness and overlapping. First, she was aware of what was going on in her classroom, so she responded immediately to Ken's and Lance's horseplay. And, at the same time that she was helping Vicki, she was monitoring the rest of the class, which illustrates the concept of overlapping.

In the responses to Items 2, 3, and 4, notice how each: (a) addresses the behavior, (b) describes the behavior in terms of its effect on the teacher, and (c) describes the teacher's feelings generated by the behavior.

2. You must get your assignments in on time. When you don't, I have to give you make-up work, and I get tired and frustrated when I have to spend my time that way.

3. Felicia, blurting out the answers is against the rules. This makes it difficult for me to try to give everyone a chance to answer, and I'm uncomfortable when I can't give everyone an equal chance.

Exercise 12.4

1. Alberto demonstrated several characteristics of effective interventions. First, he kept his encounter with Heather brief and he didn't get in an argument with her. He followed through by seeing her after class and explaining the consequences. While Heather protested to the contrary, Alberto was consistent in his dealing with her. He didn't force Heather into any admission of guilt, thereby forcing a power struggle. His consequences for misbehavior were clear and he administered them.

2. First, Alberto had clearly stated rules for which rationales were provided. This occurred in the planning phase. Second, he was firm in his dealings with Heather. Third, he communicated clearly, addressed the behavior, and was assertive in his response.

Self-Help Quiz_____

TRUE/FALSE QUESTIONS. Write T in the blank if the statement is true, and write F if it is false.

_____ 1.   The ability to manage student behavior is the number one concern of beginning teachers.
_____ 2.   The concept classroom management and the concept discipline mean the same thing.
_____ 3.   Rules are very important for beginning teachers, but veterans rarely use them.
_____ 4.   The most effective teachers are those who are quickly able to stop classroom management incidents after they occur.
_____ 5.   If rules and procedures are taught well enough at the beginning of the year, monitoring them later on should not be necessary.

MULTIPLE CHOICE: Circle the best response in each case.

6. Which of the following best describes a productive learning environment?
   a.   An environment in which learners understand and obey well-established rules
   b.   An environment that involves collaboration and cooperation between the teacher and students
   c.   An environment that involves order and well-established routines
   d.   An environment that is orderly and focuses on learning

7. Interns and beginning teachers are often more concerned about classroom management than any other aspect of teaching. As an intern, which of the following is likely to be most effective for reducing the likelihood of classroom management problems?
   a.   Be very stern and make an attempt to demonstrate that you are confident and in charge.
   b.   Be very well organized. Eliminate "dead time," such as handing back papers, during which management problems can occur.
   c.   Be very human and caring. If the students know that you care about them, the likelihood that they'll misbehave is reduced.
   d.   Organize your class into cooperative groups the first day. When students work in groups, they are less likely to be off-task than in whole-class discussions.

8. We have emphasized the importance of providing rationales for rules and procedures. Of the following, the most important reason we want to provide rationales is:
   a.   we want students to believe that the world is rational and not capricious, and rationales help establish a a sense of order and understanding.
   b.   students are unlikely to obey rules if rationales for them aren't given.
   c.   our overriding goal in classroom management is to get students to conform to our rules.
   d.   obeying rules is the primary goal of schooling, and rationales increase the likelihood that the rules will be obeyed.

9. "Man, that Mrs. Robinson must have eyes in the back of her head," Eddie comments to John. The classroom management concept most closely related to this description is:
   a.   withitness.
   b.   overlapping.
   c.   momentum.
   d.   smoothness.

10. With respect to using punishment in classroom management, which of the following statements is most accurate?
   a.   Punishment should never be used, because it can cause negative emotional reactions to school.
   b.   Punishment should be avoided, if possible, but in some cases it can be used effectively with careful professional judgment.
   c.   Punishment is generally more effective than reinforcement for being certain that students obey rules.
   d.   Punishment is effective for ensuring that procedures are followed, but it is ineffective for being sure that rules are followed.

Use the following vignette for items 11-13.

You are a 7th grade science teacher conducting a lesson on plant parts and the function of each of the parts. You begin the lesson by reaching down behind your desk and picking up a large plant that you bought at a flower shop. You show the students the different plant parts, and as you're explaining the functions of each part, Rodney begins poking Jennifer with a ruler. At the same time Jimmy is whispering to Susan across the aisle.

11. If you are withit, which of the following best describes how you should respond?
    a.   First stop Jimmy's whispering, since it is least serious, and then concentrate on Rodney.
    b.   First stop Rodney and then stop Jimmy.
    c.   Stop Rodney immediately and ignore Jimmy.
    d.   Stop the lesson and discuss the rule about keeping hands and feet to yourself with the whole class.

12. Which of the following best describes "overlapping"?
    a.   Stop the lesson and discuss the rule about keeping hands and feet to yourself with the whole class while making eye contact with Rodney.
    b.   While you're explaining the functions of the plant parts move over to Rodney, take his ruler, and continue standing by him for a moment.
    c.   Stop the lesson briefly, admonish Rodney, and then continue with the lesson.
    d.   Stop the lesson briefly, tell Rodney to put his ruler away, tell Jimmy to stop whispering, and continue with the lesson.

13. Having the plant behind your desk at the beginning of the lesson best illustrates:
    a.   lesson organization.
    b.   lesson withitness.
    c.   lesson momentum.
    d.   lesson overlapping.

14. Karen Johnson's 10th graders are working on their next day's English homework as she circulates among them. She is bending over helping Leroy when Jeff and Mike begin whispering loudly behind her.
    "Jeff. Mike. Stop talking and get started on your homework," she says glancing over her shoulder.
    The boys slow their whispering, and Karen turns back to Leroy. Soon they are whispering as loudly as ever.
    "I thought I told you to stop talking," Karen says over her shoulder again, this time with a hint of irritation in her voice.
    The boys glance at her and quickly resume whispering.

Which of the following best describes the above incident?
    a.   Karen's intervention is effective, because she attends to a management incident at the same time she conducts instruction.
    b.   Karen's intervention is ineffective, since her verbal and nonverbal behavior are incongruent.
    c.   Karen's intervention is effective, since most of the students are working diligently.
    d.   Karen's intervention is ineffective, since she didn't actively listen to the students.

15. You have a rule that prohibits talking without permission. As your 5th graders are doing seatwork, Sonja briefly whispers something across the aisle and then resumes working. Based on the discussion of the "intervention continuum" in the chapter, which of the following is the best course of action?
    a.   Ignore the behavior since it was brief.
    b.   "Desist" the behavior immediately, to prevent it from happening again.
    c.   Openly praise one of the students who is working conscientiously and diligently.
    d.   Remind Sonja of the rule, and suggest that she come to you if she has a question.

16. Mrs. Harkness is teaching the rule, "Bring all needed materials to class each day," to her students. She discusses the rule, provides examples, and then asks the students to describe some of the materials they should bring. She follows up by simulating getting ready for school and gathering the materials she needs. Of the following, the best prediction of the grade level Mrs. Harkness teaches is:
    a.   first grade.
    b.   fifth grade.
    c.   seventh grade.
    d.   tenth grade.

17. Based on the criteria for effective rules, which of the following rules is best stated?
    a.   Do not speak unless you are called on by the teacher.
    b.   Always come to class prepared.
    c.   Avoid embarrassing your classmates.
    d.   Leave your desk only when given permission.

18. A boy is caught running in a hallway, which is against the rules. If the outcome is consistent with patterns identified by research, which of the following consequences is likely to be most effective?
    a.   Give him a referral and send him to the main office.
    b.   Have him return to where he started running and then walk to where he is going.
    c.   Have the student walk backwards to his destination.
    d.   Keep the student in detention in your classroom for 15 minutes after school.

19. One of your sixth graders has been chronically disruptive. You warn him, he stops briefly, and then becomes disruptive again. You state, "Please go to the timeout area." He looks at you and says, "Do I have to?"

    Based on the suggestions of assertive discipline, of the following, your best course of action is:
    a.   Restate your demand, reminding him of the consequences for defiance.
    b.   Explain to him the reason for the no-talking rule and leave it at that.
    c.   Ask him why he is refusing to comply with your demand.
    d.   Send him a non-verbal signal to be quiet.

Use the following vignette for items 20-21.

Jan, a kindergarten teacher, Rod, a fifth grade teacher, an eighth grade physical science teacher named Dawn, and Joe, a 10th grade world history teacher are all at a party and begin talking "shop," specifically how they manage their classrooms.

    Assume their students' characteristics are consistent with patterns identified by research.

20. The one for whom establishing explicit boundaries and predictable consequences is most critical is:
    a.   Jan.
    b.   Rod.
    c.   Dawn.
    d.   Joe.

21. The one whose students need rules to be explicitly taught, practiced and reinforced is:
    a.   Jan.
    b.   Rod.
    c.   Dawn.
    d.   Joe.

22. Students finish a worksheet in Mrs. Wood's class, while she is working with a reading group. When individuals are finished, they get up from their desks and deposit the worksheet in a folder at the front of the room. Mrs. Wood continues working with the reading group without saying anything to the students doing the worksheet. This process best illustrates which of the following?

    a.   A classroom procedure
    b.   A classroom rule
    c.   Teacher withitness
    d.   Teacher overlapping

23. As Mrs. Hayes is helping Janet with one of the problems on the seatwork assignment, Rene, who has had her hand up, nearly shouts, "Mrs. Hayes, I can't do this one. I've had my hand up for five minutes."

    "Shouting out is against the rules," Mrs. Hayes responds, as she turns to Rene. "It disrupts my work with other students, and I get irritable when I'm repeatedly disrupted."

    Of the following, Mrs. Hayes behavior best illustrates which of the following?

    a.   An "I-message"
    b.   A passive response
    c.   An assertive response
    d.   A hostile response
    e.   Active listening

Use the following vignette for Items 24-25.

Cory Streger created the following set of rules for her class:

    1.   Come to class prepared each day.
    2.   No talking without permission.
    3.   Listen politely when a classmate is talking.
    4.   No complaining about assignments and other tasks.
    5.   Leave your seat only when given permission.

    Cory handed each student a copy of the rules and told them to put them in the front of their notebooks. She then said, "These are the rules we're going to follow for the year. Please keep them in mind and follow them carefully.

    "Now," Cory continued. "Let's begin today's topic," and she then turned to the lesson for the day.

24. Using the principles presented in the chapter devoted to creating and teaching rules, write an assessment of Cory's rules. Include at least one positive feature and at least one negative feature of her rules.

25. Using the principles presented in the chapter devoted to creating and teaching rules, write an assessment of the way Cory presented the rules to her class. Include at least two suggestions for improving the way the rules were presented.

Self-Help Quiz Answers_____

    1.   t
    2.   f
    3.   f
    4.   f
    5.   f
    6.   d   Productive learning environments are defined as those that are orderly and focus on learning.
    7.   b   Being well organized helps create orderly classroom environments because they reduce non-instructional time, and students are most likely to become disruptive during non-instructional time.
    8.   a   Believing that the world is orderly and makes sense helps create a sense of equilibrium in students. When students believe that the world is orderly and rules exist for a reason, they are also more likely to obey the rules.

9.   a   Having "eyes in the back of the head" indicates that Mrs. Robinson knows what is going on in her classroom, which is the definition of withitness.

10.   b   Teachers who emphasize reinforcers are more effective than those who focus on punishment. However, research indicates that the use of punishers usually cannot be completely eliminated.

11.   b   Being "withit" also includes differentiating between less and more serious infractions and dealing with the more serious matter first.

12.   b   Overlapping involves the ability to do more than one thing at once.

13.   a   One part of organization involves having materials prepared in advance and easily accessible.

14.   b   Cognitive approaches to intervention suggest that verbal and non-verbal behaviors must be congruent.

15.   a   The intervention continuum suggests using the least intrusive or disruptive technique first.

16.   a   Younger children need to be taught rules and need to have them demonstrated and explained explicitly and carefully.

17.   d   Options a and c are stated negatively; Option b isn't as clear as would be suggested.

18.   b   Research indicates that logical consequences are most effective. Having to return to where he started running and then walk to where he is going is a logical consequence.

19.   a   Assertive discipline focuses on consequences for following and breaking rules.

20.   c   Junior high or middle school students benefit most from explicit management boundaries.

21.   a   Younger children benefit most from rules being explicitly taught and practiced.

22.   a   Classroom procedures create routines that help organize classroom life.

23.   a   "I" messages identify the behavior, attempt to communicate how the student's behavior affects the teacher and the feelings generated.

24.   First, by creating only five rules Cory minimized the number, which is a positive feature. Minimizing the number increases the likelihood that students will remember the rules. On the other hand, Cory's first rule was stated in general terms, and her second and fourth rules were stated negatively. If a rule stated in general terms is carefully illustrated and taught with examples, it can be effective, but we see no evidence that Cory provided examples of obeying the rule.

25.   Cory could have presented the rules to her class much more effectively. First, she did not solicit student input into the creation of the rules. Second, and perhaps most important, she provided no rationale for the rules. Reasons for rules are at the heart of cognitive approaches to management. Third, she didn't provide examples of obeying the rules, so she didn't teach the rules as concepts. Teaching rules as concepts (by providing examples) increases students' understanding of the rules and increases the likelihood that they will obey the rules. (Since Cory had just presented the rules, we have no evidence about the extent to which she monitored the rules throughout the year.)

CHAPTER 13: CREATING PRODUCTIVE LEARNING ENVIRONMENTS: PRINCIPLES AND MODELS OF INSTRUCTION

Chapter Outline_____

I.   Planning for instruction
    A. Selecting topics
    B. Preparing learning objectives
        1. Objectives in the cognitive domain
        2. A taxonomy for cognitive objectives
    C. Preparing and organizing learning activities
        1. Task analysis: A planning tool
    D. Planning for assessment
    E. Instructional alignment
    F. Planning in a standards-based environment
II.   Implementing instruction: Essential teaching skills
    A. Attitudes
    B. Organization
    C. Communication
        1. Knowledge of content: Its role in clear communication
    D. Focus: Attracting and maintaining attention
    E. Feedback
        1. Praise
        2. Written feedback
    F. Questioning
        1. Questioning Frequency
        2. Equitable distribution
        3. Prompting
        4. Wait-time
        5. Cognitive levels of questions
    G. Review and closure
    H. Learning contexts: Instruction in urban environments
        1. Attitudes
        2. Questioning
        3. Feedback
III. Models of instruction
    A. Direct instruction
        a. Introduction and review
        b. Developing understanding
        c.. Guided practice
        d. Independent practice
        e. Homework
    B. Lecture and lecture-discussion
        1. Lectures
        2. Overcoming the weaknesses of lectures: Lecture-discussions
    C. Guided discovery
        a. Introduction and review
        b. The open-ended phase
        c. The convergent phase
        d. Closure
    D. Cooperative learning
        1. Introducing cooperative learning
        2. Cooperative learning strategies
    E. Cooperative learning: A tool for capitalizing on diversity
IV.   Assessment and learning: Using assessment as a learning tool

Chapter Objectives_____

- Describe the steps involved in planning for instruction, and identify an additional step when planning in a standards-based environment

- Identify examples of essential teaching skills in learning experiences, and analyze the role of feedback in promoting learning.

- Explain the relationships between essential teaching skills and models of instruction, and analyze the components of different models.

- Identify the characteristics of effective assessments, and explain the relationships between effective assessments and essential teaching skills.

Chapter Overview_____

In Chapters 2-5 your study centered on students, how they develop, and the ways they differ. Your efforts shifted in Chapters 6-9 to the nature of the learning process itself, and you then examined learner motivation and what teachers can do to increase it in Chapters 10 and 11.

You then turned to the development of productive learning environments, which are orderly, learning-focused classrooms. In Chapter 12 you learned ways of creating and maintaining orderly environments, and in this chapter you examined the way expert teachers plan and implement lessons and assess learner understanding.

Planning involves making decisions about the content students are expected to master, sequencing concepts, principles, and the relationships among them, preparing examples that students can use to construct understanding, and creating assessments that measure what students have learned.

As teachers implement their lessons, they should consistently demonstrate essential teaching skills, the abilities that all teachers—regardless of grade level, subject matter area, or topic—should have to promote as much learning as possible. Among them are positive and professional attitudes, efficient use of time, clear communication, informative feedback, and skilled questioning.

Models of instruction are approaches to teaching, grounded in learning theory and supported by research, that include sets of steps designed to help students reach specified learning objectives. Essential teaching skills support all instructional models. No single instructional model is most effective for all students or for helping students reach all learning objectives, and teachers should vary the way they teach. For some learning objectives explicit, teacher directed instruction is most effective, and for other objectives, more learner directed approaches are preferable.

Productive learning environments are assessment centered. This means that teachers are constantly gathering information about students' understanding of the topics they're studying. Effective assessments focus on students' thinking as much as on correct answers.

Application Exercises_____

Exercise 13.1

Laurie Zentz is an elementary teacher studying Native Americans from different regions of the country.

"At the beginning of the school year, I had decided that my students should have a better understanding and appreciation of other cultures. I hoped to spark some interest, so maybe they would read about some other cultures on their own. When I saw a chapter in the social studies book on Native Americans, I decided to focus on their culture and life-style.

"My major goal was to have the students see these different Native American tribes as people. When we're finished, they'll be able to identify the tribes when I describe their lifestyle and where they live," Laurie commented in describing her unit. "I show a couple of videos that really do a good job of illustrating the characteristics of each tribe, and then we have 'Native American Day' when kids dress up in native costume and explain how the tribe they represent worked and lived,' she went on. "I also give them a solid test on the stuff. I have some drawings and descriptions of hypothetical groups, and they have to identify the tribe based on the information I give. Then, we talk about the test in detail the next day. I want to see how much they really understand. They probably learn more in these discussions than they do in the lessons themselves.

"It's a lot of work," she commented finally. "We have to find a day when we can invite the other grades in to see our 'village,' and getting all the presentations scheduled is a mess. But it's worth it. They get a lot out of it, and they like it."

1.   Describe specifically where Laurie demonstrated pedagogical content knowledge in her lesson.

2.   Classify Laurie's objective into one of the cells of the cognitive taxonomy table.

3.   Was Laurie's classroom assessment centered? Explain why it was or was not?

4.   Describe instructional alignment. Based on the evidence in the case study, is Laurie's instruction aligned? Explain.

Respond to Exercises 13.2-13.4 based on the case study in the chapter involving Scott Sowell and his lesson on Bernoulli's principle.

Exercise 13.2

1.   Evaluate Scott's organization for his lesson. Provide evidence taken directly from the case study in making your evaluation.

2.   Explain how Scott's knowledge of content was demonstrated in his communication.

3.   Identify an example in Scott's lesson where he demonstrated effective communication by using emphasis.

Exercise 13.3

The following is some dialogue taken from Scott's lesson.

He referred the students to the first sketch and then asked, "Was I blowing on the top or the bottom? . . . Rachel?
        "The top."
        "And what happened there? . . . Heather?"
        "The paper rose up."
        He then turned to the second sketch and asked, "What did we do to these pieces of paper? . . . Shentae?"

149

"We blew in between them."
"Yes, we blew in between them didn't we," he repeated. "And what happened there? . . . Ricky?"
"They came together."

1.   What essential teaching skill is best illustrated in this excerpt of the lesson? Explain.

2.   Scott's use of his sketches on the board capitalized on which essential teaching skill? Explain.

Exercise 13.4

1.   Identify the dialogue from Scott's lesson that illustrates his closure.

2.   Describe three ways in which Scott's lesson was assessment centered.

Exercise 13.5

Consider the two following goals:

> For students to correctly simplify an arithmetic expression, following the rule: "First complete the operations in parentheses, then multiply and divide left to right, and finally add and subtract left to right."

> For students to write paragraphs using a variety of adjectives and adverbs correctly.

Describe in detail how you would use direct instruction to help your students reach the goals.

Exercise 13.6

Which model of instruction did Scott most nearly use in his lesson? Explain.

Feedback for Application Exercises_____

Exercise 13.1

1. Laurie demonstrated pedagogical content knowledge in the way she represented her topic. For example she showed a couple of videos that "really do a good job of illustrating the characteristics of each tribe," and then she had "Native American Day." Both helped make the content meaningful for the students.

2. Laurie's objective is stated near the beginning of the case study: ". . . they'll be able to identify the tribes when I describe their lifestyle and where they live." This objective would be best classified into the cell where conceptual knowledge intersects with understanding. The tribes and their characteristics are concepts, and being able to identify the tribes based on descriptions of their locations and habitats demonstrates understanding.

3. Laurie's classroom was assessment centered. The best evidence supporting this conclusion appears in her statements, "Then, we talk about the test in detail the next day. I want to see how much they really understand. They probably learn more in these discussions than they do in the lessons themselves." Using assessment as a mechanism to promote learning is an essential characteristic of an assessment-centered classroom.

4. Instructional alignment is the match between goals, learning activities, and assessment. Learning activities should be consistent with goals, and assessment should be consistent with both goals and learning activities.

Laurie's instruction was aligned. Her goal was for the students to understand the lifestyle of Native American tribes and how their lifestyle related to where they lived. Her videos illustrated Native American lifestyles and her "Native American Day" was also consistent with the goal. Her test was consistent with her goal. She gave them drawings and descriptions of hypothetical groups and they had to identify the tribes based on the information she provided.

Exercise 13.2

1. Organization is illustrated in three ways: (1) starting on time, (2) having materials ready, and (3) having well-established routines. Scott began his lesson as soon as the bell rang, his papers, and his funnels and balls were ready for distribution. We don't have a great deal of evidence about his routines.

2. Scott's knowledge of content was demonstrated in the clarity of his language. He didn't use vague terms, like *perhaps, maybe, and so on,* or *that sort of thing.* His lesson was also thematic and to a point (connected discourse). Teachers who have thorough knowledge of content use clearer language than those whose knowledge is less thorough.

3. After Scott completed his review, he used emphasis when he told the students to keep the concept of force and the principle stating that objects move in the direction of the greater force in mind as they moved through the lesson.

Scott's communication, in general, was very effective. His language was clear, the lesson was thematic and led to a point, and he used emphasis appropriately. (We didn't see a transition signal in the lesson.)

Exercise 13.3

1. Equitable distribution is the essential teaching skill best illustrated by the dialogue. Scott called on a different individual student, by name, in each of his questions.

2. Scott's use of the sketches provided a form of sensory focus in the lesson. The sketches, in addition to providing effective examples of the topic, helped maintain the students' attention, and maintaining attention is a primary purpose of sensory focus.

Exercise 13.4

1. Dialogue that illustrates Scott's closure is as follows:

Scott: Now, I want everyone to look closely. . . . Do you see a relationship between where you blew
           and which one was stronger? . . . Heather?
Heather: It seems like wherever you blew, the opposite was stronger.
Scott: So every place you blew, where was the force greater?
Heather: In the opposite direction.
Scott: So, this person named Bernoulli, who first discovered this principle, . . . he said that every time
           you increase the speed of the air, the force goes down. . . . So when I speed up the wind on the
           top of the paper (holding up the single sheet of paper), the force goes down and this force takes
           over (motioning to the force underneath the paper). Same thing when I blow between two
           sheets. The force in between goes down and the outside force takes over, . . . okay. (And he
           provided a similar description for the ball and funnel.)

Scott's closure would have been more effective if he had guided the students through the descriptions of the relationship between speed of the air and the force it exerts instead of simply explaining it to them.

2. First, Scott's assessment was an integral part of the teaching-learning process; it wasn't something tacked on sometime after the lesson. Second, Scott's assessment focused as much or more on the students' thinking as on their answers. Third, Scott carefully discussed the assessments after they had been administered and scored.

Exercise 13.5

In each case the lesson would begin with a review of the previous day's work.

In the math lesson you would review each of the operations and the operations where parentheses are involved.

In the case of writing paragraphs using adjectives and adverbs, you would review adjectives, nouns, and pronouns including examples of adjectives describing the other two parts of speech.

Then, in the *developing understanding* phase you would help the students understand the skill or ability using examples and discussion. You would model a solution to a problem, such as the following:

$$4 + 5(2 + 6) - 8/4 = 4 + 5(8) - 8/4$$

You would then show another example, and as a class, you would discuss the steps. You would ask a student to describe the first step, explain why it is first, proceed to the second, third, and so on. In each case you would call on different students, and in the questioning process, ask students *why* they believe that particular step is next.

Discussion and providing explanations are strongly emphasized in this phase of the lesson.

In the *developing understanding* phase of the lesson on adjectives and adverbs, you would present the students with an example, such as:

John and Karen, with her brown hair blowing in the wind, drove his old car to the football game. They soon met their very best friends, Latoya and Michael, at the large gate near the entrance. The game was incredibly exciting, and, because the team's running game was in high gear, the home team won by a bare margin.

You would discuss the example in detail, emphasizing adjectives such as *exciting* because it doesn't precede the noun, and *running* because it more commonly is used as a verb. You would do the same with the adverbs, emphasizing an example such as *soon* because it doesn't end in *ly*, which is the characteristic students commonly attach to the concept *adverb*.

After you are satisfied that the students have a reasonable understanding of the skill or concepts, students would be given the chance to practice, first under your supervision, and then independently.

In the math lesson, you would give the students several examples to simplify, and the English lesson, you would ask the students to write paragraphs in which examples of adjectives and adverbs were embedded.

Exercise 13.6

Scott most nearly used guided discovery in his lesson. He began by reviewing the concept *force* and the principle *objects move in the direction of the greater force.* He then presented examples and had the students observe them during the open-ended phase. He guided the students to the relationship between force and the speed of air during the convergent phase. He brought the lesson to closure by articulating the relationship between force and the speed of air and again linking the description to the examples.

Self-Help Quiz_____

TRUE/FALSE QUESTIONS. Write T in the blank if the statement is true and write F if the statement is false.

_____ 1. A teacher could possess extensive knowledge of content and still lack pedagogical content knowledge.

_____ 2. According to research, in question and answer sessions teachers typically direct questions to individual students rather than letting anyone answer who wishes to do so.

_____ 3. According to research, a thorough understanding of content is adequate to allow teachers to plan effectively

_____ 4. According to research, the major portion of classroom questions, exercises, and tests focuses on the cell where factual knowledge intersects with remember in the cognitive taxonomy table.

_____ 5. According to research, teachers who assess thoroughly and often have students who learn more than teachers whose assessments are less thorough.

MULTIPLE-CHOICE ITEMS. Circle the best response in each case.

6. Which of the following best illustrates pedagogical content knowledge?
   a. Mr. Duckworth describes the events leading up to the Spanish-American War. In the process he outlines events, such as the sinking of the battleship *Maine* in Havana harbor.
   b. Mrs. Ramos writes short case studies about the students' loyalty to their school, their language, and their favorite music and social events to be used as analogies for the concept *nationalism* as she begins a unit on the events leading up to World War I.
   c. Mr. Helmsley explains that the ocean currents run from south to north along the coast of Europe, so the climate is more moderate than would be expected for the latitude of the countries.
   d. Mrs. Armstrong shows the students a map of the United States that illustrates land forms. She then explains the agricultural areas of the country based on the information in the map.

7. Which of the following is NOT a step in a task analysis?
   a. Ms. Gardner determines that her biology students need to be able to dissect a worm during a 45 minute lab class well enough to identify major organs and systems.
   b. Mrs. Gardner lists the material she will need: worms, dissecting instruments, disinfectant, labels, charts, and lab coats for day of the dissection.
   c. Mrs. Gardner knows from a previous quiz that some of her students will need to learn to identify some of the organs while others will need help with the fine motor skills required in the actual dissection process.
   d. Ms. Gardner makes a list of all the things that her students will need to know before the lab class in order to succeed at the activity planned.

8. Which step in the planning process is best illustrated when Ms. Gardner (in item 7) decides to ask her students to draw from memory a labeled diagram of their dissections the day following the lab class?
   a. Deciding what topics are important to study
   b. Preparing objectives
   c. Preparing and organizing learning activities
   d. Planning for assessment

9. Into which cell of the cognitive taxonomy table would the following objective be most accurately classified?
   Students will use the formula $A = \pi r^2$ to find the area of several circles when they're given different radii and diameters.
   a. Remember factual knowledge
   b. Remember conceptual knowledge
   c. Apply conceptual knowledge
   d. Apply procedural knowledge

10. Jeanna Evans wants her students to write persuasive essays using correct punctuation and grammar. She presents the students with a list of sentences that use incorrect grammar and punctuation, and she has the students rewrite the sentences using correct grammar and punctuation. The next day she gives them a test in which they have to write a persuasive essay using correct grammar and punctuation.

Of the following, which is the most valid conclusion?
   a. Jeanna's instruction is aligned, because her goal was for the students to write using correct grammar and punctuation, and she had them practice writing using correct grammar and punctuation.
   b. Jeanna's instruction is not aligned, because she didn't appear to explain the rules before she gave the assignment.
   c. Jeanna's instruction is aligned, because her test was similar to her goal.
   d. Jeanna's instruction is not aligned, because she had the students write isolated sentences during her learning activity.

   Phenix Davis, a science teacher, wants her students to understand the characteristics of the solar system. She prepares a model showing the planets in their relative distances from the sun. She explains the model, pointing out that the first four planets are called the inner planets and the other five are called the outer planets.
   Loretta Wilson, a social studies teacher, wants her students to understand how geography, economy, and recreational patterns are interrelated. She shows the students a map that illustrates different geographic regions, such as mountains and plains, a matrix comparing the economies of the areas, and pictures illustrating the recreational patterns in these areas.
   Jonah Washington, a math teacher, wants his students to be able to simplify arithmetic expressions and has his students simplify a series of expression such as 3 + 5(8 - 2) - 7.
   Ruben Askew, a 4th grade teacher, wants his students to identify the correct verb in sentences, such as "Andrea and Jose (is, are) the fastest runners on the girls' and boys' track teams." He has the students complete a series of exercises in which they have to identify the correct verb.

11. The teacher whose instruction was least well aligned was:
   a. Phenix
   b. Loretta
   c. Jonah
   d. Ruben

12. Third period in Bartram Middle school begins at 10:00 a.m. and ends at 10:50. Kristy Williams, one of the teachers, typically starts her math class at 10:04. Her friend, Kevin Anderson, typically gets started about 10:10. Of the following, the best conclusion we can make based on this information is:
   a. Kristy is a more effective teacher than is Kevin.
   b. Kristy's students are on task more than are Kevin's.
   c. Kristy has more allocated time than does Kevin.
   d. Kristy is better organized than is Kevin.

13. Of the following, teachers' understanding of the content they teach is most closely related to which of the following essential teaching skills?
   a. Positive attitudes.
   b. Effective organization.
   c. Effective communication.
   d. Effective questioning.

14. A teacher in a discussion of the Northern and Southern states prior to the Civil War says, "We've looked at the economic conditions in the North in the middle 1800's. Now we're going to shift and look at the economy in the South during this same period." Of the following, the teacher's comment best illustrates:
   a. effective lesson organization.
   b. ineffective lesson organization.
   c. effective communication.
   d. ineffective communication.
   e. ineffective lesson focus.

15. A teacher displays the following sentence on the board:

Studying is important if you want to be successful.

She then asks, "How is the word 'studying' used in the sentence?. . . Ed?"
   ". . . It's a verb," Ed answers.
   She responds, "Not quite. Help him out, . . . Kathy?"

Of the following, the best assessment of the teacher's response to Ed's answer is:
   a. effective lesson organization.
   b. effective communication
   c. ineffective communication.
   d. ineffective sensory focus.
   e. ineffective feedback.

16. You are studying direct objects with your students and you display the following sentence on the board.

   Ramon kicked the ball to Jack.

You ask Alice, one of your students, "What is the direct object in the sentence?" Alice sits quietly, saying nothing. According to research, which of the following statements or questions is most effective?
   a. "Can someone help Alice out here?"
   b. "Look, Alice, the sentence says 'Ramon kicked the ball.' Ball is the direct object."
   c. "The direct object receives the action of the verb. Ball is the direct object."
   d. "What did Ramon kick, Alice?"

17. When working with urban students, which of the following is likely to be the most effective strategy for promoting learning?
   a. Allow urban students to work alone, because they may not be comfortable in traditional learning activities.
   b. Carefully practice equitable distribution in questioning to hold students accountable for paying attention and participating in learning activities.
   c. Provide students with ample seatwork to allow them to practice basic skills that they may not have fully developed.
   d. Design learning activities to provide as much control and structure as possible, since classroom management is often a challenge in urban environments.

Consider the following goals:

I. You want your students to acquire interpersonal skills and to learn to take turns in expressing their opinions as they design a procedure to investigate the effect of density on the evaporation of liquids (such as how fast does alcohol evaporate compared to water, since alcohol is less dense than water).

II. You want your students to understand that parenthetical expressions are set off by commas, and you want the students to be as involved as possible in the activity.

III. You want your students to be able to solve simultaneous equations, such as finding the values for x and y in the equations $2x + 3y = 8$, and $x + y = 4$.

18. Of the following, the instructional strategy that is likely to be most successful for reaching the first goal is:
    a. unstructured discovery.
    b. guided discovery.
    c. direct instruction.
    d. cooperative learning.

19. Of the following, the instructional strategy that is likely to be most successful for reaching the second goal is:
    a. unstructured discovery.
    b. guided discovery.
    c. direct instruction.
    d. cooperative learning.

20. Of the following, the instructional strategy that is likely to be most successful for reaching the third goal is:
    a. unstructured discovery.
    b. guided discovery.
    c. direct instruction.
    d. cooperative learning.

Use the following information for items 21-25.

    Mr. Englehart wants his students to understand similarities between the heavy influx of immigrants to the United States in the early 20th century compared to another heavy influx during the 1980s. He describes conditions in Europe in the early part of the century and he also notes that the Vietnam War that ended in 1975 resulted in many Southeast Asians coming to this country. After a few minutes he asks Felicia to summarize what has been discussed to this point. After Felicia and three other students offer comments, he adds some information about an influx of Russian immigrants after the collapse of Communism, Cambodians after the Pol Pot purges, and several other groups. He then asks Jennifer to identify similarities in some of the reasons for immigration during the two time periods, and after Jennifer responds he asks Don to make two generalizations about the reasons people immigrate.
    Mrs. Carlsen wants her students to understand Newton's second law, the law stating that when we exert a force on an object, it goes faster and faster, i.e., it accelerates. To get the students' attention, she drops a book and explains that the book accelerated until it was stopped by the floor. She then demonstrates force and acceleration by pulling a small cart across the front of the classroom using a spring scale that exerts a constant force, and the students can see that the cart accelerates. She also holds a tennis ball above her head and drops it and then shows a computer simulation that illustrates the acceleration of the dropped ball in slow motion. The students discuss what they've seen, and Mrs. Carlsen guides them with questioning until they understand that when they see the distance between the images of the ball get greater and greater, the ball is accelerating. Gradually, they begin to understand the idea of acceleration. She then gives the students an additional example. The students decide if it illustrates the law, and they discuss their thinking as they analyze the example. Mrs. Carlsen repeats the process with a second example. Finally, she

shows the students three additional examples, and in each case they must decide on their own whether or not the example illustrates the law, and explain their reasoning in writing.

Mr. Hall wants his students to learn to work with each other to gather information and solve problems. He has different students study the geography of a region, others study the climate, still others the economy, and still others the government and educational systems. The students compile their information, sharing what they've found with their peers. After the unit is complete all students individually are given a test that covers the content.

Mrs. Williams wants her students to understand the concept hyperbole. She shows the students a series of sentences, such as "I had a million pages of homework to do last night," and "His descriptions were the most beautiful prose I've ever read." Mrs. Williams has the students work in groups of three to identify what the sentences have in common, and as Mrs. Williams and the class discuss their findings, they–aided by Mrs. Williams' questioning–gradually conclude that an unrealistic exaggeration is involved, and they reach the concept hyperbole. When they're finished, all students use the classroom computers to write paragraphs in which statements of hyperbole are embedded.

Mr. Price wants his students to know what kinds of materials conduct electricity. He gives the students batteries, wire, bulbs, and packets of materials including paper clips, craft sticks, rubber bands, aluminum foil, brass buttons, bolts and nuts. He directs them to work with the batteries, bulbs, wire, and materials and see what kinds of conclusions they can make.

Mr. Polanski wants his students to be able to consider what might affect how fast water evaporates. They offer different possibilities, such as the temperature of the water (for example, being placed in a sunny window versus the refrigerator) and the size of the opening of the container (such as the water being in a cake pan versus a small-mouthed jar). They work in groups to put water in different locations in the room and in large-mouthed and small-mouthed jars and see how much the water level has gone down each day. They conclude that both the temperature and the size of the opening affect the rate of evaporation. They use their classroom computers to graph the relationship between the temperature and the rates of evaporation.

21. Based on the goal and learning activity, the teacher who was most attempting to implement unstructured discovery was:
    a. Mr. Englehart.
    b. Mrs. Carlsen.
    c. Mr. Hall.
    d. Mrs. Williams.
    e. Mr. Price.

22. Based on the goal and learning activity, the teacher who was most attempting to implement guided discovery was:
    a. Mr. Englehart.
    b. Mrs. Carlsen.
    c. Mr. Hall.
    d. Mrs. Williams.
    e. Mr. Price.

23. Based on the goal and learning activity, the teacher who was most attempting to implement direct instruction was:
    a. Mr. Englehart.
    b. Mrs. Carlsen.
    c. Mr. Hall.
    d. Mrs. Williams.
    e. Mr. Polanski.

24. Based on the goal and learning activity, the teacher who was most attempting to implement cooperative learning was:
   a. Mr. Englehart.
   b. Mrs. Carlsen.
   c. Mr. Hall.
   d. Mrs. Williams.
   e. Mr. Price.

25. Based on the goal and learning activity, the teacher who was most attempting to implement a lecture discussion was:
   a. Mr. Englehart.
   b. Mrs. Carlsen.
   c. Mr. Hall.
   d. Mrs. Williams.
   e. Mr. Price.

Self-Help Quiz Answers_____

1. t
2. f
3. f
4. t
5. t
6. b Mrs. Ramos was able to create examples that illustrated the concept *nationalism*. The ability to create meaningful examples demonstrates pedagogical content knowledge. The other three teachers merely explained or described the content they wanted the students to understand. This is typical of teachers who lack pedagogical content knowledge.
7. b Task analysis involves thinking about the presentation of a topic, breaking content down into its component parts—concepts, principles, and skills—and sequencing those components. Simply listing materials doesn't involve all these thought processes.
8. d Planning for assessment involves making decisions about how to best measure student understanding.
9. d Finding the area of a circle involves a procedure, and students are applying their understanding when they use the formula to do so.
10. d Jeanna's goal was for the students to be able to write persuasive essays using correct grammar and punctuation. During her learning activity, her students had no opportunity to practice this skill and receive feedback. Her test was congruent with her goal, but her learning activity was not.
11. a Phenix's goal was for the students to understand the characteristics of the solar system, but all she did was identify the inner and outer planets. The model and this explanation only help the students understand one characteristic of the solar system.
12. d One characteristic of the essential teaching skill, *organization*, is starting on time. This doesn't mean, however, that Kristy is a more effective teacher than Kevin, because we don't know if she demonstrates the other essential teaching skills better than he does.
13. c Teacher understanding of content is directly related to the precision of a teacher's language, and precise language is a part of communication.
14. c Signaling a transition from one topic to another is one aspect of effective communication.
15. e Effective feedback provides corrective information. By turning the question to another student, the teacher put Ed in a passive role and gave him no corrective information.
16. d In this choice you are prompting Alice. A prompt is the best response to a student non-answer. It assists the student while still moving the lesson forward.
17. b Making equitable distribution the prevailing pattern in your classroom can do more than anything else to communicate that you believe all students can learn and you expect them to do so. Having students work alone (choice a) doesn't give them the practice with articulating their understanding and developing social skills that are part of the total learning process. Students in

urban environments tend to be given too much seatwork (choice c), and teachers in urban environments tend to overemphasize activities that maintain control (choice d).

18   d   Wanting students "to acquire interpersonal skills and to learn to take turns in expressing their opinions as they design a procedure to investigate," is a goal most effectively met with cooperative learning.

19   b   Wanting your students "to understand that parenthetical expressions are set off by commas, and . . . to be as involved as possible in the activity" is a goal most effectively met with guided discovery. Unstructured discovery (choice a) is generally ineffective for meeting specific goals, and while direct instruction (choice c) could be used to reach the goal, students typically are less involved in direct instruction than in guided discovery lessons. Cooperative learning (choice d) is not an appropriate method for reaching this goal.

20.   c   Direct instruction is an effective model for teaching content that involves specific procedural skills, which are involved in solving simultaneous equations.

21.   e   Mr. Price is providing the students with materials and asking them to make any conclusions they can. There is no evidence in the description that he is providing any guidance, and there is no inquiry problem or question involved in the activity. There is also no evidence of goals related to cooperation.

22.   d   Mrs. Williams's goal is for the students to understand the concept hyperbole. The description says that she and the students discuss their findings, suggesting that she is providing some guidance. Although they work in pairs, learning to collaborate isn't the primary goal.

23.   b   Mrs. Carlsen introduced the lesson, demonstrated and explained the law, conducted guided practice with the two examples they analyzed and discussed, and then had the students practice independently on three more examples.

24.   c   Mr. Hall was implementing Jigsaw II, which is a form of cooperative learning.

25.   a   Mr. Englehart provided information when he described conditions in Europe in the early part of the century and pointed out that Southeast Asians came to this country after the Vietnam War. He monitored comprehension when he asked Felicia to summarize what has been discussed to this point. He provided more information when he talked about an influx of Russian immigrants after the collapse of Communism, Cambodians after the Pol Pot purges, and several other groups. He again monitored comprehension when he asked Jennifer to identify similarities in some of the reasons for immigration during the two time periods, and he promoted integration when he asked Don to make two generalizations about the reasons people immigrate.

CHAPTER 14: LEARNING, INSTRUCTION, AND TECHNOLOGY

Chapter Outline_____

I.   What is technology?
II.   Technology and learning
    A.   Behaviorism and technology
    B.   Technology and cognitive learning theory
        1.   Information processing
            a.   Attracting attention and creating accurate perceptions
            b.   Managing the resources of working memory
            c.   Promoting encoding into long-term memory
            d.   Managing processing with metacognitive skills
        2.   Constructivism and technology
    C.   Social cognitive theory and technology
III. Technology and instruction
    A.   Drill-and-practice software
    B.   Tutorials
        1.   Multimedia & hypermedia
        2.   Strengths of tutorials
        3.   Weaknesses of tutorials
    C.   Simulations
        1.   Benefits of simulations
            a.   Time alteration
            b.   Safety
            c.   Expense
        2.   Simulations as problem solving tools
    D.   Databases & spreadsheets
        1.   Databases
        2.   Spreadsheets
    E.   Word processing: Using technology to teach writing
        1.   Issues in the use of word processing technologies
    F.   Internet-based technologies
        1.   The Internet in problem-based learning
        2.   The Internet as a communication tool
        3.   Advantages & disadvantages of Internet communication
    G.   Distance education
    H.   Exploring diversity: Employing technology to support learners with disabilities
        1.   Adaptations to computer input devices
        2.   Adaptations to output devices
    I.   Using technology in the classroom: Instructional principles
        1.   Using technology in classrooms: Findings from research
IV.   Teacher support applications of technology
    A.   Preparing instructional materials
        1.   PowerPoint: Planning for presentation options
    B.   Classroom assessment
        1.   Planning & constructing tests
        2.   Administering tests
        3.   Scoring and interpreting tests
        4.   Maintaining student records
    C.   Communicating with Parents

Chapter Objectives_____

- Identify different views of technology in descriptions of classroom support materials.

- Explain how different theories of learning are applied to technology use in classrooms.

- Describe ways that different forms of technology are used to support instruction and identify the learning theories that support these forms of technology.

- Explain how word processing, the Internet, and assistive technology can increase learning.

- Identify different ways that technology can be used to make teachers' work more efficient.

Chapter Overview_____

One definition of technology describes it as hardware—instruments, machines, and computers. A second definition of technology describes it as a process, integrated into and an integral part of the teaching-learning process. Most experts now describe technology as a combination of hardware and process.

Behaviorist applications of technology utilize software that provides students with immediate and informative reinforcement for correct responses. Information processing applications of technology utilize the strengths and limitations of cognitive structures to maximize meaningful learning. Constructivist applications of technology emphasize the capabilities of technology to promote the knowledge construction process. Social cognitive theories of learning capitalize on the effects of observation and modeling on learning.

Drill-and-practice and tutorial software promote learning by providing practice with effective feedback. Simulations provide learners with realistic settings for problem solving. Databases and spreadsheets allow learners to organize and present information in coherent patterns.

Word processing technologies can be used to increase writing skills, allowing students to focus their cognitive energies on the meaning and organization of text. The Internet provides a rich source of information for students and allows teachers and students to connect over wide distances. Assistive technology provides accommodations for the unique needs of students with exceptionalities.

Technology provides effective ways for teachers to present information and represent difficult-to-learn ideas. Technology assists teachers in assessing student learning by allowing them to plan, construct, and administer tests, score tests and interpret results, and integrate scores into a comprehensive record keeping system. Technology makes communication with parents more efficient. E-mails, websites, and phone messages are all effective ways for teachers to communicate with parents and other caregivers.

Application Exercises_____

We encourage you to first write your responses to each of the exercises below, and then check your answers with the feedback that immediately follows the exercises.

Exercise 14.1

Read the following case study and answer the questions that follow it.

      Pete Anderson, a 5-year veteran at a middle school, is highly regarded by the principal, his students, and their parents. As we enter Pete's classroom, it appears chaotic, and we wonder how anyone could consider him a "good" teacher. One group of five students is working on a 4-by-8-foot sheet of heavy paper to be used in a presentation to their classmates. Two other groups of four students are working on different displays, and the seven computers in his room are all being used by pairs of students searching the Internet. The noise level is quite high, giving the impression that there is no order. As we walk around the room, we notice that each group of students is working intently. Pete explains that he had the students organize themselves into pairs—with one group of three, since he has 27 students—and each pair selected one of the original 13 colonies. Their task was to create a company like the Hudson Bay Trading Company for each colony. Pairs could team up and work on two related colonies together if they chose to do so, as indicated by the group of five and the two groups of four.
      Pete explains that he wanted to try something different in this unit on American history. Instead of simply presenting information to students and discussing it, he continues, he presented students with a problem—creating a company that could use the resources of the particular colony or colonies. The students went to work searching for information that would help them solve the problem. They were using the classroom's computers to gather information, and they had to collaborate in making decisions about how to present the information to their classmates. Their presentation had to include a description of how their investors could make a profit using the resources of the colony.

1.   What theory of learning was best illustrated in this example?

2.   If Pete had said to one of the groups, "Go over to Sharon's group and see how they are organizing their information," what theory of learning would be illustrated?

Exercise 14.2

Read the following case study and answer the questions that follow it.

      Fifth-grade teacher Sandy Hutton is involved in a unit on the circulatory system and wants her students to understand the functions of the heart and how blood pressure influences it. On a CD-ROM accompanying the class science textbook, Sandy finds a model that illustrates how the heart is like a bicycle pump with valves opening and closing. She shares the model with her class by using her computer to project it on a screen, and she brings in an old bicycle pump to illustrate how valves open and close to create pressure. With the help of the school nurse, she is able to find several sphygmomanometers (devices for measuring blood pressure), which students then use to measure their pulse rates and blood pressure during different types of activities. She asks the students to search for patterns in their measurements and to organize their information into charts on their computers. Finally, they share their results with the class.

Explain how Sandy could have used the following technologies to help her students achieve her learning goals:

1.   Drill-and-practice and tutorial software

2.   Database

3.   Internet

Chapter 14: Learning, Instruction, and Technology

Exercise 14.3

Read the following case study and answer the questions that follow it.

Latisha Evans, a first-year teacher at Henderson Middle School, runs into one of her colleagues and friends, Carl DeGroot, in the hallway.

"You sure look excited," Carl says with a smile. "What's happening?"

"Wow," Latisha responded, gesturing for emphasis. "They got it today; they really got it. . . . I've been trying to get my language arts classes to understand what we mean by internal conflict, and it seemed to be just too abstract for them. . . . Plus, they would only half pay attention when I would explain it. . . . So I wrote up a few little vignettes, like 'Kelly didn't know what to do. She was looking forward to the class trip, but if she went she wouldn't be able to try out for city soccer league.' Then, I put them together with a PowerPoint presentation and included some pictures of people with pensive looks on their faces and that kind of thing. . . . Neat animation tricks to make each example appear on the screen and then follow it with the pictures. It really got the students thinking, and we had a great discussion about the concept. . . It was the best I've ever done. Using PowerPoint to get their attention really made a difference."

1. Evaluate Latisha's instruction using the concept of instructional alignment.

2. Evaluate Latisha's use of PowerPoint using information from this chapter.

Feedback for Application Exercises_____

Exercise 14.1

1. Pete's instructional activities were primarily based upon constructivist theories of learning. He immersed his students in an authentic learning task and asked each group to create a trading company. They used their knowledge of the *Hudson Bay Trading Company* to construct their new company. In addition, Pete organized students into groups, using social interaction to facilitate learning.

2. Referring students to another group was an example of social cognitive theory. Pete hoped that students, by observing the other students as models, would acquire new ways to organize the information.

Exercise 14.2

1. Drill-and-practice software and tutorials could have been used to teach basic facts and concepts about the circulatory system, such as what is an *artery*, *vein*, and *capillary*.

2. Sandy could have used a database to help her students organize the information about pulse rates and blood pressure. A database would allow her students to organize and summarize information and also to search for patterns and trends.

3. Sandy could use the Internet in several ways. One is to access information from a broad array of sources for her own planning. She could also help her students do the same. Finally, her students could use the Internet to share and compare their findings with other classrooms across the country.

Exercise 14.3

1. Latisha's instruction was aligned. Her learning objective was to have her students understand the concept of internal conflict, and she used examples to illustrate the concept.

2. Latisha used PowerPoint effectively. Her use of this technology was not only aligned with her goals, it was also interactive, allowing her to actively involve students and gather feedback about their learning progress.

Self-Help Quiz

TRUE/FALSE QUESTIONS. Write T in the blank if the statement is true, and write F if the statement is false.

_____ 1.   Research on the effects of technology on learning has shown a consistent positive effect.

_____ 2.   Most of the available educational technology software focuses on problem solving.

_____ 3.   Constructivist applications of educational technology primarily focus on students acquiring facts and skills.

_____ 4.   The Internet can be a valuable source of information for both teachers and students.

_____ 5.   Research shows that PowerPoint presentations are superior to overhead projections.

MULTIPLE-CHOICE ITEMS. Circle the best response in each case.

6. As opposed to a hardware view of technology, a process view of technology:
   a.   emphasizes the teaching of content through drill and practice.
   b.   stresses connections between academic areas.
   c.   integrates technology into instruction.
   d.   attempts to remediate learner difficulties through technology.

7. A major difference between drill and practice and tutorials is that tutorials:
   a.   provide practice with feedback.
   b.   are designed for stand-alone instruction.
   c.   are aimed at basic skills.
   d.   emphasize the active involvement of students.

8. Drill-and-practice software programs can be highly motivational and are most effective when the teacher's goal is to:
   a.   develop higher-level thinking skills.
   b.   enhance fact and skill learning.
   c.   simulate real-life situations in the classroom.
   d.   provide practice in using technology.

9. The most effective types of problem-solving software:
   a.   present a problem and provide opportunities for practice.
   b.   guide learners as they attempt to solve a problem.
   c.   provide continual feedback so learners don't make mistakes.
   d.   are open-ended so students get experience in problem finding.

10. Which of the following has **not** been proven true of the benefits of word processing technologies for teaching writing?
   a.   Students write more.
   b.   Students revise more thoroughly.
   c.   Students have more positive attitudes toward writing.
   d.   Students produce better products.

11. Databases are most often used to:
   a.   edit information.
   b.   develop basic skills.
   c.   organize data.
   d.   process information.

12. Mrs. Williams is a middle school social studies teacher who wants her students to understand how physical features and climate influence where people live and how they make a living. To do this, students visit an uninhabited island and have to decide where they would live and what they would do to live. Mrs. Williams is utilizing:
    a.   drill-and-practice software.
    b.   tutorial software.
    c.   simulation software.
    d.   spreadsheet software.

13. Chatrooms differ from bulletin boards in that they allow students to:
    a.   talk over longer distances.
    b.   discuss the same topic.
    c.   talk at the same time.
    d.   record messages before responding.

14. If a teacher wanted his students to learn to respond thoughtfully to other students' comments and ideas, he would probably use a:
    a.   simulation.
    b.   bulletin board.
    c.   chatroom.
    d.   tutorial.

15. A high school foreign language teacher uses software to teach vocabulary. Students are presented with the English word and have to supply its counterpart in Spanish. This type of instruction most closely reflects which theoretical perspective?
    a.   Behaviorist
    b.   Information processing
    c.   Constructivist
    d.   Social cognitive

16. A middle school social studies teacher has students use the Internet to communicate with another class across the country about their ecology experiment. The two classes compare data and try to figure out how local conditions influenced the results. This type of instruction most closely reflects which theoretical perspective?
    a.   Behaviorist
    b.   Information processing
    c.   Constructivist
    d.   Social cognitive

17. A high school physical education instructor is trying to teach her students how to effectively hit a backhand stroke in tennis. She first shows them an expert doing this and then videotapes them practicing, pointing out excellent examples through videotape. This type of instruction most closely reflects which theoretical perspective?
    a.   Behaviorist
    b.   Information processing
    c.   Constructivist
    d.   Social cognitive

18. Adaptations to assist students with disabilities typically uses which type of technology?
    a.   Simulations
    b.   Problem-solving software
    c.   Internet
    d.   Computers

19. Which of the following is NOT an advantage of using simulations over real-life experiences like labs or field trips?
   a. Time alteration
   b. Realism
   c. Safety
   d. Expense

20. A high school physics teacher wants her students to see the effects of gravity on a falling object. She shows them a videotape segment that depicts several objects falling in slow motion. Which of the following advantages of simulations is working here?
   a. Time alteration
   b. Realism
   c. Safety
   d. Expense

21. A social studies teacher wants his students to understand how demographic factors like age and gender influence voting practices. He has his students interview a number of people and then wants the class to analyze the data for patterns and trends. He is most likely to use which type of software?
   a. Simulation
   b. Database
   c. Tutorial
   d. Spreadsheet

22. Which of the following is *not* an advantage of distance education technologies?
   a. Offering of specialized courses to small populations
   b. Opportunities to drill and practice with feedback
   c. Access to non-traditional student populations
   d. Convenience for students

23. Which of the following is *not* true of research about students and distance education?
   a. Most students are adults.
   b. Dropout rates are usually higher.
   c. Asynchronous interaction is more effective than synchronous.
   d. Clear directions are essential.

24. When designing educational technology, minimizing irrelevant visuals and omitting extraneous background sounds is most important to which aspect of the information processing model?
   a. Attention
   b. Working memory
   c. Long term memory
   d. Retrieval

25. Which of the following is *not* a potential problem for students using the Internet as an information source?
   a. Information may be too organized and structured.
   b. Information may be too easy to find.
   c. Information may not be developmentally appropriate.
   d. Information may not match specific learning goals.

Self-Help Quiz Answers_____

1.   f
2.   f
3.   f
4.   t
5.   f

6. c   A process view of technology integrates technology into instruction, rather than thinking of it as an add-on.
7. b   Tutorials contain background information in addition to questions with feedback and are designed to serve as stand-alone instruction.
8. b   Drill-and-practice software programs primarily target the learning of basic facts and skills.
9. d   When we use problem-solving software, we want to give students practice with real-world problems. These typically are ill-defined and require students to find and define the problem.
10. d   When students use word processing technologies, they write more, revise more thoroughly, have more positive attitudes toward writing, but do not necessarily produce better products. This is an area where the teacher is essential.
11. c   Databases have the capability to organize large amounts of data and consequently are very useful in problem-solving activities.
12. c   Simulation software allows students to vicariously experience places and situations outside the classroom.
13. c   Chatrooms allow students to talk synchronously, or at the same time.
14. b   Bulletin boards are asynchronous and do not require a student to respond immediately. Consequently, students have more time to consider their responses.
15. a   A high school foreign language teacher using software to teach vocabulary reflects a behaviorist view of learning in which the two terms are stimulus-response connections.
16. c   Because the students are actively involved in interpreting the data and constructing their own understanding, this type of instruction is most closely aligned with constructivist theories of learning.
17. d   This teacher relied upon modeling and observational learning, which reflects a social cognitive perspective on learning.
18. d   Adaptations to computer input and output devices are the most common changes made to help students with disabilities.
19. b   Although simulations attempt to be realistic, they can't compete with actual experiences in terms of realism. All the other options are advantages of simulations.
20. a   The ability of simulations to slow down physical processes that are too fast for the naked eye is a distinct advantage of using simulations in the sciences.
21. b   Databases are ideally suited for helping student organize data and analyze them for patterns and trends.
22. b   Drill and practice with feedback are not typically found in distance education technologies. All of the other options are advantages of distance education.
23. c   Research shows that while asynchronous interaction is more convenient, it might not provide enough structure for younger students.
24. b   A major potential problem with educational technology is that it can create sensory overload, resulting in information not being processed from working memory into long term memory.
25. b   Ease of access is typically not a problem for students when they use the Internet to access information. All the others are potential problems.

CHAPTER 15: ASSESSING CLASSROOM LEARNING

Chapter Outline_____

I. Classroom assessment
    A. Functions of classroom assessment
        1. Formal and informal assessment
        2. The need for formal assessment
    B. Validity: Making appropriate assessment decisions
    C. Reliability: Consistency in assessment
II. Traditional assessment strategies
    A. Teachers' assessment patterns
    B. Constructing valid test items: Instructional principles
        1. Multiple choice
            a. The stem
            b. Distracters
            c. Assessing higher level learning
        2. Matching items
        3. True-false items
        4. Completion items
        5. Essay items: Measuring complex outcomes
        6. Using rubrics
    C. Commercially prepared test items
III. Alternative assessment
    A. Performance assessments
    B. Designing performance assessments: Instructional principles
        1. Specifying the performance
        2. Selecting the focus of assessment
        3. Structuring the evaluation setting
        4. Designing evaluation procedures
            a. Systematic observation
            b. Checklists
            c. Rating scales
    C. Portfolio assessment: Involving students in alternative assessment
    D. Putting traditional and alternative assessment into perspective
IV. Effective assessment practices: Instructional principles
    A. Planning for assessment
        1. Tables of specifications: Increasing validity through planning
    B. Preparing students for assessments
        1. Teaching test-taking strategies
        2. Reducing test anxiety
        3. Specific test-preparation procedures
    C. Administering assessments
    D. Analyzing results
V. Grading and reporting: The total assessment system
    A. Designing a grading system
        1. Formative and summative assessments
        2. Norm-referenced and criterion-referenced grading systems
        3. Traditional and alternative assessments
        4. Homework
    B. Assigning grades: Increasing learning and motivation
        1. Points or percentages
    C. Learning contexts: Assessment in urban classrooms

Chapter Objectives_____

- Identify examples of basic assessment concepts, such as formal and informal assessments, validity, and reliability in classroom activities.

- Analyze assessment items based on criteria used to create effective assessments, and explain how rubrics can increase the validity and reliability of essay items.

- Describe applications of different forms of alternative assessments.

- Explain applications of effective assessment practices.

- Describe the components and decisions involved in designing a total assessment system

Chapter Overview_____

Your study of this text is nearing completion. To this point you have examined the nature of learning and the influence that student characteristics, motivation, classroom management, and effective instruction all have on the amount students achieve. We now turn to the process of assessment, which is an effort to answer the question, "How much have students learned?"

Assessment involves all the processes and tools teachers use to make decisions about their students' progress. Valid assessments are consistent with stated learning objectives. Reliable assessments are consistent; unreliable measurements cannot be valid. One of the strengths of objective test formats, such as multiple-choice, is their high reliability. Essay tests can be unreliable.

Teachers in the elementary grades use performance assessments; they rely more on informal measures and commercially prepared tests to a greater extent than do teachers of older students, and they also place a greater emphasis on affective goals. The tests middle and secondary school teachers prepare most commonly use completion and matching formats, and they are composed of mostly knowledge/recall items.

Alternative assessments ask students to demonstrate skills similar to those required in the real world. Systematic observations, checklists, and rating scales can all be used to increase the validity and reliability of alternative assessments. Portfolios involve students in the design, collection, and evaluation of their own work.

Effective teachers prepare their students for tests by specifying precisely what will be on the tests, giving students a chance to practice responding to items under testlike conditions, and establishing positive expectations for student performance.

Effective teachers are sensitive to the possibility of bias as they design and implement their assessment systems. Bias can result from students' lack of experience with evaluation procedures, unequal access to relevant content knowledge, and problems with language.

Decisions about the relative weight of tests, quizzes, homework, and performance measures are left up to individual teachers. These factors together with the processes of preparing students for tests and administering them make up the teacher's total assessment system.

Application Exercises_____

Exercise 15.1

Use the following case study to respond to the questions below.

> Ginger Kelly's second graders have finished subtraction of one-digit from two-digit numbers without regrouping and are now working on subtraction of one-digit from two-digit numbers with regrouping. Her goal is for them to be skilled at identifying and solving problems that both do and do not require regrouping. She has four students working problems at the board while the others do the same problems at their seats.
> "Now let's try one more," she directs, seeing that the four students have gotten the problem right. She then gives the class another problem.
> As they work, she notices Erin gazing out the window instead of working. She goes to Erin's desk and, to her delight, finds that Erin has already correctly finished the problem.
> "Good work, Erin!" she exclaims after seeing Erin's paper.
> "They've got it," she says to herself, seeing that the students at the board have again done the problem correctly.
> Ginger then tells her students they will have a quiz the next day on problems similar to these.
> The next day, Ginger gives her students a 10-problem quiz involving subtraction of one-digit from two-digit numbers, 7 of which require regrouping. The students are told to show all their work on the work sheet.

1.   Identify at least two examples of informal assessment and at least one example of formal assessment in the case study.

2.   Ginger concluded, "They've got it," as she watched the students work. Based on the information in the case study, evaluate the extent to which the conclusion was valid at that point in her instruction. Give reasons for your evaluation.

3.   Based on the information in the case study, assess the extent to which Ginger's quiz was valid and how likely it was to be reliable. Give reasons for your answer.

4.   What is the primary advantage of informal assessment? What is the primary danger in using informal assessments?

5.   What is the primary function of formal assessment?

Exercise 15.2

Examine each of the following items and analyze them according to the criteria specified for multiple-choice items. An item may be effective according to the criteria, or it may be inconsistent with one or more than one of the guidelines. (For the purposes of these exercises, we have *italicized* the correct answer.)

1. Of the following, the best explanation for why the South lost the Civil War is:
   a.   the North had better military leadership.
   b.   there were more big cities in the north.
   c.   *the North had more industry that could support an army, whereas the South was mostly agricultural.*
   d.   it was too hot in the South.

2. Which of the following is a characteristic of young, rugged mountains?
   a.   They always have U-shaped valleys.
   b.   They have gently flowing streams.
   c.   *They have rugged, rocky peaks that extend above the tree line.*
   d.   All of the above.

3. Which of the following best illustrates an omnivore?
    a. *Ben is an animal of the forest. He spends most of his time in the winter in a long sleep. He roams around searching for the berries he loves to eat. When he is near a stream, he will also sometimes catch fish.*
    b. Billy is a high mountain animal. He has a thick coat to protect him from the cold. He has to scrape and scratch through the snow to get to the tender mosses that make up most of his diet.
    c. Sylvia lives in a nest near the top of a huge tree. She spends much of her time soaring through the air searching with her keen eyes for the rabbits and rodents that she brings back for her young.
    d. Sally spends most of her time in the water in the far north. On warm days, she lies near the water to sun herself before diving for the fish that make up her diet.

Look at the following sample items taken from a commercially prepared test and analyze them according to the criteria specified in this section of the chapter. In cases of inconsistency, describe specifically how the items fail to meet the criterion.

A. Complete each sentence below by filling in the blanks.
    1. About _____ percent of the earth's surface is covered by water.
    2. The strength of earthquakes is measured on the _____ scale.
    3. Very dry regions of the earth are called _____.

B. Underline the word or group of words that will make each sentence read correctly.
    1. A landmass almost entirely surrounded by water is called a(an) (isthmus, peninsula).
    2. Mountains are areas of (high, low) relief.
    3. The outer layer of the earth is called the (crust, mantle).

4. The completion items

5. The alternative response items

Exercise 15.3

Abdul Kalif was attempting to teach his middle school students to write persuasive essays. To motivate his students he focused their essays on the new school's search for a school mascot. As he planned for his instruction he decided to provide several models and use students to give feedback about first drafts. To assist the students in their evaluation of each others' essays he developed a scoring rubric that had written descriptions of key elements (e.g. "Explicitly stated position at beginning of essay."). When the projects were done he presented them to a panel of experts (other teachers) who decided which ones would appear in the school newspaper. In addition, he encouraged students to include these in their growing collection of personal writing samples.

1. What efforts did Abdul make to increase the authenticity of his assessment efforts?

2. What forms of authentic assessment did Abdul use to measure his students' writing ability?

3. What steps did Abdul take during planning to increase the validity and reliability of his assessments?

4. What evidence is there that Abdul utilized portfolio assessment?

Exercise 15.4

1. Your students are taking a test, and the intercom breaks in saying, "Ms. . . . , a parent, is on the phone. She needs to talk to you. She says it's important. Can you come to the office for a moment?"
    Using the information in this section as a basis, describe the most appropriate response to the request.

2. You have worked harder than you thought possible to get your students ready for an important test. "They have to be ready," you say to yourself. "Nobody could do a better job of teaching than I did here." To your chagrin, most of the class do very poorly on the test, and many of the responses seem to indicate a lack of effort on the part of the students.

    Based on the information in this section, which of the following is the best response to the students? (Provide a rationale for your decision.)

    a. We did a good job on the test. Now let's try and keep it up.
    b. Here are your test results. I believe if we work a little harder we can probably improve on the next test.
    c. We didn't do as well as I had hoped considering that we prepared so much. Let's try and redouble our efforts for the next test.
    d. I'm quite disappointed in the test results. Considering how hard I worked to get you ready, it doesn't look like some of you studied as much as you could have.

Exercise 15.5

Look again at Ginger Kelly's work with her second graders in Exercise 15.1. Suppose that in Ginger's grading system 94% to 100% was an A, and 86% to 93% was a B. Suppose further that six students got an A on the quiz because they got all the problems right, and eight more got a B because they missed only one problem. Is Ginger's system norm-referenced or criterion-referenced? Explain why.

Feedback for Application Exercises_____

Exercise 15.1

1. Ginger was using information assessment when she watched the students doing the practice problems at the board. While they might appear to be formal assessments, she wasn't getting the same information from all the students under the same conditions, so they were informal. She was also making an informal assessment when she noticed that Erin was gazing out the window rather than working. The quiz was an example of a formal assessment.

2. At that point in the lesson, Ginger's conclusion was not valid. Her conclusion was based only on the performance of the four students at the board (and Erin). She didn't have any information about the performance of the other students.

3. Ginger's quiz was both valid and reliable. Her goal was for the students to identify and solve problems that require regrouping, and 7 of the problems she gave required regrouping while 3 did not. (The only uncertainty in the relationship between the goal and assessment is that technically the students are not solving problems; they're merely applying an algorithm.) Reliability would be dependent upon scoring consistency as well as the length and the appropriate difficulty of the quiz.

4. Informal assessments are valuable for making routine decisions, such as whom to call on and when, how long to conduct an activity, how much review is needed, and when to intervene if students are off-task. Since informal assessments are not always reliable, grading decisions based on them may not be valid, and teachers must be careful to include assessments for grading purposes that are formal and systematic.

5. Formal assessments are used for important decisions, such as when to move on to a new topic or assigning grades.

Exercise 15.2

1. Item 1 can be criticized on the basis of the following criteria:
   a) Choice *d* is implausible, and putting an implausible distracter at choice d is particularly unwise since test-wise students are unlikely to choose it anyway.
   b) Choice *c* is the answer. Having some of the answers as choice *c* is appropriate, of course, but it is often overused.
   c) The correct answer is longer than the other distracters.

2. Item 2 can be criticized on the basis of the following criteria:
   a) It uses "all of the above" as a distracter.
   b) The absolute term "always" appears in choice *a*.
   c) The right answer is again choice *c*.
   d) The right answer is longer than the other distracters.
   e) The term "rugged" appears in both the stem and the right answer.

3. Other than the fact that each distracter is lengthy and requires that students are capable readers, item 3 meets the criteria. It is particularly effective in that the characteristics of omnivore are illustrated rather than merely giving the names of animals. For instance, suppose the item was written as follows:

Which of the following best illustrates an omnivore?
   a. Bear
   b. Mountain goat
   c. Eagle
   d. Seal

As written, it requires students to know the diet of each animal. They could understand the concept of omnivore but not know that a bear is one, and miss the item for that reason. That would make the item invalid.

4. The Completion Items: While the blanks are of equal length, two of the three items have the blank in the body of the sentence. Items 2 and 3 are not phrased in such a way that only one possible answer is correct.

5. Alternative Response Items: Numbers 2 and 3 are "give aways" for a test-wise student. Students with only a vague understanding of mountains would likely choose "high" over "low," even if they had no idea of what "relief" meant. The notion of "crust" being the outer layer can be determined from experiences, such as the "crust" of a piece of bread.

Exercise 15.3

1. Abdul did several things to try to make his assessment task more authentic. First, he focused on an issue that was important to students. Second, he used a panel of experts to judge the essays. Finally, he had students submit their essays to the school paper.

2. Basically Abdul used a performance assessment. At the end he encouraged students to include their essays in their portfolios.

3. During planning Abdul used a scoring rubric that he developed into a rating scale for students to use.

4. Portfolios have two essential characteristics: (1) they collect and display samples of students' work, and (2) they involve students in the planning. Both aspects were present in Abdul's lesson.

Exercise 15.4

1. While there is no single "correct" response, teachers should make every effort to remain in the classroom and carefully monitor their tests. On this basis an appropriate response would be, "My students are taking a test and I can't leave them. Please take a message, and I'll call Mrs. _____ as soon as I can." In the case of an extreme emergency, either the principal should handle it, or the principal should come down to your classroom to monitor your students while you go to the front office.

2. As with item 1, there is no absolute right or wrong answer. However, based on the background material and the information in the item, choice *b* is preferred.

The rationale is as follows:

Choice *a* is misleading and could even be called dishonest. In order to maintain credibility the teacher must remain "real."

Choice *c* is not a "bad" response. The only advantage in choice *b* by comparison is that it is stated in positive terms.

Choice *d* is undesirable. The implication is that "I" worked hard, but "you" didn't come through. Even if this is true, it doesn't help student performance, and may even detract from effort on subsequent tests.

Exercise 15.5

Ginger's system is criterion-referenced. Getting all the problems right is a 100%, and missing one is a 90% (9 out of 10 correct). The students are evaluated according to a pre-set standard and are not compared to each other.

Self-Help Quiz_____

TRUE-FALSE QUESTIONS: Mark T in the blank for a true statement and mark F for a false statement.

_____ 1. A test item could be invalid and still be reliable.
_____ 2. A test item could be unreliable and still be valid.
_____ 3. According to research examining the effects of assessment on learning, teachers should give fewer tests in lower achieving classes than in higher achieving classes.
_____ 4. Formal assessments are usually less reliable than are informal assessments.
_____ 5. If students understand a topic, and they respond incorrectly to a test item measuring the topic, the test item is invalid.

MULTIPLE-CHOICE QUESTIONS: Circle the best choice in each case.

6. Which of the following is the best definition of classroom assessment?
   a. All the processes involved in gathering information about student learning
   b. The decisions teachers make about student learning
   c. The quizzes, tests, and performance measures teachers use to determine how much students have learned.
   d. All the processes involved in making decisions about students' learning progress

Use the following information for items 7 and 8.

1. A teacher gives a 20 item quiz on flowering plants.
2. A teacher sees a student squint as she looks at the chalkboard.
3. A teacher calls on a student.
4. A teacher marks B+ on a student's essay.

7. The formal assessment(s) is/are:
   a. 1, 4.
   b. 2, 3.
   c. 1, 2, 3.
   d. 1.
   e. 4.

8. The informal assessment(s) is/are:
   a. 1, 2, 3.
   b. 2, 3.
   c. 1, 3.
   d. 2.
   e. 3.

Use the following information for items 9-12.

A goal for the 10th grade English department at Geneva Lakes High School is for all the students in the 10th grade to be able to write essays in which they make and defend an argument. Different teachers approach assessment of the goal differently.
    After discussing arguments and supporting evidence and giving a series of examples, Mrs. Baldwin gives the students in her class five written essays and asks the students to decide which essay best makes and defends an argument and which essay makes and defends an argument least well.
    Mr. Brannan has all the students in his class write essays in which they make and defend an argument.
    Mrs. Duncan has a class discussion in which individual students take a position. Some of the other students defend the position, while others take issue with the position. In all cases the individuals must provide evidence when they defend or take issue with the position. Mrs. Duncan then evaluates the students based on their responses in the discussion.

Mr. Combs describes the process of making and defending an argument. He then gives some examples of arguments and asks the students to write a series of statements that supports the argument.

9. The teacher whose assessments are likely to be *most* valid is:
    a. Mrs. Baldwin.
    b. Mr. Brannan.
    c. Mrs. Duncan.
    d. Mr. Combs.

10. The teacher whose assessments are likely to be *least* valid is:
    a. Mrs. Baldwin.
    b. Mr. Brannan.
    c. Mrs. Duncan.
    d. Mr. Combs.

11. The teacher whose assessments are *most likely* to be reliable is:
    a. Mrs. Baldwin.
    b. Mr. Brannan.
    c. Mrs. Duncan.
    d. Mr. Combs.

12. The teacher whose assessments are *least likely* to be reliable is:
    a. Mrs. Baldwin.
    b. Mr. Brannan.
    c. Mrs. Duncan.
    d. Mr. Combs.

Use the following information for items 13-15.

You are conducting a question and answer activity to review the parts of the cell with your class of 27 students. In your review you call on about two-thirds of the students, and most of them answer the questions correctly. You conclude that the class understands the material.

13. Of the following, noticing that the students answer most of the questions correctly best illustrates:
    a. a formal assessment.
    b. an informal assessment.
    c. a summative assessment.
    d. an assessment system.

14. Of the following, concluding that the class understands the material best illustrates:
    a. a formal assessment.
    b. an informal assessment.
    c. a formative assessment.
    d. an assessment system.

15. Which of the following best describes your conclusion?
    a. It is reliable but not valid.
    b. It is both reliable and valid.
    c. It is unreliable and therefore invalid.
    d. It is invalid and therefore unreliable.

16. Joe Williams and David Negge both have "the students' ability to assess a conclusion" as a goal for their students. They both assign an essay where the students assess the conclusion that Spain's, Britain's, and France's goal in exploring the New World in the 16th and 17th centuries was primarily economic. Joe constructs a set of criteria to be used in scoring the essay. David does not. They both score the essays and assign students grades. Of the following, which is the most accurate statement?
   a. David's assessment is likely to be less reliable than Joe's and therefore less valid as well.
   b. David's assessment is likely to be less reliable than Joe's but they are equally valid.
   c. Both teachers' assessments are likely to be invalid, since they are essays.
   d. Both teachers' assessments are valid and reliable since the assessments are consistent with their goals.

Use the following information for items 17 and 18.

Four teachers were discussing their test-anxious students:

   Mrs. Rowe commented, "I have them practice on items that are similar to those that will be on the test. Then I try to motivate them by mentioning in passing that some of the items on the test will challenge them, and they're going to have to do some thinking."
   "I do the same thing, meaning I have them practice," Mr. Potter comments, "but I don't say anything one way or the other about how difficult the test will be."
   "I do stress reduction activities with my class," Mrs. Richards adds. "Just before we begin the test, I have them close their eyes, visualize themselves doing well on the test, and take a few deep breaths. Then we start."
   "I do something a little different, "Mr. Lareau adds. "I tell them that I know they will do well, and I tell them to be ready for a test every day, because I'm not going to tell them when we're having it, except that it will be sometime during the week. It keeps them on their toes."

17. Based on research, the teacher *most effective* in reducing test anxiety in her students is likely to be:
   a. Mrs. Rowe.
   b. Mr. Potter.
   c. Mrs. Richards.
   d. Mr. Lareau.

18. Based on research, the teacher *least effective* in reducing test anxiety in her students is likely to be:
   a. Mrs. Rowe.
   b. Mr. Potter.
   c. Mrs. Richards.
   d. Mr. Lareau.

Use the following information for items 19-20.

Gigi Parker is emphasizing grammatically correct writing and expression of thought in writing with her students. She has begun using portfolios, where systematic collections of her students' are placed for review and evaluation. She puts work samples in the portfolio at least three days a week, and she is careful to date the samples to help in assessing her students' progress. In examining her students' work, she checks for grammar, punctuation, spelling, and clear expression of thought, and she assigns grades on that basis.

19. If Gigi is consistent with patterns identified by research, which of the following is most likely?
   a. Gigi is an elementary teacher.
   b. Gigi is a middle school teacher.
   c. Gigi is a high school teacher.

20. Based on the information about Gigi's assessments, which of the following is the most accurate statement?
    a. They are likely to be both reliable and valid.
    b. They are likely to be reliable but not valid.
    c. They are likely to be valid but not reliable.
    d. They are likely to be both invalid and unreliable.

Look at the four following goals and assessments.

Mrs. Andrews, a seventh-grade teacher, wants her students to be able to solve problems involving percentages. She gives her students several problems such as:

John had $45 and he spent $35 on a new shirt. What percentage of his money did he spend on the shirt?

Mr. Bowden, a fourth grade teacher, wants his students to write grammatically correct paragraphs that accurately obey grammar and punctuation rules. He gives his students several exercises in which they have to put in correct verb forms to maintain subject-verb agreement and other exercises that they punctuate properly.

Mrs. Fisher, a third grade teacher, wants her students to understand the concept *insect*. She brings in several "bugs" and has them identify those that are insects (versus spiders and other animals).

Mr. Morgan, a fifth-grade teacher, wants her students to understand the function of maps. He has his students design and draw a map of their school to a scale that they choose.

21. The teacher whose assessment is *most* nearly authentic is:
    a. Mrs. Andrews.
    b. Mr. Bowden.
    c. Mrs. Fisher.
    d. Mr. Morgan.

22. The teacher whose assessment is *least* authentic is:
    a. Mrs. Andrews.
    b. Mr. Bowden.
    c. Mrs. Fisher.
    d. Mr. Morgan.

Use the following information for items 23 and 24.

Four teachers are discussing their assessment procedures:

Mr. Ganyo comments, "I give the tests back, we go over them, and then I tell the kids to put them in their notebooks."

Mrs. Anderson responds, "I give them their scores and tell them that they can come in and discuss the tests in detail with me in one-on-one sessions before or after school if they want to."

Mr. Wilson adds, "I give the tests back, but we don't discuss them. I've gotten tired of putting up with the students' arguments about the way they've been scored."

Mrs. Mashima nods, "I give them back and we go over them. Then I collect them, because I revise and use the items again. I tell them they can come in and discuss them with me one-on-one if they are confused."

23. Based on research examining effective assessment practices, the teacher whose assessment procedure is *most* effective is:
    a. Mr. Ganyo.
    b. Mrs. Anderson.
    c. Mr. Wilson.
    d. Mrs. Mashima.

24. Based on research examining effective assessment practices, the teacher whose assessment procedure is *least* effective is:
   a. Mr. Ganyo.
   b. Mrs. Anderson.
   c. Mr. Wilson.
   d. Mrs. Mashima.

25. Look at the following test item. (For purposes of this item, we have italicized the correct answer.)

Which of the following is a function of the digestive system?
   a. To circulate the blood
   b. To protect vital body organs
   c. *To digest the food we eat and turn it into usable fuel for our bodies*
   d. To transfer nerve impulses

There are at least three problems with this item. Identify the problems. Then rewrite the item to make it more effective.

Self-Help Quiz Answers_____

1. t
2. f
3. f
4. f
5. t
6. d   Classroom assessment includes all the processes involved in making decisions about students' learning progress. It includes *both* the processes involved in gathering information about student learning *and* the decisions made based on that information. So, it is more than "All the processes involved in gathering information about student learning" (choice a), or "The decisions teachers make about student learning" (choice b). And, "The quizzes, tests, and performance measures teachers use to determine how much students have learned" (choice c) includes only the information gathering part of the process; it does not include the decisions involved.
7. a   Formal assessments include systematically gathering information and making decisions based on that information.
8. b   Informal assessments include gathering information in an incidental way during the course of a lesson or day and making decisions based on that information.
9. b   Having each student make and defend an argument in an essay is most consistent with the objective.
10. a   Judging others' arguments is not the same as making and defending your own argument. In each of the other cases the students were involved to a certain extent in defending an argument. Providing essays and having the students judge the extent to which the essay effectively makes and defends an argument, as Mrs. Baldwin did, would be an excellent learning activity that would be designed to help the students reach the goal.
11. a   Evaluating the five essays is a convergent task and could be scored reliably.
12. c   Evaluating oral discussions would be highly unreliable.
13. b   An informal measurement gathers information incidentally during the course of the lesson.
14. c   An evaluation is a decision based on measurement.
15. c   Since you didn't ask for the same information from all students and didn't systematically tap their knowledge, your conclusion would be both unreliable and therefore invalid.
16. a   Essays are often unreliable. The absence of scoring criteria suggests unreliability leading to lack of validity.

17. b Providing them with practice will help reduce test anxiety. Practice together with suggesting that some of the items will be challenging, as Mrs. Rowe did, can be effective in increasing motivation and self-efficacy, but it can increase anxiety for highly test-anxious students. Efforts at stress reduction, in and of themselves, are generally ineffective.
18. d Surprise or pop quizzes tend to increase rather than decrease anxiety.
19. a Elementary teachers tend to use more work samples than do teachers at higher levels.
20. a They are consistent with her goals, she collects them systematically and she makes evaluation decisions based on pre-established criteria.
21. d Drawing their own map of a school would be the most authentic.
22. b Artificial exercises taken out of context are least authentic.
23. d Going over items, collecting and revising them for re-use and allowing students to come in again are all effective practices.
24. c Lack of feedback on specific items greatly decreases the instructional value of tests and quizzes. While Mrs. Anderson's procedure isn't particularly effective, the option of going over the test in detail remains open to the students who will take the initiative to do so.
25. Potential problems include: (1) the correct answer is *c* (this is appropriate if choice *c* isn't overused); (2) the correct answer contains the word "digest," and the word "digest" is also in the stem; and (3) the correct choice is significantly longer than the distracters.

An improved item might appear as follows:

Which of the following best describes the function of the digestive system?
a. To circulate the blood
b. *To turn food into usable fuel*
c. To protect vital body organs
d. To transfer nerve impulses to various parts of the body

CHAPTER 16: ASSESSMENT THROUGH STANDARDIZED TESTING

Chapter Outline_____

I.   Standardized tests
    A.   Functions of standardized tests
        1.   Assessment and diagnosis of learning
        2.   Selection and placement
        3.   Program evaluation and accountability
    B.   Types of standardized tests
        1.   Achievement tests
        2.   Diagnostic tests
        3.   Intelligence tests
            a.   The Stanford-Binet
            b.   The Wechsler Scales
        4.   Aptitude tests
    C.   Evaluating standardized tests: Validity revisited
        1.   Content validity
        2.   Predictive validity
        3.   Construct validity
    D.   The teacher's role in standardized testing: Instructional principles
        1.   Matching tests and learning objectives
        2.   Preparing students
        3.   Administering tests
        4.   Interpreting results
II.   Understanding and interpreting standardized test scores
    A.   Descriptive statistics
        1.   Frequency distributions
        2.   Measures of central tendency
        3.   Measures of variability
        4.   The normal distribution
    B.   Interpreting standardized test results
        1.   Raw scores
        2.   Percentiles
        3.   Stanines
        4.   Grade equivalents
        5.   Standard scores
        6.   Standard error of measurement
III. Accountability issues in standardized testing
    A.   Standards-based education and accountability
        1.   No Child Left Behind
        2.   High-stakes tests
    B.   Testing teachers
        1.   The Praxis series
IV.   Diversity issues in standardized testing
    A.   Student diversity and test bias
        1.   Bias in content
        2.   Bias in testing procedures
        3.   Bias in test use
    B.   Eliminating bias in standardized testing: Instructional principles
        1.   Analyze test content
        2.   Adapt testing procedures
        3.   Use alternate assessment data sources
    C.   Issues in standardized testing: Implications for teachers

Chapter Objectives_____

- Identify functions and types of standardized tests in descriptions of decisions made by school officials and the types of validity addressed by the decisions.

- Explain standardized test results using statistics and standard scores.

- Describe the relationships between standards-based education, accountability, and high-stakes testing

- Describe potential types of testing bias and strategies teachers can use to minimize bias in the use of standardized tests with their students.

Chapter Overview_____

Standardized tests are given to large groups under uniform conditions, and they are scored with uniform procedures. An individual's performance is then compared to a norming group consisting of comparable people who have taken the test under similar testing conditions. Standardized testing is very important and somewhat controversial. The calls for national reforms in education are virtually all based on the fact that American students perform less well on standardized tests than do their counterparts in other industrialized countries.

Achievement tests measure student learning in different content areas; diagnostic tests give detailed descriptions of students' strengths and weaknesses in particular skill areas; intelligence tests attempt to measure an individual's ability to think in the abstract, solve problems, and the capacity to acquire knowledge. Aptitude tests are designed to predict a student's potential for future learning, and they measure general abilities developed over long periods of time. The high school SAT and ACT are two examples of aptitude tests.

Validity is a central concern in evaluating and selecting standardized tests. Content validity represents the overlap or match between what is taught and what is tested. Predictive validity is an indicator of a test's ability to gauge future performance. Construct validity examines the extent to which a test actually measures what it is designed to measure.

Teachers use statistical methods to understand and interpret the vast amount of information gathered on standardized tests. Measures of central tendency–the mean, median, and mode–describe a group's performance as a whole, and the range and standard deviation give an indication of the variability in the scores.

For large samples, standardized test scores tend to approximate a normal distribution. In normal distributions, the mean, median, and mode are the same score, about 68% of all scores are within one standard deviation from the mean, and about 98% of the scores lie within two standard deviations from the mean.

Students' performances on standardized tests are commonly reported in several ways: percentiles, a ranking compared to all others who have taken the test; stanines, which describe scores in bands distributed from the mean; grade equivalents, which compare students to average scores for a particular age group; or standard scores, which describe scores in standardized deviation units from the mean. The standard error of measurement on a test gives a range of scores into which a student's true score is likely to fall.

Application Exercises_____

Exercise 16.1

Analyze the following to determine whether an achievement, aptitude, diagnostic or intelligence test is being considered. In addition decide whether content, predictive, or construct validity is involved.

1.   Teachers at Jefferson Elementary School were trying to decide whether Ken Bradbury needed supplemental resource help. To gather information to be used in making this decision a standardized test was administered to determine his overall potential for learning. One of the teachers objected to the use of the test, questioning whether test content accurately matched the school's curriculum.

2.   Teachers at Westlake Middle School were trying to decide which of their students should be recommended for an accelerated science program. One of the counselors mentioned the Science Process Test and said that it had been successfully used at other schools in the district. One of the teachers asked if the items on the test would be worth the trouble and really tell them anything that grades wouldn't.

3.   Second grade teachers were attempting to ascertain their students' strengths and weaknesses so that they could do a better job of steering students to the appropriate learning centers designed to augment different areas of the curriculum. One of the teachers mentioned a detailed district-wide assessment instrument that measured literacy and math skills. Another teacher questioned whether the test matched the specific things they were doing at their school.

4.   Controversy raged at Lincoln Elementary School. The school had moved to a whole language approach to language arts that stressed writing and novels. Some parents wondered if their children were still learning "basics" like grammar and punctuation. The ad hoc committee decided to use a standardized test to compare Lincoln students' performance in these areas with other schools, but one teacher objected, stating that the curriculum wasn't designed to teach isolated skills.

Exercise 16.2

Students are given a standardized test, and the results indicated that Tamara scored in the 50th percentile, Joey scored in the 70th, and Helen in the 90th.

1.   Identify the stanine for each student.

2.   Identify the approximate z-score and T-score for each student.

3.   What is each student's IQ according to the Wechsler scales?

4.   Maria takes the Scholastic Aptitude Test and finds that she scored an 1100, 600 in math and 500 in English. What is her approximate percentile rank in math and English?

5.   Rhonda scores a 62 on a test with a mean of 50 and a standard deviation of 8. If the test results approximate a normal distribution, what is Rhonda's:
      a.   Approximate percentile rank?
      b.   Stanine?
      c.   z-score?

6. A test is given with a mean of 60, a median of 60, a mode of 60 and a standard deviation of 5. Approximately half the group of students who took the test scored from 55 to 65 on the test. Of the following, which is the best conclusion?
   a. The scores fit a normal distribution.
   b. The scores do not fit a normal distribution.
   c. We don't have enough information to determine whether or not the scores fit a normal distribution.
   Explain your answer.

7. Joanne scores a 45, Franklin scores a 40, and Monica scores a 35 on a test with a standard error of 3. Which of the following statements are true? (More than one answer may be true.)
   a. Joanne's true score is higher than both Franklin's and Monica's.
   b. Franklin's true score is higher than both Joanne's and Monica's.
   c. Franklin's true score might be higher than both Joanne's and Monica's.
   d. Monica's true score might be higher than both Joanne's and Franklin's.
   e. Joanne's true score is higher than Monica's and might be higher than Franklin's.
   Explain your answer in each case.

Feedback for Application Exercises

Exercise 16.1

1. Overall potential for learning is one characteristic of an intelligence test. The match with the school's curriculum suggests a concern with content validity.

2. The teachers at Westlake were interested in a content-specific aptitude test. The teacher's concern centered around predictive validity.

3. A detailed assessment aimed at content is characteristic of a diagnostic test. The teacher questioned whether the test had content validity and whether it matched the content of the curriculum at that school.

4. The test could be either a standardized achievement or diagnostic test, depending upon the degree of detail and specificity. The teacher was questioning its content validity, or the match with their curriculum.

Exercise 16.2

1. Tamara is in stanine 5, Joey in stanine 6, and Helen in stanine 8.

2. Tamara has a z-score of 0 and a T-score of 50, Joey a z-score of approximately .5 and a T-score of 55, and Helen a z-score of approximately 1.4 and a T-score of 64.

3. Tamara's IQ is 100, Joey's is approximately 107, and Helen's approximately 120.

4. Maria's approximate percentile rank in math is 84, and her approximate percentile rank in English is 50.

5. Rhonda's score indicates that she is 1.5 standard deviations above the mean. On this basis: (a) her approximate percentile rank would be 92, (b) she would be in stanine 8, and (c) her z-score would be 1.5.

6. The best conclusion is that the scores do not approximate a normal distribution. While the mean, median, and mode are all the same, a normal distribution has approximately 68% of all scores falling from one standard deviation below the mean to one standard deviation above the mean. This distribution has half the scores falling from one standard deviation below to one standard deviation above the mean.

7. Because the standard error is 3, Joanne's true score is probably between 42 and 48, Franklin's is between 37 and 43, and Monica's is between 32 and 38.

This means choices c and e are true.

Self-Help Quiz_____

TRUE-FALSE QUESTIONS: Mark T in the blank for a true statement and mark F for a false statement.

_____ 1.   Standardized tests tend to be less reliable than are teacher-made tests.
_____ 2.   Grade equivalents indicate the grade in which a learner should be placed.
_____ 3.   Standardized tests typically are not used as a basis for assigning grades to students.
_____ 4.   Aptitude and intelligence are synonymous terms.
_____ 5.   The mean of a distribution of scores is more strongly influenced by extremely high or extremely low scores than is the median in a distribution of scores.

MULTIPLE-CHOICE QUESTIONS: Circle the best choice in each case.

6. Your school has implemented a new math curriculum in the fourth grade that emphasizes the National Council of Teachers of Mathematics Curriculum and Evaluation Standards. The four fourth-grade teachers are somewhat uneasy about some of emphasis in the curriculum and are concerned about whether or not the students are "getting" what they need to be getting at the fourth grade level. Of the following, to answer their question, which of the following would be the school's most valid decision?
     a.   Have the four math teachers create a series of exercises that are consistent with the curriculum objectives, administer the exercises, and compare the four grades.
     b.   Select a standardized achievement test in math, administer the test to the four classes and analyze the results.
     c.   Select a standardized diagnostic test in math, administer the test to the four classes and analyze the results.
     d.   Combine the results of the teacher-made exercises and the diagnostic test and analyze both.

7. You are on a team that is making decisions about placing students in a program for the gifted. Of the following, which measure would you be least likely to consider in this process?
     a.   Teacher recommendations
     b.   Achievement test results
     c.   Aptitude test results
     d.   Diagnostic test results

8. Of the following, the two that are most closely related are:
     a.   aptitude and achievement tests.
     b.   aptitude and diagnostic tests.
     c.   intelligence and diagnostic tests.
     d.   achievement and diagnostic tests.
     e.   achievement and intelligence tests.

9. Your school has been focusing on higher-order and critical thinking in your students, and you have measured your students' abilities in that area. To see how much progress you've made in that area you want to give another standardized test that measures the students' present critical thinking abilities. In selecting the test, which of the following is your school's primary concern?
     a.   Content validity
     b.   Construct validity
     c.   Predictive validity
     d.   Face validity

10. The horizontal axis of a normal distribution at any particular point best represents which of the following?
    a. The raw score on a test.
    b. The number of people who attained a particular score on a test.
    c. The mean score of the people who took the test.
    d. The standard deviation of the scores on the test.

Use the following information for items 11-13.

A student takes a 60-item subtest of a standardized test. The subtest has a mean of 48 with a standard deviation of 6. The student gets a 54 on the subtest.

11. The 54 on the subtest is best described as the:
    a. raw score.
    b. standard error.
    c. standard score.
    d. stanine score.

12. Of the following, the best estimate of the student's percentile ranking is:
    a. 96.
    b. 90.
    c. 84.
    d. 50.

13. Of the following, the best estimate of the student's stanine ranking is:
    a. 5.
    b. 6.
    c. 7.
    d. 8.
    e. 9.

Use the following information for items 14-17.

A subtest of a standardized test has a mean of 40 with a standard deviation of 4. (Assume a very large sample so the test results nearly fit a normal distribution.) George scores a 46 on the subtest.

14. Based on this information, which of the following is the best approximation of George's percentile rank?
    a. 40th.
    b. 44th.
    c. 84th.
    d. 90th.
    e. 98th.

15. Cory scores a 44 on the same subtest. Of the following the best description of Cory's stanine is:
    a. 5.
    b. 6.
    c. 7.
    d. 8.
    e. 9.

16. On this test George's T-score would be:
   a. 45.
   b. 46.
   c. 55.
   d. 60.
   e. 65.

17. On this test George's z-score would be:
   a. -1.0.
   b. -1.5.
   c. 1.0.
   d. 1.5.
   e. 4.6.

18. Ellen scores a 77 on a standardized test that has a standard error of 4. Of the following, which is the most valid conclusion?
   a. Ellen's true score is likely to be somewhere between 77 and 81.
   b. Ellen's true score is likely to be somewhere between 73 and 77.
   c. Ellen's true score is likely to be somewhere between 73 and 81.
   d. Ellen's true score is likely to be somewhere between 75 and 79.

19. Diane is in the 55th percentile, Jerome is in the 65th percentile, and Juanita is in the 75th percentile of a standardized test. Of the following, which is the most valid conclusion?
   a. The difference between Diane's and Jerome's raw scores is greater than the difference between Juanita's and Jerome's raw scores.
   b. The difference between Jerome's and Juanita's raw scores is greater than the difference between Jerome's and Diane's raw scores.
   c. The difference between Diane's and Jerome's raw scores is equal to the difference between Juanita's and Jerome's raw scores.
   d. We can't make a conclusion about differences in raw scores when we only have access to information about percentiles.

20. Deanna, a beginning third grader, has a grade equivalent score of 5.5 on a standardized reading achievement test. Of the following, which is the most valid conclusion?
   a. Deanna is an advanced reader.
   b. If one exists, Deanna should be placed in a reading program for gifted students.
   c. Deanna should be placed in fifth grade reading.
   d. Deanna's parents should be advised to consider having Deanna skip the third grade and move into the fourth grade.

21. On a subtest of a standardized test Warren scores at the 88th percentile. The year before he had scored at the 80th percentile on the same test. Of the following, which is the most valid conclusion?
   a. Warren scored as high or higher than 88 percent of the people who took the test during this year's administration of the test.
   b. Warren answered exactly 88 percent of the items on the test correctly during this year's administration of the test.
   c. Warren answered approximately 88 percent of the items on the subtest correctly during this year's administration of the test.
   d. Warren answered 8 percent more of the items correctly on this year's administration of the test than he answered correctly on last year's administration of the test.

22. You have two sets of scores, which are as follows:

Set A: Mean–40 Median–40 Standard deviation–4
Set B: Mean–40 Median–41 Standard deviation–6

Of the following, which is the most accurate statement?
   a. The students' performance for both sets was equal since the means are the same.
   b. The scores in Set B tend to be spread out more than the scores in Set A.
   c. The students in Set B actually performed better, according to the test, than those in Set A since the standard deviation is higher than in Set A.
   d. The students in Set B actually performed better, according to the test, than those in Set A since both the median and standard deviation are higher than they are in Set A.

23. Kathy, one of Mrs. Mahoney's students in 10th grade honors English, got a high B the first grading period and an A- the second grading period. Mrs. Mahoney commented periodically on Kathy's good work on her essays. However, Kathy didn't score particularly highly on the PSAT (Preliminary Scholastic Aptitude Test), scoring in the 48th percentile on the verbal section. By comparison, most of the rest of the class scored in the 80th percentile or higher. The results were sent to Mrs. Mahoney, who then passed them along to Kathy.

Kathy's father proofread her essays as she had done the first two grading periods, but Kathy got a C the third grading period. "I'll bring it back up, Dad," she vowed. However, she got another C the fourth grading period and also got a C for the year.

Based on the information in the case study, which of the following is the most likely explanation for the decline in Kathy's grades?
   a. Her motivation declined, and with it, the quality of her work.
   b. Kathy's self-esteem was lowered as a result of her modest performance on the PSAT and as a result her performance suffered.
   c. Having scored lower than her peers, Kathy no longer felt capable of competing with them and her efforts were reduced.
   d. Mrs. Mahoney's perception of Kathy's ability was adversely affected by Kathy's PSAT results.

24. An item from the WISC-III shows students pictures with a missing element in each, such as a scissors with the bolt that holds the two parts of the scissors together missing. Suppose some of the students taking the test have virtually no experience with scissors. Which of the following is the most valid conclusion?
   a. Since the ability to acquire experience is a characteristic of intelligence, the item is valid for all students.
   b. For students lacking experience, content bias exists in the item.
   c. For students lacking experience, bias in testing procedures is likely to exist.
   d. The ability to identify missing elements of pictures is unrelated to intelligence, so the item is invalid for all students.

25. Identify three important differences between standardized and teacher-made tests.

Self-Help Quiz Answers_____

1. f
2. f
3. t
4. f
5. t
6. d By comparing the results of the teacher-made exercises and the diagnostic test the teachers would have two different perspectives on the question of what students were learning.
7. d Diagnostic tests are useful for identifying specific deficiencies and strengths in a content area.
8. d Achievement and diagnostic tests both measure mastery of content; diagnostic tests are more detailed and specific in their focus.

9.   a   Content validity refers to the relationship between what is taught and what is tested. Since the school's goal is to "... see how much progress you've made in that area ..." you're concerned about that relationship. (If you were concerned about whether or not the items on the test actually measured higher-order and critical thinking, you would be concerned with construct validity.)

10.   a   The horizontal axis represents the raw score; the vertical axis represents the number of people attaining a score.

11.   a   The raw score on a test is the number of items answered correctly.

12.   c   The student is one standard deviation above the mean, which corresponds to the 84th percentile.

13.   c   One standard deviation above the mean corresponds to stanine 7.

14.   d   George's score of 46 is one and one half standard deviation units above the mean; this would translate into a percentile of about 90.

15.   c   One standard deviation above the mean corresponds to a stanine of 7.

16.   e   One standard deviation above the mean corresponds to a T-score of 60, and two standard deviations above the mean corresponds to a T-score of 70, so George's T-score would be 65.

17.   d   A z-score is the number of standard deviation units.

18.   c   A standard error of 4 suggests a band of possible scores of 4 above and below the raw score.

19.   b   Differences between raw scores result in greater differences in percentiles at the ends of the continuum.

20.   a   The score indicates that Deanna is an advanced reader; the remaining options are quite speculative.

21.   a   Percentile scores describe a person's relative position in a group compared to others taking the exam.

22.   b   A greater standard deviation suggests a greater distribution of scores. The fact that the median is one point higher for the second distribution tells us very little about the differences in overall achievement, particularly when the means are equal.

23.   d   One of the negative side effects of standardized scores is their potential adverse affects on teacher expectations. All the other options were quite similar, focusing on adverse affects to Kathy's perceptions of herself.

24.   b   The item unduly penalizes students for their lack of experience with scissors.

25.   Some differences include: purposes, number of items, how they are developed, and how scores are reported.

Publisher's Note

Michael Cole is a leading British illustrator whose long standing ambition to produce a fully illustrated version of Charles Dickens' *A Christmas Carol*, a story for which he declares a veritable passion, has at last been fulfilled.

Visualization of this nineteenth century masterpiece of English literature has been meticulously researched. And here, too, lies a tale. For Cole's depictions are not only true to Dickens' own vivid character portrayals, they are also modeled on several of the residents of Cole's own charming Somerset village, Norton St. Philip, near Bath.

Having painstakingly drafted the pagination, Cole cast the roles, dressing everyone in suitable costumes from the wardrobe of the local dramatic society. Next, he carefully set the stage for each frame of the storyboard, with masterful use of photographic reference provided by his wife, Sue. All joined in enthusiastically, daunted neither by the nature nor, in some instances, the proportions, of the characters played: Scrooge, a local solicitor; Fezziwig, a retired customs and excise officer; Bob Cratchit, a company director; and in the Ghost of Christmas Present, the artist's self-portrait. A number of minor characters are based on his daughter, Selby.

The resulting artwork, inspired in many respects by Leech's original illustrations, is splendidly rich in color and detail, with many dramatic large illustrations and superb double-page spreads varying the pace to remarkable effect. Magnificent endpapers – both clearly allegorical panoramas – open and close the rendering. Presentation of the text has been most carefully considered, too, and Cole has worked from the original manuscript. Narrative is typeset, while the hand-written dialogue, in the style of the cartoons of the time, captures the spirit of the period.

We, as the publishers, trust that many readers, young and old, will find great enjoyment in this edition of a well-loved book. We hope, too, that its many delights will be savored not only as a magnificent piece of Christmas fare but all throughout the year.

For
Sue Larner

Charles Dickens

A CHRISTMAS CAROL

Fully Illustrated by
Michael Cole

BARRON'S
Woodbury, New York · Toronto

To everyone who has assisted with the creation and publication of this work, including the residents of Norton St. Philip and in particular Jeremy Towler, my warmest thanks.

Michael Cole

First edition published in the United States and Canada in 1985 by Barron's Educational Series, Inc.

All inquiries should be addressed to:
Barron's Educational Series, Inc.
113 Crossways Park Drive
Woodbury, New York 11797

Library of Congress Catalog Card No. 85–15815

International Standard Book No. 0-8120-5705-8

Narrative typeset in Garamond Original by Tradespools Ltd.
Originated, printed, and bound
by Sagdos in Italy
56789 987654321

I have endeavoured in this Ghostly little book, to raise the Ghost of an Idea, which shall not put my readers out of humour with themselves, with each other, with the season, or with me. May it haunt their houses pleasantly, and no one wish to lay it.

Their faithful Friend and Servant,

Charles Dickens

December, 1843.

STAVE I

MARLEY'S GHOST

Marley was dead: to begin with. There is no doubt whatever about that. The register of his burial was signed by the clergyman, the clerk, the undertaker, and the chief mourner. Scrooge signed it: and Scrooge's name was good upon 'Change, for anything he chose to put his hand to. Old Marley was as dead as a door-nail.

Mind! I don't mean to say that I know, of my own knowledge, what there is particularly dead about a door-nail. I might have been inclined, myself, to regard a coffin-nail as the deadest piece of ironmongery in the trade. But the wisdom of our ancestors is in the simile; and my unhallowed hands shall not disturb it, or the Country's done for. You will therefore permit me to repeat, emphatically, that Marley was as dead as a door-nail.

Scrooge knew he was dead? Of course he did. How could it be otherwise? Scrooge and he were partners for I don't know how many years. Scrooge was his sole executor, his sole administrator, his sole assign, his sole residuary legatee, his sole friend and sole mourner. And even Scrooge was not so dreadfully cut up by the sad event, but that he was an excellent man of business on the very day of the funeral, and solemnised it with an undoubted bargain.

The mention of Marley's funeral brings me back to the point I started from. There is no doubt that Marley was dead. This must be distinctly understood, or nothing wonderful can come of the story I am going to relate. If we were not perfectly convinced that Hamlet's Father died before the play began, there would be nothing more remarkable in his taking a stroll at night, in an easterly wind, upon his own ramparts, than there would be in any other middle-aged gentleman rashly turning out after dark in a breezy spot—say Saint Paul's Churchyard for instance—literally to astonish his son's weak mind.

Scrooge never painted out Old Marley's name. There it stood, years afterwards, above the warehouse door: Scrooge and Marley. The firm was known as Scrooge and Marley. Sometimes people new to the business called Scrooge Scrooge, and sometimes Marley, but he answered to both names: it was all the same to him.

Oh! But he was a tight-fisted hand at the grindstone, Scrooge! a squeezing, wrenching, grasping, scraping, clutching, covetous old sinner! Hard and sharp as flint, from which no steel had ever struck out generous fire; secret, and self-contained, and solitary as an oyster. The cold within him froze his old features, nipped his pointed nose, shrivelled his cheek, stiffened his gait; made his eyes red, his thin lips blue; and spoke out shrewdly in his grating voice. A frosty rime was on his head, and on his eyebrows, and his wiry chin. He carried his own low temperature always about him; he iced his office in the dog-days; and didn't thaw it one degree at Christmas.

External heat and cold had little influence on Scrooge. No warmth could warm, nor wintry weather chill him. No wind that blew was bitterer than he, no falling snow was more intent upon its purpose, no pelting rain less open to entreaty. Foul weather didn't know where to have him. The heaviest rain, and snow, and hail, and sleet, could boast of the advantage over him in only one respect. They often "came down" handsomely, and Scrooge never did.

Nobody ever stopped him in the street to say, with gladsome looks, "My dear Scrooge, how are you? when will you come to see me?" No beggars implored him to bestow a trifle, no children asked him what it was o'clock, no man or woman ever once in all his life inquired the way to such and such a place, of Scrooge. Even the blindmen's dogs appeared to know him; and when they saw him coming on, would tug their owners into doorways and up courts; and then would wag their tails as though they said, "no eye at all is better than an evil eye, dark master!"

But what did Scrooge care? It was the very thing he liked. To edge his way along the crowded paths of life, warning all human sympathy to keep its distance, was what the knowing ones call "nuts" to Scrooge.

Once upon a time—of all the good days in the year, on Christmas Eve—old Scrooge sat busy in his counting-house. It was cold, bleak, biting weather: foggy withal: and he could hear the people in the court outside go wheezing up and down, beating their hands upon their breasts, and stamping their feet upon the pavement-stones to warm them. The city clocks had only just gone three, but it was quite dark already: it had not been light all day: and candles were flaring in the windows of the neighbouring offices, like ruddy smears upon the palpable brown air. The fog came pouring in at every chink and keyhole, and was so dense without, that although the court was of the narrowest, the houses opposite were mere phantoms. To see the dingy cloud come drooping down, obscuring everything, one might have thought that Nature lived hard by, and was brewing on a large scale.

The door of Scrooge's counting-house was open that he might keep his eye upon his clerk, who in a dismal little cell beyond, a sort of tank, was copying letters. Scrooge had a very small fire, but the clerk's fire was so very much smaller that it looked like one coal. But he couldn't replenish it, for Scrooge kept the coal-box in his own room; and so surely as the clerk came in with the shovel, the master predicted that it would be necessary for them to part. Wherefore the clerk put on his white comforter, and tried to warm himself at the candle; in which effort, not being a man of a strong imagination, he failed.

> A merry Christmas, uncle! God save you!

It was the voice of Scrooge's nephew, who came upon him so quickly that this was the first intimation he had of his approach.

> Bah! Humbug!

> Christmas, a humbug, uncle! You don't mean that, I am sure.

> I do. Merry Christmas! What right have you to be merry? What reason have you to be merry? You're poor enough.

He had so heated himself with rapid walking in the fog and frost, this nephew of Scrooge's, that he was all in a glow; his face was ruddy and handsome; his eyes sparkled, and his breath smoked again.

Scrooge having no better answer ready on the spur of the moment, said, "Bah!" again; and followed it up with "Humbug."

> Don't be cross, uncle.

> Come, then, what right have you to be dismal? What reason have you to be morose? You're rich enough.

> What else can I be when I live in such a world of fools as this? Merry Christmas! Out upon Merry Christmas! What's Christmas time to you but a time for paying bills without money; a time for finding yourself a year older, and not an hour richer; a time for balancing your books and having every item in 'em through a round dozen of months presented dead against you? If I could work my will, every idiot who goes about with 'Merry Christmas', on his lips, should be boiled with his own pudding, and buried with a stake of holly through his heart. He should!

Uncle!

Nephew! Keep Christmas in your own way, and let me keep it in mine.

Keep it! But you don't keep it!

Let me leave it alone, then. Much good may it do you! Much good it has ever done you!

There are many things from which I might have derived good by which I have not profited, I dare say, Christmas among the rest. But I am sure I have always thought of Christmas time, when it has come round— apart from the veneration due to its sacred name and origin, if anything belonging to it can be apart from that — as a good time: a kind, forgiving charitable, pleasant time: the only time I know of, in the long calendar of the year, when men and women seem by one consent to open their shut up hearts freely, and to think of people below them as if they really were fellow passengers to the grave, and not another race of creatures bound on other journeys. And therefore, Uncle, though it has never put a scrap of gold or silver in my pocket, I believe that it has done me good, and **will** do me good; and I say, God bless it!

The clerk in the tank involuntarily applauded: becoming immediately sensible of the impropriety, he poked the fire, and extinguished the last frail spark for ever.

Let me hear another sound from **you** and you'll keep your Christmas by losing your situation.

You're quite a powerful speaker, sir. I wonder you don't go into Parliament.

But why? Why?

Why did you get married?

Because I fell in love.

Because you fell in love!

. . . growled Scrooge, as if that were the only one thing in the world more ridiculous than a merry Christmas.

Good afternoon!

Don't be angry Uncle. Come! Dine with us to-morrow.

Scrooge said that he would see him—yes, indeed he did. He went the whole length of the expression, and said that he would see him in that extremity first.

Nay, Uncle, but you never came to see me before that happened. Why give it as a reason for not coming now?

Good afternoon!

I want nothing from you; I ask nothing of you; Why cannot we be friends?

Good afternoon!

I am sorry with all my heart, to find you so resolute. We have never had any quarrel, to which I have been a party. But I have made the trial in homage to Christmas, and I'll keep my Christmas humour to the last. So, A Merry Christmas, uncle!

And A Happy New Year!

Good afternoon!

Good afternoon!

His nephew left the room without an angry word, notwithstanding. He stopped at the outer door to bestow the greetings of the season on the clerk, who, cold as he was, was warmer than Scrooge; for he returned them cordially.

There's another fellow my clerk, with fifteen shillings a week and a wife and a family, talking about a merry Christmas. I'll retire to Bedlam.

This lunatic, in letting Scrooge's nephew out, had let two other people in. They were portly gentlemen, pleasant to behold, and now stood, with their hats off, in Scrooge's office. They had books and papers in their hands, and bowed to him.

Scrooge and Marley's I believe. Have I the pleasure of addressing Mr Scrooge or Mr Marley?

Mr Marley has been dead these seven years. He died seven years ago, this very night.

We have no doubt his liberality is well represented by his surviving partner.

It certainly was; for they had been two kindred spirits. At the ominous word "liberality," Scrooge frowned, and shook his head, and handed the credentials back.

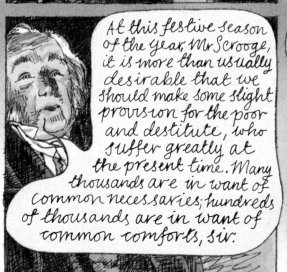
At this festive season of the year, Mr Scrooge, it is more than usually desirable that we should make some slight provision for the poor and destitute, who suffer greatly at the present time. Many thousands are in want of common necessaries; hundreds of thousands are in want of common comforts, sir.

Are there no prisons?

Plenty of prisons.

And the Union workhouses, are they still in operation?

They are. Still. I wish I could say they were not.

Meanwhile the fog and darkness thickened so, that people ran about with flaring links, proffering their services to go before horses in carriages, and conduct them on their way. The ancient tower of a church, whose gruff old bell was always peeping slily down at Scrooge out of a gothic window in the wall, became invisible, and struck the hours and quarters in the clouds, with tremulous vibrations afterwards, as if its teeth were chattering in its frozen head up there. The cold became intense. In the main street, at the corner of the court, some labourers were repairing the gas-pipes, and had lighted a great fire in a brazier, round which a party of ragged men and boys were gathered: warming their hands and winking their eyes before the blaze in rapture. The waterplug being left in solitude, its overflowings sullenly congealed, and turned to misanthropic ice. The brightness of the shops where holly sprigs and berries crackled in the lamp-heat of the windows, made pale faces ruddy as they passed. Poulterers' and grocers' trades became a splendid joke: a glorious pageant, with which it was next to impossible to believe that such dull principles as bargain and sale had anything to do. The Lord Mayor, in the stronghold of the mighty Mansion House, gave orders to his fifty cooks and butlers to keep Christmas as a Lord Mayor's household should; and even the little tailor, whom he had fined five shillings on the previous Monday for being drunk and blood-thirsty in the streets, stirred up to-morrow's pudding in his garret, while his lean wife and the baby sallied out to buy the beef.

Foggier yet, and colder! Piercing, searching, biting cold. If the good Saint Dunstan had but nipped the Evil Spirit's nose with a touch of such weather as that, instead of using his familiar weapons, then indeed he would have roared to lusty purpose.

The owner of one scant young nose, gnawed and mumbled by the hungry cold as bones are gnawed by dogs, stooped down at Scrooge's keyhole to regale him with a Christmas carol: but at the first sound of –
"God bless you merry gentleman!"
"May nothing you dismay!"

Scrooge seized the ruler with such energy of action, that the singer fled in terror, leaving the keyhole to the fog and even more congenial frost.

At length the hour of shutting up the counting-house arrived. With an ill-will Scrooge dismounted from his stool, and tacitly admitted the fact to the expectant clerk in the tank, who instantly snuffed his candle out, and put on his hat.

You'll want all day to-morrow, I suppose?

If quite convenient, sir.

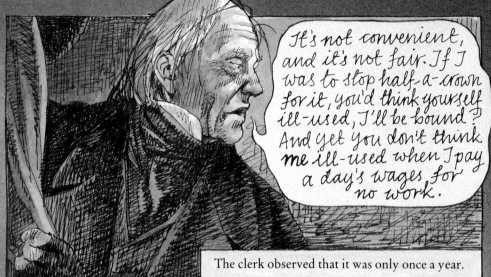

It's not convenient, and it's not fair. If I was to stop half-a-crown for it, you'd think yourself ill-used, I'll be bound? And yet you don't think me ill-used when I pay a day's wages for no work.

The clerk observed that it was only once a year.

A poor excuse for picking a man's pocket every twenty-fifth of December! But I suppose you must have the whole day. Be here all the earlier next morning!

The clerk promised that he would; and Scrooge walked out with a growl.

The office was closed in a twinkling, and the clerk, with the long ends of his white comforter dangling below his waist (for he boasted no great-coat), went down a slide on Cornhill, at the end of a lane of boys, twenty times, in honour of its being Christmas-eve, and then ran home to Camden Town as hard as he could pelt, to play at blindman's-buff.

Scrooge took his melancholy dinner in his usual melancholy tavern; and having read all the newspapers, and beguiled the rest of the evening with his banker's-book, went home to bed.

He lived in chambers which had once belonged to his deceased partner. They were a gloomy suite of rooms, in a lowering pile of building up a yard, where it had so little business to be, that one could scarcely help fancying it must have run there when it was a young house, playing at hide-and-seek with other houses, and have forgotten the way out again. It was old enough now, and dreary enough, for nobody lived in it but Scrooge, the other rooms being all let out as offices. The yard was so dark that even Scrooge, who knew its every stone, was fain to grope with his hands. The fog and frost so hung about the black old gateway of the house, that it seemed as if the Genius of the Weather sat in mournful meditation on the threshold.

Now, it is a fact, that there was nothing at all particular about the knocker on the door, except that it was very large. It is also a fact that Scrooge had seen it night and morning during his whole residence in that place; also that Scrooge had as little of what is called fancy about him as any man in the City of London, even including—which is a bold word—the corporation, aldermen, and livery. Let it also be borne in mind that Scrooge had not bestowed one thought on Marley, since his last mention of his seven-years' dead partner that afternoon. And then let any man explain to me, if he can, how it happened that Scrooge, having his key in the lock of the door, saw in the knocker, without its undergoing any intermediate process of change: not a knocker, but Marley's face.

Marley's face. It was not in impenetrable shadow as the other objects in the yard were, but had a dismal light about it, like a bad lobster in a dark cellar. It was not angry or ferocious, but looked at Scrooge as Marley used to look: with ghostly spectacles turned up upon its ghostly forehead. The hair was curiously stirred, as if by breath or hot-air; and though the eyes were wide open, they were perfectly motionless. That, and its livid colour, made it horrible; but its horror seemed to be, in spite of the face and beyond its control, rather than a part of its own expression.

As Scrooge looked fixedly at this phenomenon, it was a knocker again.

To say that he was not startled, or that his blood was not conscious of a terrible sensation to which it had been a stranger from infancy, would be untrue. But he put his hand upon the key he had relinquished, turned it sturdily, walked in, and lighted his candle.

He *did* pause, with a moment's irresolution, before he shut the door; and he *did* look cautiously behind it first, as if he half-expected to be terrified with the sight of Marley's pigtail sticking out into the hall. But there was nothing on the back of the door, except the screws and nuts that held the knocker on; so he said "Pooh, pooh!" and closed it with a bang.

The sound resounded through the house like thunder. Every room above, and every cask in the wine-merchant's cellars below, appeared to have a separate peal of echoes of its own. Scrooge was not a man to be frightened by echoes. He fastened the door, and walked across the hall, and up the stairs: slowly too: trimming his candle as he went.

You may talk vaguely about driving a coach-and-six up a good old flight of stairs, or through a bad young Act of Parliament; but I mean to say you might have got a hearse up that staircase, and taken it broadwise, with the splinter-bar towards the wall, and the door towards the balustrades: and done it easy.

There was plenty of width for that, and room to spare; which is perhaps the reason why Scrooge thought he saw a locomotive hearse going on before him in the gloom. Half a dozen gas-lamps out of the street wouldn't have lighted the entry too well, so you may suppose that it was pretty dark with Scrooge's dip.

Up Scrooge went, not caring a button for that: darkness is cheap, and Scrooge liked it. But before he shut his heavy door, he walked through his rooms to see that all was right. He had just enough recollection of the face to desire to do that.

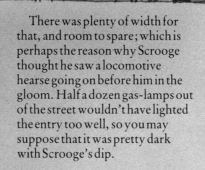

Sitting room, bed-room, lumber-room. All as they should be. Nobody under the table, nobody under the sofa; a small fire in the grate; spoon and basin ready; and the little saucepan of gruel (Scrooge had a cold in his head) upon the hob. Nobody under the bed; nobody in the closet; nobody in his dressing-gown, which was hanging up in a suspicious attitude against the wall. Lumber-room as usual. Old fire-guard, old shoes, two fish-baskets, washing-stand on three legs, and a poker.

Quite satisfied, he closed his door, and locked himself in; double-locked himself in, which was not his custom. Thus secured against surprise, he took off his cravat; put on his dressing-gown and slippers, and his night-cap; and sat down before the fire to take his gruel.

It was a very low fire indeed; nothing on such a bitter night. He was obliged to sit close to it, and brood over it, before he could extract the least sensation of warmth from such a handful of fuel. The fire-place was an old one, built by some Dutch merchant long ago, and paved all round with quaint Dutch tiles, designed to illustrate the Scriptures. There were Cains and Abels; Pharaoh's daughters, Queens of Sheba, Angelic messengers descending through the air on clouds like feather-beds, Abrahams, Belshazzars, Apostles putting off to sea in butter-boats, hundreds of figures to attract his thoughts; and yet that face of Marley, seven years dead, came like the ancient Prophet's rod, and swallowed up the whole. If each smooth tile had been a blank at first, with power to shape some picture on its surface from the disjointed fragments of his thoughts, there would have been a copy of old Marley's head on every one.

"Humbug!" said Scrooge; and walked across the room.

After several turns, he sat down again. As he threw his head back in the chair, his glance happened to rest upon a bell, a disused bell, that hung in the room, and communicated for some purpose now forgotten with a chamber in the highest story of the building. It was with great astonishment, and with a strange, inexplicable dread, that as he looked, he saw this bell begin to swing. It swung so softly in the outset that it scarcely made a sound; but soon it rang out loudly, and so did every bell in the house.

This might have lasted half a minute, or a minute, but it seemed an hour. The bells ceased as they had begun, together. They were succeeded by a clanking noise, deep down below; as if some person were dragging a heavy chain over the casks in the wine-merchant's cellar. Scrooge then remembered to have heard that ghosts in haunted houses were described as dragging chains.

The cellar-door flew open with a booming sound, and then he heard the noise much louder, on the floors below; then coming up the stairs; then coming straight towards his door.

It's humbug still! I won't believe it.

His colour changed though, when, without a pause, it came on through the heavy door, and passed into the room before his eyes. Upon its coming in, the dying flame leaped up, as though it cried "I know him! Marley's Ghost!" and fell again.

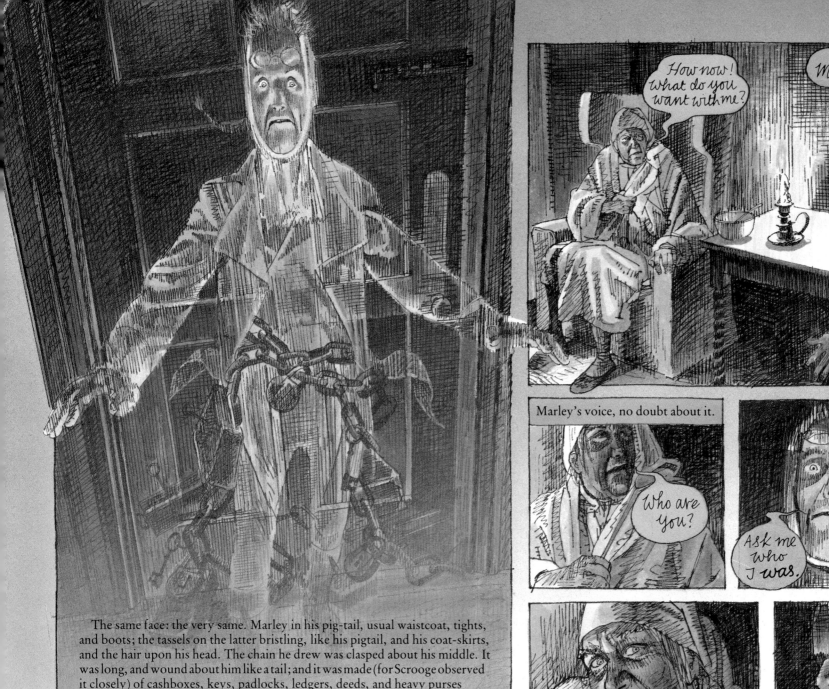

The same face: the very same. Marley in his pig-tail, usual waistcoat, tights, and boots; the tassels on the latter bristling, like his pigtail, and his coat-skirts, and the hair upon his head. The chain he drew was clasped about his middle. It was long, and wound about him like a tail; and it was made (for Scrooge observed it closely) of cashboxes, keys, padlocks, ledgers, deeds, and heavy purses wrought in steel. His body was transparent: so that Scrooge, observing him, and looking through his waistcoat, could see the two buttons on his coat behind.

Scrooge had often heard it said that Marley had no bowels, but he had never believed it until now.

No, nor did he believe it even now. Though he looked the phantom through and through, and saw it standing before him; though he felt the chilling influence of its death-cold eyes; and marked the very texture of the folded kerchief bound about its head and chin, which wrapper he had not observed before: he was still incredulous, and fought against his senses.

"Can you — can you sit down?"

"I can"

"Do it then."

Scrooge asked the question, because he didn't know whether a ghost so transparent might find himself in a condition to take a chair; and felt that in the event of its being impossible, it might involve the necessity of an embarrassing explanation. But the ghost sat down on the opposite side of the fire-place, as if he were quite used to it.

"I don't."

"You don't believe in me."

"What evidence would you have of my reality, beyond that of your senses?"

"I don't know."

"Why do you doubt your senses?"

"Because a little thing affects them. A slight disorder of the stomach makes them cheats. You may be an undigested bit of beef, a blot of mustard, a crumb of cheese, a fragment of under-done potato. There's more of gravy than of grave about you, whatever you are!"

Scrooge was not much in the habit of cracking jokes, nor did he feel, in his heart, by any means waggish then. The truth is, that he tried to be smart, as a means of distracting his own attention, and keeping down his terror; for the spectre's voice disturbed the very marrow in his bones.

To sit, staring at those fixed, glazed eyes, in silence for a moment, would play, Scrooge felt, the very deuce with him. There was something very awful, too, in the spectre's being provided with an infernal atmosphere of its own. Scrooge could not feel it himself, but this was clearly the case; for though the Ghost sat perfectly motionless, its hair, and skirts, and tassels, were still agitated as by the hot vapour from an oven.

"You see this toothpick?"

... said Scrooge, returning quickly to the charge, for the reason just assigned; and wishing, though it were only for a second, to divert the vision's stony gaze from himself.

"I do."

"You are not looking at it."

"But I see it, notwithstanding"

"Well! I have but to swallow this, and be for the rest of my days persecuted by a legion of goblins, all of my own creation. Humbug, I tell you — humbug!"

At this, the spirit raised a frightful cry, and shook its chain with such a dismal and appalling noise, that Scrooge held on tight to his chair, to save himself from falling in a swoon. But how much greater was his horror, when the phantom taking off the bandage round its head, as if it were too warm to wear in-doors, its lower jaw dropped down upon its breast!

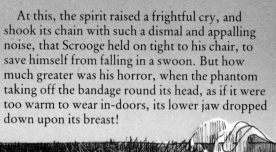

Scrooge fell upon his knees, and clasped his hands before his face.

Mercy! Dreadful apparition, why do you trouble me?

Man of the worldly mind! Do you believe in me or not?

I do, I must. But why do the spirits walk the earth, and why do they come to me?

It is required of every man that the spirit within him should walk abroad among his fellow-men, and travel far and wide; and if that spirit goes not forth in life, it is condemned to do so after death. It is doomed to wander through the world — Oh, woe is me! — and witness what it cannot share, but might have shared on earth, and turned to happiness!

Again the spectre raised a cry, and shook its chain, and wrung its shadowy hands.

You are fettered. Tell me why?

I wear the chain I forged in life. I made it link by link and yard by yard; I girded it on of my own free will, and of my own free will I wore it. Is its pattern strange to you?

Scrooge trembled more and more.

Or would you know the weight and length of the strong coil you bear yourself? It was full as heavy and as long as this seven Christmas Eves ago. You have laboured on it, since. It is a ponderous chain!

Scrooge glanced about him on the floor, in the expectation of finding himself surrounded by some fifty or sixty fathoms of iron cable: but he could see nothing.

Jacob, Old Jacob Marley, tell me more. Speak comfort to me, Jacob.

I have none to give. It comes from other regions, Ebenezer Scrooge, and is conveyed by other ministers, to other kinds of men. Nor can I tell you what I would. A very little more is all permitted to me. I cannot rest, I cannot stay, I cannot linger anywhere. My spirit never walked beyond our counting-house — mark me! — in life my spirit never roved beyond the narrow limits of our money-changing hole; and weary journeys lie before me!

It was a habit with Scrooge, whenever he became thoughtful, to put his hands in his breeches pockets. Pondering on what the Ghost had said, he did so now, but without lifting up his eyes, or getting off his knees.

You must have been very slow about it, Jacob.

Slow!

Seven years dead, and travelling all the time?

The whole time. No rest, no peace. Incessant torture of remorse.

You travel fast?

On the wings of the wind.

You might have got over a great quantity of ground in seven years.

The Ghost, on hearing this, set up another cry, and clanked its chain so hideously in the dead silence of the night, that the Ward would have been justified in indicting it for a nuisance.

Oh, captive, bound, and double-ironed, not to know, that ages of incessant labour by immortal creatures, for this earth must pass into eternity before the good of which it is susceptible is all developed. Not to know that any Christian spirit working kindly in its little sphere, whatever it may be, will find its mortal life too short for its vast means of usefulness. Not to know that no space of regret can make amends for one life's opportunities misused! Yet such was I! Oh such was I!

But you were always a good man of business, Jacob.

Business! Mankind was my business. The common welfare was my business; charity, mercy, forbearance, and benevolence, were, all, my business. The dealings of my trade were but a drop of water in the comprehensive ocean of my business!

It held up its chain at arm's length, as if that were the cause of all its unavailing grief, and flung it heavily upon the ground again.

At this time of the rolling year I suffer most. Why did I walk through the crowds of fellow-beings with my eyes turned down, and never raise them to that blessed Star which led the Wise Men to a poor abode? Were there no poor homes to which it's light would have conducted me!

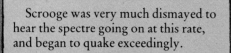

Scrooge was very much dismayed to hear the spectre going on at this rate, and began to quake exceedingly.

It was not an agreeable idea. Scrooge shivered, and wiped the perspiration from his brow.

Scrooge's countenance fell almost as low as the Ghost's had done.

When it had said these words, the spectre took its wrapper from the table, and bound it round its head, as before. Scrooge knew this, by the smart sound its teeth made, when the jaws were brought together by the bandage. He ventured to raise his eyes again, and found his supernatural visitor confronting him in an erect attitude, with its chain wound over and about its arm.

The apparition walked backward from him; and at every step it took, the window raised itself a little, so that when the spectre reached it, it was wide open. It beckoned Scrooge to approach, which he did. When they were within two paces of each other, Marley's Ghost held up its hand, warning him to come no nearer. Scrooge stopped.

Not so much in obedience, as in surprise and fear: for on the raising of the hand, he became sensible of confused noises in the air; incoherent sounds of lamentation and regret; wailings inexpressibly sorrowful and self-accusatory. The spectre, after listening for a moment, joined in the mournful dirge; and floated out upon the bleak, dark night.

Scrooge followed to the window: desperate in his curiosity. He looked out.

The air was filled with phantoms, wandering hither and thither in restless haste, and moaning as they went. Every one of them wore chains like Marley's Ghost; some few (they might be guilty governments) were linked together; none were free. Many had been personally known to Scrooge in their lives. He had been quite familiar with one old ghost, in a white waistcoat, with a monstrous iron safe attached to its ankle, who cried piteously at being unable to assist a wretched woman with an infant, whom it saw below, upon a door-step. The misery with them all was, clearly, that they sought to interfere, for good, in human matters, and had lost the power for ever.

Whether these creatures faded into mist, or mist enshrouded them, he could not tell. But they and their spirit voices faded together; and the night became as it had been when he walked home.

Scrooge closed the window, and examined the door by which the Ghost had entered. It was double-locked, as he had locked it with his own hands, and the bolts were undisturbed. He tried to say "Humbug!" but stopped at the first syllable. And being, from the emotion he had undergone, or the fatigues of the day, or his glimpse of the Invisible World, or the dull conversation of the Ghost, or the lateness of the hour, much in need of repose; went straight to bed, without undressing, and fell asleep upon the instant.

STAVE II.

THE FIRST OF THE THREE SPIRITS.

When Scrooge awoke, it was so dark, that looking out of bed, he could scarcely distinguish the transparent window from the opaque walls of his chamber. He was endeavouring to pierce the darkness with his ferret eyes, when the chimes of a neighbouring church struck the four quarters. So he listened for the hour.

To his great astonishment the heavy bell went on from six to seven, and from seven to eight, and regularly up to twelve; then stopped. Twelve! It was past two when he went to bed. The clock was wrong. An icicle must have got into the works. Twelve!

He touched the spring of his repeater, to correct this most preposterous clock. Its rapid little pulse beat twelve; and stopped.

Why it isn't possible that I can have slept through a whole day and far into another night. It isn't possible that anything has happened to the Sun and this is twelve at noon!

The idea being an alarming one, he scrambled out of bed, and groped his way to the window. He was obliged to rub the frost off with the sleeve of his dressing-gown before he could see anything; and could see very little then. All he could make out was, that it was still very foggy and extremely cold, and that there was no noise of people running to and fro, and making a great stir, as there unquestionably would have been if night had beaten off bright day, and taken possession of the world. This was a great relief, because "three days after sight of this First of Exchange pay to Mr. Ebenezer Scrooge or his order," and so forth, would have become a mere United States' security if there were no days to count by.

Scrooge went to bed again, and thought, and thought, and thought it over and over and over, and could make nothing of it. The more he thought, the more perplexed he was; and the more he endeavoured not to think, the more he thought. Marley's Ghost bothered him exceedingly. Every time he resolved within himself, after mature inquiry, that it was all a dream, his mind flew back again like a strong spring released, to its first position, and presented the same problem to be worked all through, "Was it a dream or not?"

Scrooge lay in this state until the chimes had gone three quarters more, when he remembered, on a sudden, that the Ghost had warned him of a visitation when the bell tolled one. He resolved to lie awake until the hour was past; and considering that he could no more go to sleep than go to Heaven, this was perhaps the wisest resolution in his power.

The quarter was so long, that he was more than once convinced he must have sunk into a doze unconsciously, and missed the clock. At length it broke upon his listening ear.

Ding, Dong!

A quarter past!

Ding Dong!

Half past.

Ding Dong!

A quarter to it

Ding, Dong

The hour itself and nothing else!

He spoke before the hour bell sounded, which it now did with a deep, dull, hollow, melancholy ONE.

Light flashed up in the room upon the instant, and the curtains of his bed were drawn. The curtains of his bed were drawn aside, I tell you, by a hand.

Not the curtains at his feet, nor the curtains at his back, but those to which his face was addressed. The curtains of his bed were drawn aside; and Scrooge, starting up into a half-recumbent attitude, found himself face to face with the unearthly visitor who drew them: as close to it as I am now to you, and I am standing in the spirit at your elbow.

It was a strange figure—like a child: yet not so like a child as like an old man, viewed through some supernatural medium, which gave him the appearance of having receded from the view, and being diminished to a child's proportions. Its hair, which hung about its neck and down its back, was white as if with age; and yet the face had not a wrinkle in it, and the tenderest bloom was on the skin. The arms were very long and muscular; the hands the same, as if its hold were of uncommon strength. Its legs and feet, most delicately formed, were, like those upper members, bare. It wore a tunic of the purest white; and round its waist was bound a lustrous belt, the sheen of which was beautiful. It held a branch of fresh green holly in its hand; and, in singular contradiction of that wintry emblem, had its dress trimmed with summer flowers. But the strangest thing about it was, that from the crown of its head there sprung a bright clear jet of light, by which all this was visible; and which was doubtless the occasion of its using, in its duller moments, a great extinguisher for a cap, which it now held under its arm.

Even this, though, when Scrooge looked at it with increasing steadiness, was *not* its strangest quality. For as its belt sparkled and glittered now in one part and now in another, and what was light one instant, at another time was dark, so the figure itself fluctuated in its distinctness: being now a thing with one arm, now with one leg, now with twenty legs, now a pair of legs without a head, now a head without a body: of which dissolving parts, no outline would be visible in the dense gloom wherein they melted away. And in the very wonder of this, it would be itself again; distinct and clear as ever.

As the words were spoken, they passed through the wall, and stood upon an open country road, with fields on either hand. The city had entirely vanished. Not a vestige of it was to be seen. The darkness and the mist had vanished with it, for it was a clear, cold, winter day, with snow upon the ground.

Good Heaven! I was bred in this place. I was a boy here!

The Spirit gazed upon him mildly. Its gentle touch, though it had been light and instantaneous, appeared still present to the old man's sense of feeling. He was conscious of a thousand odours floating in the air, each one connected with a thousand thoughts, and hopes, and joys, and cares long, long, forgotten!

Your lip is trembling. And what is that upon your cheek?

You recollect the way?

Remember it! I could walk it blindfold.

Scrooge muttered, with an unusual catching in his voice, that it was a pimple; and begged the Ghost to lead him where he would.

Strange to have forgotten it for so many years! Let us go on.

They walked along the road; Scrooge recognising every gate, and post, and tree; until a little market-town appeared in the distance, with its bridge, its church, and winding river. Some shaggy ponies now were seen trotting towards them with boys upon their backs, who called to other boys in country gigs and carts, driven by farmers. All these boys were in great spirits, and shouted to each other, until the broad fields were so full of merry music, that the crisp air laughed to hear it.

These are but shadows of the things that have been. They have no consciousness of us.

The jocund travellers came on; and as they came, Scrooge knew and named them every one. Why was he rejoiced beyond all bounds to see them! Why did his cold eye glisten, and his heart leap up as they went past! Why was he filled with gladness when he heard them give each other Merry Christmas, as they parted at cross-roads and bye-ways, for their several homes! What was merry Christmas to Scrooge? Out upon merry Christmas! What good had it ever done to him?

The school is not quite deserted. A solitary child, neglected by his friends, is left there still.

Scrooge said he knew it. And he sobbed.

They left the high-road, by a well remembered lane, and soon approached a mansion of dull red brick, with a little weathercock-surmounted cupola, on the roof, and a bell hanging in it. It was a large house, but one of broken fortunes; for the spacious offices were little used, their walls were damp and mossy, their windows broken, and their gates decayed. Fowls clucked and strutted in the stables; and the coach-houses and sheds were overrun with grass. Nor was it more retentive of its ancient state, within; for entering the dreary hall, and glancing through the open doors of many rooms, they found them poorly furnished, cold, and vast. There was an earthy savour in the air, a chilly bareness in the place, which associated itself somehow with too much getting up by candle-light, and not too much to eat.

They went, the Ghost and Scrooge, across the hall, to a door at the back of the house. It opened before them, and disclosed a long, bare, melancholy room, made barer still by lines of plain deal forms and desks. At one of these a lonely boy was reading near a feeble fire; and Scrooge sat down upon a form and wept to see his poor forgotten self as he had used to be.

Not a latent echo in the house, not a squeak and scuffle from the mice behind the panelling, not a drip from the half-thawed water-spout in the dull yard behind, not a sigh among the leafless boughs of one despondent poplar, not the idle swinging of an empty store-house door, no, not a clicking in the fire, but fell upon the heart of Scrooge with softening influence, and gave a freer passage to his tears.

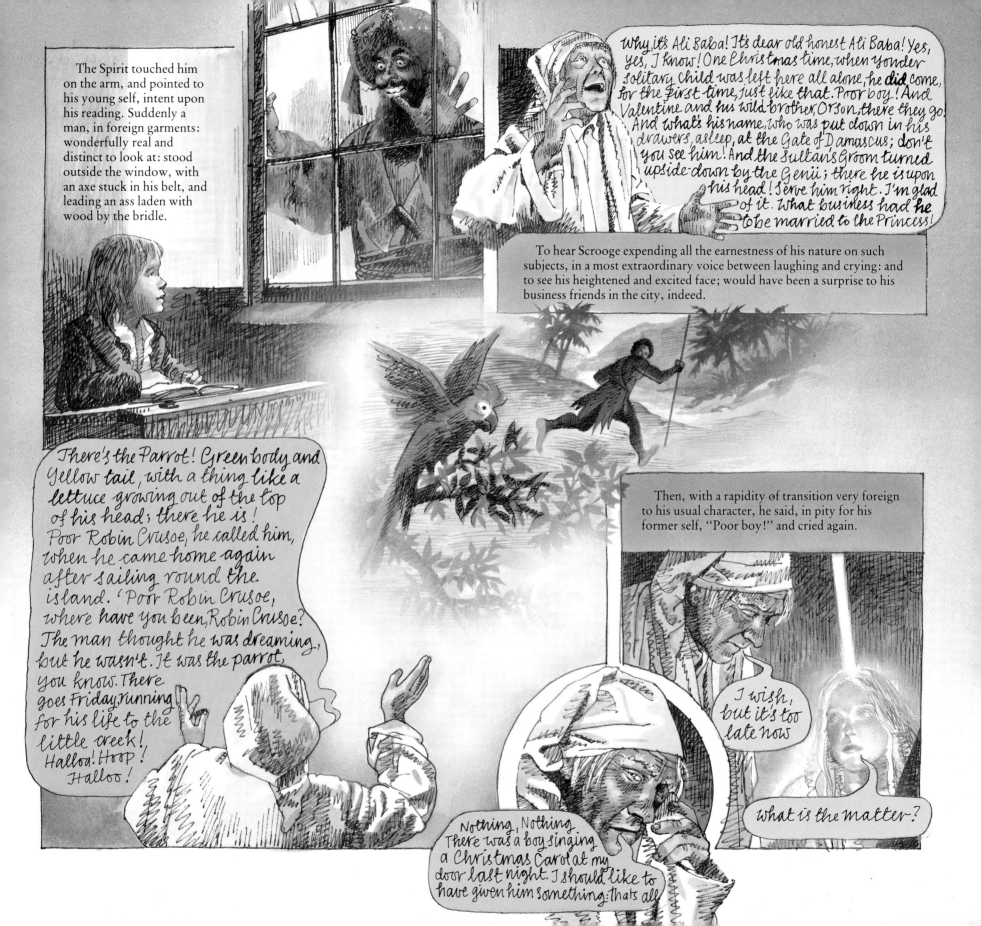

The Spirit touched him on the arm, and pointed to his young self, intent upon his reading. Suddenly a man, in foreign garments: wonderfully real and distinct to look at: stood outside the window, with an axe stuck in his belt, and leading an ass laden with wood by the bridle.

Why, it's Ali Baba! It's dear old honest Ali Baba! Yes, yes, I know! One Christmas time, when yonder solitary child was left here all alone, he **did** come, for the first time, just like that. Poor boy! And Valentine and his wild brother, Orson, there they go! And what's his name, who was put down in his drawers, asleep, at the Gate of Damascus; don't you see him! And the Sultan's Groom turned upside-down by the Genii; there he is upon his head! Serve him right. I'm glad of it. What business had **he** to be married to the Princess!

To hear Scrooge expending all the earnestness of his nature on such subjects, in a most extraordinary voice between laughing and crying: and to see his heightened and excited face; would have been a surprise to his business friends in the city, indeed.

There's the Parrot! Green body and Yellow tail, with a thing like a lettuce growing out of the top of his head; there he is! Poor Robin Crusoe, he called him, when he came home again after sailing round the island. 'Poor Robin Crusoe, where have you been, Robin Crusoe? The man thought he was dreaming, but he wasn't. It was the parrot, you know. There goes Friday, running for his life to the little creek! Halloa! Hoop! Halloo!

Then, with a rapidity of transition very foreign to his usual character, he said, in pity for his former self, "Poor boy!" and cried again.

I wish, but it's too late now

What is the matter?

Nothing, Nothing. There was a boy singing a Christmas Carol at my door last night. I should like to have given him something; that's all

The Ghost smiled thoughtfully, and waved its hand: saying as it did so,

Let us see another Christmas!

Scrooge's former self grew larger at the words, and the room became a little darker and more dirty. The panels shrunk, the windows cracked; fragments of plaster fell out of the ceiling, and the naked laths were shown instead; but how all this was brought about, Scrooge knew no more than you do. He only knew that it was quite correct; that everything had happened so; that there he was, alone again, when all the other boys had gone home for the jolly holidays.

He was not reading now, but walking up and down despairingly.

Scrooge looked at the Ghost, and with a mournful shaking of his head, glanced anxiously towards the door.

It opened; and a little girl, much younger than the boy, came darting in, and putting her arms about his neck, and often kissing him, addressed him as her "Dear, dear brother."

I have come to bring you home dear brother! To bring you home, home, home!

Home, little Fan?

Yes! Home, for good and all. Home, for ever and ever. Father is so much kinder than he used to be, that home's like Heaven! He spoke so gently to me one dear night when I was going to bed, that I was not afraid to ask him once more if you might come home; and he said, Yes, you should; and sent me in a coach to bring you. And you're to be a man! and are never to come back here; but first, we're to be together all the Christmas long and have the merriest time in all the world.

Although they had but that moment left the school behind them, they were now in the busy thoroughfares of a city, where shadowy passengers passed and repassed; where shadowy carts and coaches battled for the way, and all the strife and tumult of a real city were. It was made plain enough, by the dressing of the shops, that here too it was Christmas time again; but it was evening, and the streets were lighted up.

The Ghost stopped at a certain warehouse door, and asked Scrooge if he knew it.

Know it! Was I apprenticed here?

They went in. At sight of an old gentleman in a Welch wig, sitting behind such a high desk, that if he had been two inches taller he must have knocked his head against the ceiling, Scrooge cried in great excitement:

Why, it's old Fezziwig! Bless his heart; it's Fezziwig alive again!

Old Fezziwig laid down his pen, and looked up at the clock, which pointed to the hour of seven. He rubbed his hands; adjusted his capacious waistcoat; laughed all over himself, from his shoes to his organ of benevolence; and called out in a comfortable, oily, rich, fat, jovial voice:

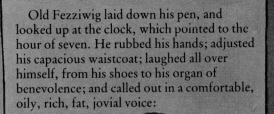

Yo ho, there! Ebenezer! Dick!

Scrooge's former self, now grown a young man, came briskly in, accompanied by his fellow-'prentice.

Dick Wilkins, to be sure! Bless me, yes. There he is. He was very much attached to me, was Dick. Poor Dick! Dear, dear!

Yo ho, my boys! No more work to-night. Christmas Eve, Dick. Christmas, Ebenezer! Let's have the shutters up, before a man can say, Jack Robinson!

You wouldn't believe how those two fellows went at it! They charged into the street with the shutters—one, two, three—had 'em up in their places—four, five, six—barred 'em and pinned 'em—seven, eight, nine—and came back before you could have got to twelve, panting like race-horses.

Hilli-Ho! Clear away, my lads, and let's have lots of room here! Hilli-ho, Dick! Chirrup, Ebenezer!

Clear away! There was nothing they wouldn't have cleared away, or couldn't have cleared away, with old Fezziwig looking on. It was done in a minute. Every movable was packed off, as if it were dismissed from public life for evermore; the floor was swept and watered, the lamps were trimmed, fuel was heaped upon the fire; and the warehouse was as snug, and warm, and dry, and bright a ball-room, as you would desire to see upon a winter's night.

In came a fiddler with a music-book, and went up to the lofty desk, and made an orchestra of it, and tuned like fifty stomach-aches. In came Mrs. Fezziwig, one vast substantial smile. In came the three Miss Fezziwigs, beaming and lovable. In came the six young followers whose hearts they broke. In came all the young men and women employed in the business. In came the housemaid, with her cousin, the baker. In came the cook, with her brother's particular friend, the milkman. In came the boy from over the way, who was suspected of not having board enough from his master; trying to hide himself behind the girl from next door but one, who was proved to have had her ears pulled by her Mistress. In they all came, one after another; some shyly, some boldly, some gracefully, some awkwardly, some pushing, some pulling; in they all came, anyhow and everyhow. Away they all went, twenty couple at once, hands half round and back again the other way; down the middle and up again; round and round in various stages of affectionate grouping; old top couple always turning up in the wrong place; new top couple starting off again, as soon as they got there; all top couples at last, and not a bottom one to help them. When this result was brought about, old Fezziwig, clapping his hands to stop the dance, cried out, "Well done!" and the fiddler plunged his hot face into a pot of porter, especially provided for that purpose. But scorning rest upon his reappearance, he instantly began again, though there were no dancers yet, as if the other fiddler had been carried home, exhausted, on a shutter; and he were a bran-new man resolved to beat him out of sight, or perish.

There were more dances, and there were forfeits, and more dances, and there was cake, and there was negus, and there was a great piece of Cold Roast, and there was a great piece of Cold Boiled, and there were mince-pies, and plenty of beer. But the great effect of the evening came after the Roast and Boiled, when the fiddler (an artful dog, mind! The sort of man who knew his business better than you or I could have told it him!) struck up "Sir Roger de Coverley." Then old Fezziwig stood out to dance with Mrs. Fezziwig. Top couple, too; with a good stiff piece of work cut out for them; three or four and twenty pair of partners; people who were not to be trifled with; people who *would* dance, and had no notion of walking.

But if they had been twice as many: ah, four times: old Fezziwig would have been a match for them, and so would Mrs. Fezziwig. As to *her*, she was worthy to be his partner in every sense of the term. If that's not high praise, tell me higher, and I'll use it. A positive light appeared to issue from Fezziwig's calves. They shone in every part of the dance like moons. You couldn't have predicted, at any given time, what would become of 'em next. And when old Fezziwig and Mrs. Fezziwig had gone all through the dance; advance and retire, hold hands with your partner; bow and curtsey; corkscrew; thread-the-needle, and back again to your place; Fezziwig "cut"—cut so deftly, that he appeared to wink with his legs, and came upon his feet again without a stagger.

When the clock struck eleven, this domestic ball broke up. Mr. and Mrs. Fezziwig took their stations, one on either side the door, and shaking hands with every person individu' as he or she went out, wished him or her a Merry Christmas. When everybody had retired but the two 'prentices, they did the same to them; and thus the cheerful voices died away, and the lads were left to their beds; which were under a counter in the back-shop.

During the whole of this time, Scrooge had acted like a man out of his wits. His heart and soul were in the scene, and with his former self. He corroborated everything, remembered everything, enjoyed everything, and underwent the strangest agitation. It was not until now, when the bright faces of his former self and Dick were turned from them, that he remembered the Ghost, and became conscious that it was looking full upon him, while the light upon its head burnt very clear.

A small matter, to make these silly folks so full of gratitude.

Small!

The Spirit signed to him to listen to the two apprentices, who were pouring out their hearts in praise of Fezziwig: and when he had done so, said,

Why! Is it not? He has spent but a few pounds of your mortal money: three or four, perhaps. Is that so much that he deserves this praise?

Heated by the remark, and speaking unconsciously like his former, not his latter, self,

It isn't that, Spirit. He has the power to render us happy or unhappy: to make our service light or burdensome; a pleasure or a toil. Say that his power lies in words and looks; in things so slight and insignificant that it is impossible to add and count 'em up: what then? The happiness he gives is quite as great as if it cost a fortune.

He felt the Spirit's glance, and stopped.

What is the matter?

Nothing particular.

Something, I think?

No, no. I should like to be able to say a word or two to my clerk just now! That's all.

His former self turned down the lamps as he gave utterance to the wish; and Scrooge and the Ghost again stood side by side in the open air.

My time grows short. Quick!

This was not addressed to Scrooge, or to any one whom he could see, but it produced an immediate effect. For again Scrooge saw himself. He was older now; a man in the prime of life. His face had not the harsh and rigid lines of later years; but it had begun to wear the signs of care and avarice. There was an eager, greedy, restless motion in the eye, which showed the passion that had taken root, and where the shadow of the growing tree would fall.

He was not alone, but sat by the side of a fair young girl in a mourning-dress: in whose eyes there were tears, which sparkled in the light that shone out of the Ghost of Christmas Past.

What Idol has displaced you?

It matters little. To you, very little. Another idol has displaced me; and if it can cheer and comfort you in time to come, as I would have tried to do, I have no just cause to grieve.

A golden one.

This is the even-handed dealing of the world! There is nothing on which it is so hard as poverty; and there is nothing it professes to condemn with such severity as the pursuit of wealth!

You fear the world too much. All your other hopes have merged into the hope of being beyond the chance of its sordid reproach. I have seen your nobler aspirations fall off one by one, until the master-passion, Gain, engrosses you. Have I not?

What then? Even if I have grown so much wiser, what then? I am not changed towards you.

She shook her head.

Am I?

Our contract is an old one. It was made when we were both poor and content to be so, until, in good season, we could improve our worldly fortune by our patient industry. You **are** changed. When it was made, you were another man.

I was a boy.

"Your own feeling tells you that you were not what you are. I am. That which promised happiness when we were one in heart, is fraught with misery now that we are two. How often and how keenly I have thought of this, I will not say. It is enough that I **have** thought of it, and can release you.

"Have I ever sought release?"

"In words. No. Never."

"In what, then?"

"In a changed nature; in an altered spirit; in another atmosphere of life; another Hope as its great end. In everything that made my love of any worth or value in your sight. If this had never been between us, tell me, would you seek me out and try to win me now? Ah, no!"

He seemed to yield to the justice of this supposition, in spite of himself. But he said, with a struggle,

"You think not."

"I would gladly think otherwise if I could. Heaven knows! When I have learned a Truth like this, I know how strong and irresistible it must be. But if you were free today, tomorrow, yesterday, can even I believe that you would choose a dowerless girl — you who, in your very confidence with her, weigh everything by Gain: or, choosing her, if for a moment you were false enough to your one guiding principle to do so, do I not know that your repentance and regret would surely follow? I do; and I release you. With a full heart for the love of him you once were."

He was about to speak; but with her head turned from him, she resumed.

"You may — the memory of what is past half makes me hope you will — have pain in this. A very, very brief time, and you will dismiss the recollection of it, gladly, as an unprofitable dream, from which it happened well that you awoke. May you be happy in the life you have chosen!"

She left him; and they parted.

"Spirit, show me no more! Conduct me home. Why do you delight to torture me?"

"One shadow more!"

"No more! No more. I don't wish to see it. Show me no more!"

But the relentless Ghost pinioned him in both his arms, and forced him to observe what happened next.

They were in another scene and place: a room, not very large or handsome, but full of comfort. Near to the winter fire sat a beautiful young girl, so like the last that Scrooge believed it was the same, until he saw *her*, now a comely matron, sitting opposite her daughter. The noise in this room was perfectly tumultuous, for there were more children there, than Scrooge in his agitated state of mind could count; and, unlike the celebrated herd in the poem, they were not forty children conducting themselves like one, but every child was conducting itself like forty. The consequences were uproarious beyond belief; but no one seemed to care; on the contrary, the mother and daughter laughed heartily, and enjoyed it very much; and the latter, soon beginning to mingle in the sports, got pillaged by the young brigands most ruthlessly. What would I not have given to be one of them! Though I never could have been so rude, no, no! I wouldn't for the wealth of all the world have crushed that braided hair, and torn it down; and for the precious little shoe, I wouldn't have plucked it off, God bless my soul! to save my life. As to measuring her waist in sport, as they did, bold young brood, I couldn't have done it; I should have expected my arm to have grown round it for a punishment, and never come straight again. And yet I should have dearly liked, I own, to have touched her lips; to have questioned her, that she might have opened them; to have looked upon the lashes of her downcast eyes, and never raised a blush; to have let loose waves of hair, an inch of which would be a keep-sake beyond price: in short, I should have liked, I do confess, to have had the lightest licence of a child, and yet been man enough to know its value.

But now a knocking at the door was heard, and such a rush immediately ensued that she with laughing face and plundered dress was borne towards it the centre of a flushed and boisterous group, just in time to greet the father, who, came home attended by a man laden with Christmas toys and presents. Then the shouting and the struggling, and the onslaught that was made on the defenceless porter! The scaling him, with chairs for ladders, to dive into his pockets, despoil him of brown-paper parcels, hold on tight by his cravat, hug him round the neck, pommel his back, and kick his legs in irrepressible affection! The shouts of wonder and delight with which the development of every package was received! The terrible announcement that the baby had been taken in the act of putting a doll's frying-pan into his mouth, and was more than suspected of having swallowed a fictitious turkey, glued on a wooden platter! The immense relief of finding this a false alarm! The joy, and gratitude, and ecstacy! They are all indescribable alike. It is enough that by degrees the children and their emotions got out of the parlour and by one stair at a time, up to the top of the house; where they went to bed, and so subsided.

And now Scrooge looked on more attentively than ever, when the master of the house, having his daughter leaning fondly on him, sat down with her and her mother at his own fireside; and when he thought that such another creature, quite as graceful and as full of promise, might have called him father, and been a springtime in the haggard winter of his life, his sight grew very dim indeed.

Belle, I saw an old friend of yours this afternoon.

Who was it?

Guess!

How can I? Tut, don't I know, Mr Scrooge.

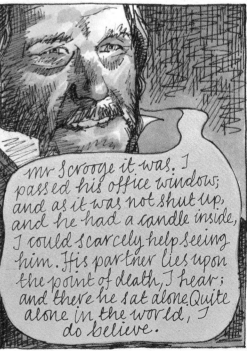

Mr Scrooge it was. I passed his office window; and as it was not shut up, and he had a candle inside, I could scarcely help seeing him. His partner lies upon the point of death, I hear; and there he sat alone. Quite alone in the world, I do believe.

Said Scrooge in a broken voice,

I told you these were shadows of the things that have been. That they are what they are, do not blame me!

Spirit! Remove me from this place.

Remove me! I cannot bear it.

He turned upon the Ghost, and seeing that it looked upon him with a face, in which in some strange way there were fragments of all the faces it had shown him, wrestled with it.

Leave me! Take me back. Haunt me no longer!

In the struggle, if that can be called a struggle in which the Ghost with no visible resistance on its own part was undisturbed by any effort of its adversary, Scrooge observed that its light was burning high and bright; and dimly connecting that with its influence over him, he seized the extinguisher-cap, and by a sudden action pressed it down upon its head.

The Spirit dropped beneath it, so that the extinguisher covered its whole form; but though Scrooge pressed it down with all his force, he could not hide the light: which streamed from under it, in an unbroken flood upon the ground.

He was conscious of being exhausted, and overcome by an irresistible drowsiness; and, further, of being in his own bedroom. He gave the cap a parting squeeze, in which his hand relaxed; and had barely time to reel to bed, before he sank into a heavy sleep.

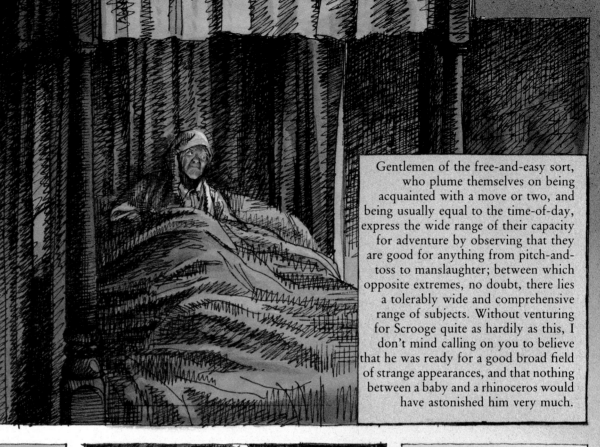

STAVE III

THE SECOND OF THE THREE SPIRITS

Awaking in the middle of a prodigiously tough snore, and sitting up in bed to get his thoughts together, Scrooge had no occasion to be told that the bell was again upon the stroke of One. He felt that he was restored to consciousness in the right nick of time, for the especial purpose of holding a conference with the second messenger despatched to him through Jacob Marley's intervention. But finding that he turned uncomfortably cold when he began to wonder which of his curtains this new spectre would draw back, he put them every one aside with his own hands; and lying down again, established a sharp look-out all round the bed. For he wished to challenge the Spirit on the moment of its appearance, and did not wish to be taken by surprise and made nervous.

Gentlemen of the free-and-easy sort, who plume themselves on being acquainted with a move or two, and being usually equal to the time-of-day, express the wide range of their capacity for adventure by observing that they are good for anything from pitch-and-toss to manslaughter; between which opposite extremes, no doubt, there lies a tolerably wide and comprehensive range of subjects. Without venturing for Scrooge quite as hardily as this, I don't mind calling on you to believe that he was ready for a good broad field of strange appearances, and that nothing between a baby and a rhinoceros would have astonished him very much.

Now, being prepared for almost anything, he was not by any means prepared for nothing; and, consequently, when the Bell struck One, and no shape appeared, he was taken with a violent fit of trembling. Five minutes, ten minutes, a quarter of an hour went by, yet nothing came. All this time, he lay upon his bed, the very core and centre of a blaze of ruddy light, which streamed upon it when the clock proclaimed the hour; and which being only light, was more alarming than a dozen ghosts, and he was powerless to make out what it meant, or would be at; and was sometimes apprehensive that he might be at that very moment an interesting case of spontaneous combustion, without having the consolation of knowing it.

At last, however, he began to think—as you or I would have thought at first; for it is always the person not in the predicament who knows what ought to have been done in it, and would unquestionably have done it too–at last, I say, he began to think that the source and secret of this ghostly light might be in the adjoining room: from whence, on further tracing it, it seemed to shine. This idea taking full possession of his mind, he got up softly and shuffled in his slippers to the door.

The moment Scrooge's hand was on the lock, a strange voice called him by his name, and bade him enter. He obeyed.

It was his own room. There was no doubt about that. But it had undergone a surprising transformation. The walls and ceiling were so hung with living green, that it looked a perfect grove, from every part of which, bright gleaming berries glistened. The crisp leaves of holly, mistletoe, and ivy reflected back the light, as if so many little mirrors had been scattered there; and such a mighty blaze went roaring up the chimney, as that dull petrifaction of a hearth had never known in Scrooge's time, or Marley's, or for many and many a winter season gone. Heaped up upon the floor, to form a kind of throne, were turkeys, geese, game, poultry, brawn, great joints of meat, sucking-pigs, long wreaths of sausages, mince-pies, plum-puddings, barrels of oysters, red-hot chestnuts, cherry-cheeked apples, juicy oranges, luscious pears, immense twelfth-cakes, and seething bowls of punch, that made the chamber dim with their delicious steam. In easy state upon this couch, there sat a jolly Giant, glorious to see; who bore a glowing torch, in shape not unlike Plenty's horn, and held it up, high up, to shed its light on Scrooge, as he came peeping round the door.

Scrooge entered timidly, and hung his head before this Spirit. He was not the dogged Scrooge he had been; and though its eyes were clear and kind, he did not like to meet them.

I am the Ghost of Christmas Present. Look upon me!

Scrooge reverently did so. It was clothed in one simple deep green robe, or mantle, bordered with white fur. This garment hung so loosely on the figure, that its capacious breast was bare, as if disdaining to be warded or concealed by any artifice. Its feet, observable beneath the ample folds of the garment, were also bare; and on its head it wore no other covering than a holly wreath set here and there with shining icicles. Its dark brown curls were long and free: free as its genial face, its sparkling eye, its open hand, its cheery voice, its unconstrained demeanour, and its joyful air. Girded round its middle was an antique scabbard; but no sword was in it, and the ancient sheath was eaten up with rust.

The Ghost of Christmas Present rose.

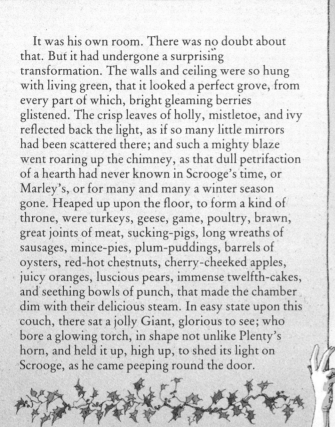

You have never seen the like of me before!

Never.

Have never walked forth with the younger members of my family; meaning, for I am very young, my elder brothers born in these later years?

I don't think I have. I am afraid I have not. Have you had many brothers, Spirit?

more than eighteen hundred.

A tremendous family to provide for!

Spirit, conduct me where you will. I went forth last night on compulsion and I learnt a lesson which is working now. Tonight, if you have aught to teach me, let me profit by it.

Touch my robe!

Scrooge did as he was told, and held it fast.

Holly, mistletoe, red berries, ivy, turkeys, geese, game, poultry, brawn, meat, pigs, sausages, oysters, pies, puddings, fruit, and punch, all vanished instantly. So did the room, the fire, the ruddy glow, the hour of night, and they stood in the city streets on Christmas morning, where (for the weather was severe) the people made a rough, but brisk and not unpleasant kind of music, in scraping the snow from the pavement in front of their dwellings, and from the tops of their houses: whence it was mad delight to the boys to see it come plumping down into the road below, and splitting into artificial little snowstorms.

The house fronts looked black enough, and the windows blacker, contrasting with the smooth white sheet of snow upon the roofs, and with the dirtier snow upon the ground; which last deposit had been ploughed up in deep furrows by the heavy wheels of carts and waggons; furrows that crossed and recrossed each other hundreds of times where the great streets branched off, and made intricate channels, hard to trace, in the thick yellow mud and icy water. The sky was gloomy, and the shortest streets were choked up with a dingy mist, half thawed half frozen, whose heavier particles descended in a shower of sooty atoms, as if all the chimneys in Great Britain had, by one consent, caught fire, and were blazing away to their dear hearts' content. There was nothing very cheerful in the climate or the town, and yet was there an air of cheerfulness abroad that the clearest summer air and brightest summer sun might have endeavoured to diffuse in vain.

For the people who were shovelling away on the house-tops were jovial and full of glee; calling out to one another from the parapets, and now and then exchanging a facetious snowball—better-natured missile far than many a wordy jest—laughing heartily if it went right, and not less heartily if it went wrong. The poulterers' shops were still half open, and the fruiterers' were radiant in their glory. There were great, round, pot-bellied baskets of chestnuts, shaped like the waistcoats of jolly old gentlemen, lolling at the doors, and tumbling out into the street in their apoplectic opulence. There were ruddy, brown-faced, broad-girthed Spanish Onions, shining in the fatness of their growth like Spanish Friars; and winking from their shelves in wanton slyness at the girls as they went by, and glanced demurely at the hung-up mistletoe. There were pears and apples, clustered high in blooming pyramids; there were bunches of grapes, made, in the shopkeepers' benevolence, to dangle from conspicuous hooks, that people's mouths might water gratis as they passed; there were piles of filberts, mossy and brown, recalling, in their fragrance, ancient walks among the woods, and pleasant shufflings ankle deep through withered leaves; there were Norfolk Biffins, squab and swarthy, setting off the yellow of the oranges and lemons, and, in the great compactness of their juicy persons, urgently entreating and beseeching to be carried home in paper bags and eaten after dinner.

The very gold and silver fish, set forth among these choice fruits in a bowl, though members of a dull and stagnant-blooded race, appeared to know that there was something going on; and, to a fish, went grasping round and round their little world in slow and passionless excitement.

The Grocers'! oh the Grocers'! nearly closed, with perhaps two shutters down, or one; but through those gaps such glimpses! It was not alone that the scales descending on the counter made a merry sound, or that the twine and roller parted company so briskly, or that the canisters were rattled up and down like juggling tricks, or even that the blended scents of tea and coffee were so grateful to the nose, or even that the raisins were so plentiful and rare, the almonds so extremely white, the sticks of cinnamon so long and straight, the other spices so delicious, the candied fruits so caked and spotted with molten sugar as to make the coldest lookers-on feel faint and subsequently bilious. Nor was it that the figs were moist and pulpy, or that the French plums blushed in modest tartness from their highly-decorated boxes, or that everything was good to eat and in its Christmas dress: but the customers were all so hurried and so eager in the hopeful promise of the day, that they tumbled up against each other at the door, clashing their wicker baskets wildly, and left their purchases upon the counter, and came running back to fetch them, and committed hundreds of the like mistakes in the best humour possible; while the Grocer and his people were so frank and fresh that the polished hearts with which they fastened their aprons behind might have been their own, worn outside for general inspection, and for Christmas daws to peck at if they chose.

But soon the steeples called good people all, to church and chapel, and away they came, flocking through the streets in their best clothes, and with their gayest faces. And at the same time there emerged from scores of bye streets, lanes, and nameless turnings, innumerable people, carrying their dinners to the bakers' shops. The sight of these poor revellers appeared to interest the Spirit very much, for he stood with Scrooge beside him in a baker's doorway, and taking off the covers as their bearers passed, sprinkled incense on their dinners from his torch. And it was a very uncommon kind of torch, for once or twice when there were angry words between some dinner-carriers who had jostled with each other, he shed a few drops of water on them from it, and their good humour was restored directly. For they said, it was a shame to quarrel upon Christmas Day. And so it was! God love it, so it was!

Scrooge promised that he would; and they went on, invisible, as they had been before, into the suburbs of the town. It was a remarkable quality of the Ghost (which Scrooge had observed at the baker's) that notwithstanding his gigantic size, he could accommodate himself to any place with ease: and that he stood beneath a low roof quite as gracefully and like a supernatural creature, as it was possible he could have done in any lofty hall.

And perhaps it was the pleasure the good Spirit had in showing off this power of his, or else it was his own kind, generous, hearty nature, and his sympathy with all poor men, that led him straight to Scrooge's clerks; for there he went, and took Scrooge with him, holding to his robe; and on the threshold of the door the Spirit smiled, and stopped to bless Bob Cratchit's dwelling with the sprinklings of his torch. Think of that! Bob had but fifteen "Bob" a-week himself; he pocketed on Saturdays but fifteen copies of his Christian name; and yet the Ghost of Christmas Present blessed his four-roomed house!

Then up rose Mrs. Cratchit, Cratchit's wife, dressed out but poorly in a twice-turned gown, but brave in ribbons, which are cheap and make a goodly show for sixpence; and she laid the cloth, assisted by Belinda Cratchit, second of her daughters, also brave in ribbons; while Master Peter Cratchit plunged a fork into the saucepan of potatoes, and getting the corners of his monstrous shirt-collar (Bob's private property, conferred upon his son and heir in honour of the day) into his mouth, rejoiced to find himself so gallantly attired, and yearned to show his linen in the fashionable Parks. And now two smaller Cratchits, boy and girl, came tearing in, screaming that outside the baker's they had smelt the goose, and known it for their own; and basking in luxurious thoughts of sage-and-onion, these young Cratchits danced about the table, and exalted Master Peter Cratchit to the skies, while he (not proud, although his collars nearly choked him) blew the fire, until the slow potatoes bubbling up, knocked loudly at the saucepan-lid to be let out and peeled.

"What has ever got your precious father then. And your brother Tiny Tim; and Martha warn't as late last Christmas Day by half-an-hour!"

"Here's Martha, mother!"

"Here's Martha, mother Hurrah! there's such a goose, Martha!"

"Why, bless your heart alive, my dear, how late you are!"

... said Mrs. Cratchit, kissing her a dozen times, and taking off her shawl and bonnet for her, with officious zeal.

"We'd a deal of work to finish up last night and had to clear away this morning, mother!"

"Well! Never mind so long as you are come. Sit ye down before the fire, my dear, and have a warm, Lord bless ye!"

"No, no! There's father coming,"

"Hide Martha, hide!"

So Martha hid herself, and in came little Bob, the father, with at least three feet of comforter exclusive of the fringe, hanging down before him; and his thread-bare clothes darned up and brushed, to look seasonable; and Tiny Tim upon his shoulder. Alas for Tiny Tim, he bore a little crutch, and had his limbs supported by an iron frame!

"Why, where's our Martha?"

"Not coming,"

"Not coming! Not coming upon Christmas Day!"

... with a sudden declension in his high spirits; for he had been Tim's blood horse all the way from church, and had come home rampant.

Martha didn't like to see him disappointed, if it were only in joke; so she came out prematurely from behind the closet door, and ran into his arms, while the two young Cratchits hustled Tiny Tim, and bore him off into the wash-house, that he might hear the pudding singing in the copper.

"And how did little Tim behave?"

... asked Mrs. Cratchit, when she had rallied Bob on his credulity and Bob had hugged his daughter to his heart's content.

"As good as gold, and better. Somehow he gets thoughtful sitting by himself so much, and thinks the strangest things you ever heard. He told me, coming home, that he hoped the people saw him in the church, because he was a cripple, and it might be pleasant to them to remember upon Christmas Day, who made lame beggars walk and blind men see."

Bob's voice was tremulous when he told them this, and trembled more when he said that Tiny Tim was growing strong and hearty.

His active little crutch was heard upon the floor, and back came Tiny Tim before another word was spoken, escorted by his brother and sister to his stool beside the fire; and while Bob, turning up his cuffs—as if, poor fellow, they were capable of being made more shabby—compounded some hot mixture in a jug with gin and lemons, and stirred it round and round and put it on the hob to simmer; Master Peter and the two ubiquitous young Cratchits went to fetch the goose, with which they soon returned in high procession.

Such a bustle ensued that you might have thought a goose the rarest of all birds; a feathered phenomenon, to which a black swan was a matter of course: and in truth it was something very like it in that house. Mrs. Cratchit made the gravy (ready beforehand in a little saucepan) hissing hot; Master Peter mashed the potatoes with incredible vigour; Miss Belinda sweetened up the apple-sauce; Martha dusted the hot plates; Bob took Tiny Tim beside him in a tiny corner at the table; the two young Cratchits set chairs for everybody, not forgetting themselves, and mounting guard upon their posts, crammed spoons into their mouths, lest they should shriek for goose before their turn came to be helped. At last the dishes were set on, and grace was said. It was succeeded by a breathless pause, as Mrs. Cratchit, looking slowly all along the carving-knife, prepared to plunge it in the breast; but when she did, and when the long expected gush of stuffing issued forth, one murmur of delight arose all round the board, and even Tiny Tim, excited by the two young Cratchits, beat on the table with the handle of his knife, and feebly cried Hurrah!

There never was such a goose. Bob said he didn't believe there ever was such a goose cooked. Its tenderness and flavour, size and cheapness, were the themes of universal admiration. Eked out by the apple-sauce and mashed potatoes, it was sufficient dinner for the whole family; indeed, as Mrs. Cratchit said with a great delight (surveying one small atom of a bone upon the dish), they hadn't ate it all at last! Yet every one had had enough, and the youngest Cratchits in particular, were steeped in sage and onion to the eyebrows! But now, the plates being changed by Miss Belinda, Mrs. Cratchit left the room alone—too nervous to bear witnesses—to take the pudding up, and bring it in.

Suppose it should not be done enough! Suppose it should break in turning out! Suppose somebody should have got over the wall of the back-yard, and stolen it, while they were merry with the goose: a supposition at which the two young Cratchits became livid! All sorts of horrors were supposed.

Hallo! A great deal of steam! The pudding was out of the copper. A smell like a washing-day! That was the cloth. A smell like an eating-house, and a pastry cook's next door to each other, with a laundress's next door to that! That was the pudding. In half a minute Mrs. Cratchit entered: flushed, but smiling proudly; with the pudding, like a speckled cannon-ball, so hard and firm, blazing in half of half-a-quartern of ignited brandy, and bedight with Christmas holly stuck into the top.

Oh, a wonderful pudding! Bob Cratchit said, and calmly too, that he regarded it as the greatest success achieved by Mrs. Cratchit since their marriage. Mrs. Cratchit said that now the weight was off her mind, she would confess she had had her doubts about the quantity of flour. Everybody had something to say about it, but nobody said or thought it was at all a small pudding for a large family. It would have been flat heresy to do so. Any Cratchit would have blushed to hint at such a thing.

At last the dinner was all done, the cloth was cleared, the hearth swept, and the fire made up. The compound in the jug being tasted and considered perfect, apples and oranges were put upon the table, and a shovel-full of chestnuts on the fire. Then all the Cratchit family drew round the hearth, in what Bob Cratchit called a circle, meaning half a one; and at Bob Cratchit's elbow stood the family display of glass; two tumblers, and a custard-cup without a handle.

These held the hot stuff from the jug, however, as well as golden goblets would have done; and Bob served it out with beaming looks, while the chestnuts on the fire sputtered and crackled noisily. Then Bob proposed:

A Merry Christmas to us all, my dears. God bless us!

God bless us every one!

Which all the family re-echoed.

He sat very close to his father's side, upon his little stool. Bob held his withered little hand in his, as if he loved the child, and wished to keep him by his side, and dreaded that he might be taken from him.

tell me if Tiny Tim will live.

Spirit,

... said Scrooge, with an interest he had never felt before. ...

I see a vacant seat in the poor chimney corner, and a crutch without an owner, carefully preserved. If these shadows remain unaltered by the Future, the child will die.

No, no. Oh no, kind Spirit! say he will be spared.

If these shadows remain unaltered by the Future, none other of my race will find him here. What then? If he be like to die, he had better do it, and decrease the surplus population.

Scrooge hung his head to hear his own words quoted by the Spirit, and was overcome with penitence and grief.

Man, if man you be in heart, not adamant, forbear that wicked cant until you have discovered What the surplus is, and Where it is. Will you decide what men shall live, what men shall die? It may be, that in the sight of Heaven, you are more worthless and less fit to live than millions like this poor man's child. Oh God! to hear the Insect on the leaf pronouncing on the too much life among his hungry brothers in the dust!

Scrooge bent before the Ghost's rebuke, and trembling cast his eyes upon the ground. But he raised them speedily, on hearing his own name.

Mr. Scrooge!

I'll give you Mr. Scrooge, the Founder of the Feast!

The Founder of the Feast indeed! I wish I had him here. I'd give him a piece of my mind to feast upon, and I hope he'd have a good appetite for it.

My dear, the children; Christmas Day.

It should be Christmas Day, I am sure, on which one drinks the health of such an odious, stingy, hard, unfeeling man as Mr. Scrooge. You know he is, Robert! Nobody knows it better than you do, poor fellow!

My dear, Christmas Day.

I'll drink his health for your sake and the Day's, not for his. Long life to him! A merry Christmas and a happy new year! —he'll be very merry and very happy I have no doubt!

The children drank the toast after her. It was the first of their proceedings which had no heartiness in it. Tiny Tim drank it last of all, but he didn't care twopence for it. Scrooge was the Ogre of the family. The mention of his name cast a dark shadow on the party, which was not dispelled for full five minutes.

After it had passed away, they were ten times merrier than before, from the mere relief of Scrooge the Baleful being done with. Bob Cratchit told them how he had a situation in his eye for Master Peter, which would bring in, if obtained, full five-and-sixpence weekly. The two young Cratchits laughed tremendously at the idea of Peter's being a man of business; and Peter himself looked thoughtfully at the fire from between his collars, as if he were deliberating what particular investments he should favour when he came into the receipt of that bewildering income. Martha, who was a poor apprentice at a milliner's, then told them what kind of work she had to do, and how many hours she worked at a stretch, and how she meant to lie a-bed tomorrow morning for a good long rest; tomorrow being a holiday she passed at home. Also how she had seen a countess and a lord some days before, and how the lord "was much about as tall as Peter;" at which Peter pulled up his collars so high that you couldn't have seen his head if you had been there. All this time the chesnuts and the jug went round and round; and bye and bye they had a song, about a lost child travelling in the snow, from Tiny Tim; who had a plaintive little voice, and sang it very well indeed.

There was nothing of high mark in this. They were not a handsome family; they were not well dressed; their shoes were far from being waterproof; their clothes were scanty; and Peter might have known, and very likely did, the inside of a pawnbroker's. But they were happy, grateful, pleased with one another, and contented with the time; and when they faded, and looked happier yet in the bright sprinklings of the Spirit's torch at parting, Scrooge had his eye upon them, and especially on Tiny Tim, until the last.

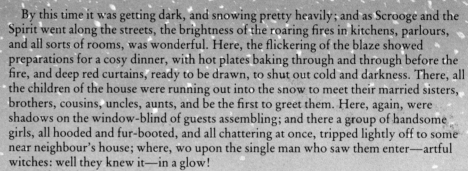

By this time it was getting dark, and snowing pretty heavily; and as Scrooge and the Spirit went along the streets, the brightness of the roaring fires in kitchens, parlours, and all sorts of rooms, was wonderful. Here, the flickering of the blaze showed preparations for a cosy dinner, with hot plates baking through and through before the fire, and deep red curtains, ready to be drawn, to shut out cold and darkness. There, all the children of the house were running out into the snow to meet their married sisters, brothers, cousins, uncles, aunts, and be the first to greet them. Here, again, were shadows on the window-blind of guests assembling; and there a group of handsome girls, all hooded and fur-booted, and all chattering at once, tripped lightly off to some near neighbour's house; where, wo upon the single man who saw them enter—artful witches: well they knew it—in a glow!

But if you had judged from the numbers of people on their way to friendly gatherings, you might have thought that no one was at home to give them welcome when they got there, instead of every house expecting company, and piling up its fires half-chimney high. Blessings on it, how the Ghost exulted! How it bared its breadth of breast, and opened its capacious palm, and floated on, outpouring, with a generous hand, its bright and harmless mirth on everything within its reach! The very lamplighter, who ran on before dotting the dusky street with specks of light, and who was dressed to spend the evening somewhere, laughed out loudly as the Spirit passed: though little kenned the lamplighter that he had any company but Christmas!

And now, without a word of warning from the Ghost, they stood upon a bleak and desert moor, where monstrous masses of rude stone were cast about, as though it were the burial-place of giants; and water spread itself wheresoever it listed—or would have done so, but for the frost that held it prisoner; and nothing grew but moss and furze, and coarse, rank grass. Down in the west the setting sun had left a streak of fiery red, which glared upon the desolation for an instant, like a sullen eye, and frowning lower, lower, lower yet, was lost in the thick gloom of darkest night.

What place is this?

A place where miners live, who labour in the bowels of the earth. But they know me, see!

A light shone from the window of a hut, and swiftly they advanced towards it.

Passing through the wall of mud and stone, they found a cheerful company assembled round a glowing fire. An old, old man and woman, with their children and their children's children, and another generation beyond that, all decked out gaily in their holiday attire. The old man, in a voice that seldom rose above the howling of the wind upon the barren waste, was singing them a Christmas song; it had been a very old song when he was a boy; and from time to time they all joined in the chorus. So surely as they raised their voices, the old man got quite blithe and loud; and so surely as they stopped, his vigour sank again.

The Spirit did not tarry here, but bade Scrooge hold his robe, and passing on above the moor, sped whither? Not to sea? To sea. To Scrooge's horror, looking back, he saw the last of the land, a frightful range of rocks, behind them; and his ears were deafened by the thundering of water, as it rolled, and roared, and raged among the dreadful caverns it had worn, and fiercely tried to undermine the earth.

Built upon a dismal reef of sunken rocks, some league or so from shore, on which the waters chafed and dashed, the wild year through, there stood a solitary lighthouse. Great heaps of sea-weed clung to its base, and storm-birds—born of the wind one might suppose, as sea-weed of the water—rose and fell about it, like the waves they skimmed.

But even here, two men who watched the light had made a fire, that through the loophole in the thick stone wall shed out a ray of brightness on the awful sea. Joining their horny hands over the rough table at which they sat, they wished each other Merry Christmas in their can of grog; and one of them: the elder, too, with his face all damaged and scarred with hard weather, as the figure-head of an old ship might be: struck up a sturdy song that was like a Gale in itself.

They stood beside the helmsman at the wheel, the look-out in the bow, the officers who had the watch; dark, ghostly figures in their several stations; but every man among them hummed a Christmas tune, or had a Christmas thought, or spoke below his breath to his companion of some bygone Christmas Day, with homeward hopes belonging to it. And every man on board, waking or sleeping, good or bad, had had a kinder word for another on that day than on any day in the year; and had shared to some extent in its festivities; and had remembered those he cared for at a distance, and had known that they delighted to remember him.

Again the Ghost sped on, above the black and heaving sea—on, on—until, being far away, as he told Scrooge, from any shore, they lighted on a ship.

Ha, ha! Ha, ha, ha!

It was a great surprise to Scrooge, while listening to the moaning of the wind, and thinking what a solemn thing it was to move on through the lonely darkness over an unknown abyss, whose depths were secrets as profound as Death: it was a great surprise to Scrooge, while thus engaged, to hear a hearty laugh. It was a much greater surprise to Scrooge to recognise it as his own nephew's, and to find himself in a bright, dry, gleaming room, with the Spirit standing smiling by his side, and looking at that same nephew with approving affability!

If you should happen, by any unlikely chance, to know a man more blest in a laugh than Scrooge's nephew, all I can say is, I should like to know him too. Introduce him to me, and I'll cultivate his acquaintance. It is a fair, even-handed, noble adjustment of things, that while there is infection in disease and sorrow, there is nothing in the world so irresistibly contagious as laughter and good-humour. When Scrooge's nephew laughed in this way: holding his sides, rolling his head, and twisting his face into the most extravagant contortions: Scrooge's niece, by marriage, laughed as heartily as he. And their assembled friends being not a bit behindhand, roared out, lustily "Ha, ha! Ha, ha, ha, ha!"

He said that Christmas was a humbug, as I live! He believed it too!

Bless those women; they never do anything by halves. They are always in earnest.

She was very pretty: exceedingly pretty. With a dimpled, surprised-looking, capital face; a ripe little mouth, that seemed made to be kissed—as no doubt it was; all kinds of good little dots about her chin, that melted into one another when she laughed; and the sunniest pair of eyes you ever saw in any little creature's head. Altogether she was what you would have called provoking, you know; but satisfactory, too. Oh, perfectly satisfactory!

More shame for him, Fred!

He's a comical old fellow, that's the truth: and not so pleasant as he might be. However, his offences carry their own punishment, and I have nothing to say against him.

I am sure he is very rich Fred, At least you always tell me so

What of that, my dear! His wealth is of no use to him. He don't do any good with it. He don't make himself comfortable with it. He hasn't the satisfaction of thinking—ha, ha, ha!—that he is ever going to benefit Us with it.

I have no patience with him.

Scrooge's niece's sisters, and all the other ladies, expressed the same opinion.

Oh, I have! I am sorry for him; I couldn't be angry with him if I tried. Who suffers by his ill whims! Himself, always. Here, he takes it into his head to dislike us, and he won't come and dine with us. What's the consequence? He don't lose much of a dinner.

Indeed, I think he loses a very good dinner.

Everybody else said the same, and they must be allowed to have been competent judges, because they had just had dinner; and, with the dessert upon the table, were clustered round the fire, by lamplight.

"Well! I am very glad to hear it, because I haven't any great faith in these young housekeepers. What do you say, Topper?"

Topper had clearly got his eye upon one of Scrooge's niece's sisters, for he answered that a bachelor was a wretched outcast, who had no right to express an opinion on the subject. Whereat Scrooge's niece's sister—the plump one with the lace tucker: not the one with the roses—blushed.

"Do go on, Fred. He never finishes what he begins to say! He is such a ridiculous fellow!"

Scrooge's nephew revelled in another laugh, and as it was impossible to keep the infection off; though the plump sister tried hard to do it with aromatic vinegar; his example was unanimously followed.

"I was only going to say, that the consequence of his taking a dislike to us, and not making merry with us, is, as I think, that he loses some pleasant moments, which could do him no harm. I am sure he loses pleasanter companions than he can find in his own thoughts, either in his mouldy old office or his dusty chambers. I mean to give him the same chance every year whether he likes it or not, for I pity him. He may rail at Christmas till he dies, but he can't help thinking better of it—I defy him—if he finds me going there, in good temper, year after year and saying Uncle Scrooge, how are you? If it only puts him in the vein to leave his poor clerk fifty pounds, **that's** something; and I think I shook him, yesterday."

It was their turn to laugh now, at the notion of his shaking Scrooge. But being thoroughly good-natured, and not much caring what they laughed at, so that they laughed at any rate, he encouraged them in their merriment, and passed the bottle, joyously.

After tea, they had some music. For they were a musical family, and knew what they were about, when they sung a Glee or Catch, I can assure you: especially Topper, who could growl away in the bass like a good one, and never swell the large veins in his forehead, or get red in the face over it. Scrooge's niece played well upon the harp; and played among other tunes a simple little air (a mere nothing: you might learn to whistle it in two minutes), which had been familiar to the child who fetched Scrooge from the boarding-school, as he had been reminded by the Ghost of Christmas Past. When this strain of music sounded, all the things that Ghost had shown him, came upon his mind; he softened more and more; and thought that if he could have listened to it often, years ago, he might have cultivated the kindnesses of life for his own happiness with his own hands, without resorting to the sexton's spade that buried Jacob Marley.

But they didn't devote the whole evening to music. After a while they played at forfeits; for it is good to be children sometimes, and never better than at Christmas, when its mighty Founder was a child himself. Stop! There was first a game at blind-man's buff. Of course there was. And I no more believe Topper was really blind than I believe he had eyes in his boots. My opinion is, that it was a done thing between him and Scrooge's nephew; and that the Ghost of Christmas Present knew it. The way he went after that plump sister in the lace tucker, was an outrage on the credulity of human nature. Knocking down the fire-irons, tumbling over the chairs, bumping up against the piano, smothering himself among the curtains, wherever she went, there went he. He always knew where the plump sister was. He wouldn't catch anybody else. If you had fallen up against him, as some of them did, and stood there; he would have made a feint of endeavouring to seize you, which would have been an affront to your understanding; and would instantly have sidled off in the direction of the plump sister. She often cried out that it wasn't fair; and it really was not. But when at last, he caught her; when, in spite of all her silken rustlings, and her rapid flutterings past him, he got her into a corner whence there was no escape; then his conduct was the most execrable.

For his pretending not to know her; his pretending that it was necessary to touch her head-dress, and further to assure himself of her identity by pressing a certain ring upon her finger, and a certain chain about her neck; was vile, monstrous! No doubt she told him her opinion of it, when, another blind-man being in office, they were so very confidential together, behind the curtains.

Scrooge's niece was not one of the blind-man's buff party, but was made comfortable with a large chair and a footstool, in a snug corner, where the Ghost and Scrooge were close behind her. But she joined in the forfeits, and loved her love to admiration with all the letters of the alphabet. Likewise at the game of How, When, and Where, she was very great, and to the secret joy of Scrooge's nephew, beat her sisters hollow: though they were sharp girls too, as Topper could have told you. There might have been twenty people there, young and old, but they all played, and so did Scrooge; for, wholly forgetting in the interest he had in what was going on, that his voice made no sound in their ears, he sometimes came out with his guess quite loud, and very often guessed right, too; for the sharpest needle, best Whitechapel, warranted not to cut in the eye, was not sharper than Scrooge: blunt as he took it in his head to be.

The Ghost was greatly pleased to find him in this mood, and looked upon him with such favour that he begged like a boy to be allowed to stay until the guests departed. But this the Spirit said could not be done.

Here's a new game. One half hour, Spirit, only one!

It was a Game called Yes and No, where Scrooge's nephew had to think of something, and the rest must find out what; he only answering to their questions yes or no as the case was. The brisk fire of questioning to which he was exposed, elicited from him that he was thinking of an animal, a live animal, rather a disagreeable animal, a savage animal, an animal that growled and grunted sometimes, and talked sometimes, and lived in London, and walked about the streets, and wasn't made a show of, and wasn't led by anybody, and didn't live in a menagerie, and was never killed in a market, and was not a horse, or an ass, or a cow, or a bull, or a tiger, or a dog, or a pig, or a cat, or a bear. At every fresh question that was put to him, this nephew burst into a fresh roar of laughter; and was so inexpressibly tickled, that he was obliged to get up off the sofa and stamp.

At last the plump sister, falling into a similar state, cried out:

I have found it out! I know what it is, Fred! I know what it is!

What is it?

It's your Uncle Scro-o-o-ooge!

Which it certainly was. Admiration was the universal sentiment, though some objected that the reply to "Is it a bear?" ought to have been "Yes;" inasmuch as an answer in the negative was sufficient to have diverted their thoughts from Mr. Scrooge, supposing they had ever had any tendency that way.

He has given us plenty of merriment, I am sure, and it would be ungrateful not to drink his health. Here is a glass of mulled wine ready to our hand at the moment; and I say 'Uncle Scrooge'!

Well! Uncle Scrooge!

A Merry Christmas and a Happy New Year to the old man, whatever he is! He wouldn't take it from me, but may he have it, nevertheless, Uncle Scrooge!

Uncle Scrooge had imperceptibly become so gay and light of heart, that he would have pledged the unconscious company in return, and thanked them in an inaudible speech, if the Ghost had given him time. But the whole scene passed off in the breath of the last word spoken by his nephew; and he and the Spirit were again upon their travels.

Much they saw, and far they went, and many homes they visited, but always with a happy end. The Spirit stood beside sick beds, and they were cheerful; on foreign lands, and they were close at home; by struggling men, and they were patient in their greater hope; by poverty, and it was rich. In almshouse, hospital, and jail, in misery's every refuge, where vain man in his little brief authority had not made fast the door, and barred the Spirit out, he left his blessing, and taught Scrooge his precepts.

It was a long night, if it were only a night; but Scrooge had his doubts of this, because the Christmas Holidays appeared to be condensed into the space of time they passed together. It was strange, too, that while Scrooge remained unaltered in his outward form, the Ghost grew older, clearly older. Scrooge had observed this change, but never spoke of it, until they left a children's Twelfth Night party, when, looking at the Spirit as they stood together in an open place, he noticed that its hair was gray.

Are spirits' lives so short?

My life upon this globe, is very brief. It ends to-night.

To-night!

Tonight at midnight. Hark! The time is drawing near.

The chimes were ringing the three quarters past eleven at that moment.

STAVE IV

THE LAST OF THE SPIRITS

The Phantom slowly, gravely, silently, approached. When it came near him, Scrooge bent down upon his knee; for in the very air through which this Spirit moved it seemed to scatter gloom and mystery.

It was shrouded in a deep black garment, which concealed its head, its face, its form, and left nothing of it visible save one outstretched hand. But for this it would have been difficult to detach its figure from the night, and separate it from the darkness by which it was surrounded.

He felt that it was tall and stately when it came beside him, and that its mysterious presence filled him with a solemn dread. He knew no more, for the Spirit neither spoke nor moved.

The Spirit answered not, but pointed downward with its hand.

I am in the presence of the Ghost of Christmas Yet to Come?

You are about to show me shadows of the things that have not happened, but will happen in the time before us. Is that so Spirit?

The upper portion of the garment was contracted for an instant in its folds, as if the Spirit had inclined its head. That was the only answer he received.

Although well used to ghostly company by this time, Scrooge feared the silent shape so much that his legs trembled beneath him, and he found that he could hardly stand when he prepared to follow it. The Spirit paused a moment, as observing his condition, and giving him time to recover. But Scrooge was all the worse for this. It thrilled him with a vague uncertain horror, to know that behind the dusky shroud there were ghostly eyes intently fixed upon him, while he, though he stretched his own to the utmost, could see nothing but a special hand and one great heap of black.

Ghost of the future! I fear you more than any Spectre I have seen. But, as I know your promise is to do me good, and as I hope to live to be another man from what I was, I am prepared to bear you company, and do it with a thankful heart. Will you not speak to me?

It gave him no reply. The hand was pointed straight before them.

Lead on! Lead on! The night is waning fast! and it is precious time to me, I know. Lead on, Spirit!

The Phantom moved away as it had come towards him. Scrooge followed in the shadow of its dress, which bore him up, he thought, and carried him along.

They scarcely seemed to enter the city; for the city rather seemed to spring up about them, and encompass them of its own act. But there they were, in the heart of it; on 'Change, amongst the merchants; who hurried up and down, and chinked the money in their pockets, and conversed in groups, and looked at their watches, and trifled thoughtfully with their great gold seals; and so forth, as Scrooge had seen them often.

The Spirit stopped beside one little knot of business men. Observing that the hand was pointed to them, Scrooge advanced to listen to their talk.

No, I don't know much about it, either way: I only know he's dead.

When did he die?

Last night, I believe.

Why, what was the matter with him? I thought he'd never die.

God knows.

What has he done with his money?

... asked a red-faced gentleman with a pendulous excrescence on the end of his nose, that shook like the gills of a turkey-cock.

I haven't heard. Left it to his Company, perhaps. He hasn't left it to me. That's all I know.

This pleasantry was received with a general laugh.

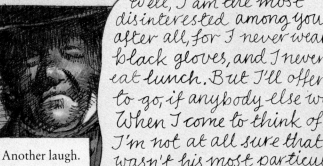

I don't mind going if a lunch is provided, but I must be fed, if I make one.

It's likely to be a very cheap funeral, for upon my life I don't know of anybody to go to it. Suppose we make up a party and volunteer?

Another laugh.

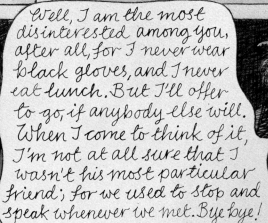

Well, I am the most disinterested among you, after all, for I never wear black gloves, and I never eat lunch. But I'll offer to go, if anybody else will. When I come to think of it, I'm not at all sure that I wasn't his most particular friend; for we used to stop and speak whenever we met. Bye bye!

Speakers and listeners strolled away, and mixed with other groups. Scrooge knew the men, and looked towards the Spirit for an explanation.

The Phantom glided on into a street. Its finger pointed to two persons meeting. Scrooge listened again, thinking that the explanation might lie here.

He knew these men, also, perfectly. They were men of business: very wealthy, and of great importance. He had made a point always of standing well in their esteem: in a business point of view, that is; strictly in a business point of view.

How are you?

How are you?

Well! Old Scratch has got his own at last, hey?

So I'm told. Cold isn't it?

No. No. Something else to think of. Good Morning!

Seasonable for Christmas time. Your'e not a skaiter, I suppose?

Not another word. That was their meeting, their conversation, and their parting.

Scrooge was at first inclined to be surprised that the Spirit should attach importance to conversations apparently so trivial; but feeling assured that they must have some hidden purpose, he set himself to consider what it was likely to be. They could scarcely be supposed to have any bearing on the death of Jacob, his old partner, for that was Past, and this Ghost's province was the Future. Nor could he think of any one immediately connected with himself, to whom he could apply them. But nothing doubting that to whomsoever they applied they had some latent moral for his own improvement, he resolved to treasure up every word he heard, and everything he saw; and especially to observe the shadow of himself when it appeared. For he had an expectation that the conduct of his future self would give him the clue he missed, and would render the solution of these riddles easy.

He looked about in that very place for his own image; but another man stood in his accustomed corner, and though the clock pointed to his usual time of day for being there, he saw no likeness of himself among the multitudes that poured in through the Porch. It gave him little surprise, however; for he had been revolving in his mind a change of life, and thought and hoped he saw his new-born resolutions carried out in this.

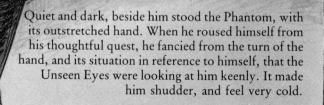

Quiet and dark, beside him stood the Phantom, with its outstretched hand. When he roused himself from his thoughtful quest, he fancied from the turn of the hand, and its situation in reference to himself, that the Unseen Eyes were looking at him keenly. It made him shudder, and feel very cold.

They left the busy scene, and went into an obscure
part of the town, where Scrooge had never penetrated
before, although he recognised its situation, and its bad
repute. The ways were foul and narrow; the shops and
houses wretched; the people half-naked, drunken,
slipshod, ugly. Alleys and archways, like so many
cesspools, disgorged their offences of smell, and dirt,
and life, upon the straggling streets; and the whole
quarter reeked with crime, with filth, and misery.

Far in this den of infamous resort, there was a low-browed, beetling shop, below a pent-house roof, where iron, old rags, bottles, bones, and greasy offal, were bought. Upon the floor within, were piled up heaps of rusty keys, nails, chains, hinges, files, scales, weights, and refuse iron of all kinds. Secrets that few would like to scrutinise were bred and hidden in mountains of unseemly rags, masses of corrupted fat, and sepulchres of bones. Sitting in among the wares he dealt in, by a charcoal-stove, made of old bricks, was a gray-haired rascal, nearly seventy years of age; who had screened himself from the cold air without, by a frousy curtaining of miscellaneous tatters, hung upon a line; and smoked his pipe in all the luxury of calm retirement.

Scrooge and the Phantom came into the presence of this man, just as a woman with a heavy bundle slunk into the shop. But she had scarcely entered, when another woman, similarly laden, came in too; and she was closely followed by a man in faded black, who was no less startled by the sight of them, than they had been upon the recognition of each other. After a short period of blank astonishment, in which the old man with the pipe had joined them, they all three burst into a laugh.

You couldn't have met in a better place. Come into the parlour. You were made free of it long ago, you know; and the other two an't strangers. Stop till I shut the door of the shop.

Let the charwoman alone to be the first! Let the laundress alone to be the second; and let the undertaker's man alone be third. Look here, old Joe, here's a chance! If we haven't all three met here without meaning it!

Ah! How it skreeks! There an't such a rusty bit of metal in the place as its own hinges, I believe; and I'm sure there's no such old bones here as mine. Ha, ha! We're all suitable to our calling, we're well matched. Come into the parlour. Come into the parlour.

The parlour was the space behind the screen of rags. The old man raked the fire together with an old stair-rod, and having trimmed his smoky lamp (for it was night), with the stem of his pipe, put it in his mouth again.

While he did this, the woman who had already spoken threw her bundle on the floor and sat down in a flaunting manner on a stool; crossing her elbows on her knees, and looking with a bold defiance at the other two.

What odds then! What odds, Mrs Dilber? Every person has a right to take care of themselves. He always did!

That's true, indeed! No man more so.

Why, then, don't stand staring as if you was afraid woman; who's the wiser? We're not going to pick holes in each other's coats I suppose?

No, indeed! We should hope not.

Very well, then! That's enough. Who's the worse for the loss of a few things like these? Not a dead man, I suppose.

No, indeed.

If he wanted to keep 'em after he was dead, a wicked old screw, why wasn't he natural in his lifetime? If he had been, he'd have had somebody to look after him when he was struck with Death, instead of lying gasping out his last there, alone by himself.

It's the truest word that ever was spoke. It's a judgement on him.

I wish it was a little heavier one, and it should have been, you may depend upon it, if I could have laid my hands on anything else. Open that bundle, old Joe, and let me know the value of it. Speak out plain. I'm not afraid to be the first, nor afraid of them to see it. We knew pretty well that we were helping ourselves, before we met here, I believe. It's no sin. Open the bundle, Joe.

But the gallantry of her friends would not allow of this; and the man in faded black, mounting the breach first, produced *his* plunder. It was not extensive. A seal or two, a pencil-case, a pair of sleeve-buttons, and a brooch of no great value, were all. They were severally examined and appraised by old Joe, who chalked the sums he was disposed to give for each upon the wall, and added them up into a total when he found that there was nothing more to come.

That's your account, and I wouldn't give another sixpence, if I was to be boiled for not doing it. Who's next?

Mrs. Dilber was next. Sheets and towels, a little wearing apparel, two old-fashioned silver teaspoons, a pair of sugar-tongs, and a few boots. Her account was stated on the wall in the same manner.

Joe went down on his knees for the greater convenience of opening it, and having unfastened a great many knots, dragged out a large and heavy roll of some dark stuff.

Yes I do. Why not?

I always give too much to ladies. It's a weakness of mine and that's the way I ruin myself. That's your account. If you asked me for another penny, and made it an open question, I'd repent of being so liberal and knock off half-a-crown!

And now undo my bundle, Joe.

What do you call this? Bed-curtains!

Ah! Bed-Curtains!

You don't mean to say you took 'em down, rings and all, with him lying there?

You were born to make your fortune, and you'll certainly do it.

I certainly shan't hold my hand, when I can get anything in it by reaching it out, for the sake of such a man as He was, I promise you, Joe. Don't drop that oil upon the blankets, now.

His blankets?

Whose else's do you think? He isn't likely to take cold without 'em, I dare say.

I hope he didn't die of anything catching? eh?

Don't you be afraid of that. I ain't so fond of his company that I'd loiter about him for such things, if he did. Ah! you may look through that shirt till your eyes ache; but you won't find a hole in it, nor a threadbare place. It's the best he had, and a fine one too. They'd have wasted it, if it hadn't been for me.

What do you call wasting of it?

Putting it on him to be buried in, to be sure. Somebody was fool enough to do it, but I took it off again. If calico an't good enough for such a purpose, it isn't good enough for anything. It's quite as becoming to the body. He can't look uglier than he did in that one.

`Scrooge listened to this dialogue in horror. As they sat grouped about their spoil, in the scanty light afforded by the old man's lamp, he viewed them with a detestation and disgust, which could hardly have been greater, though they had been obscene demons, marketing the corpse itself.

"Ha, ha!" laughed the same woman, when old Joe, producing a flannel bag with money in it, told out their several gains upon the ground.

This is the end of it, you see! He frightened every one away from him when he was alive, to profit us when he was dead! Ha, ha, ha!

Spirit! I see, I see. The case of this unhappy man might be my own. My life tends that way, now. Merciful Heaven, what is this!

He recoiled in terror, for the scene had changed, and now he almost touched a bed: a bare, uncurtained bed: on which, beneath a ragged sheet, there lay a something covered up, which, though it was dumb, announced itself in awful language.

The room was very dark, too dark to be observed with any accuracy, though Scrooge glanced round it in obedience to a secret impulse, anxious to know what kind of room it was. A pale light, rising in the outer air, fell straight upon the bed; and on it, plundered and bereft, unwatched, unwept, uncared for, was the body of this man.

Scrooge glanced towards the Phantom. Its steady hand was pointed to the head. The cover was so carelessly adjusted that the slightest raising of it, the motion of a finger upon Scrooge's part, would have disclosed the face. He thought of it, felt how easy it would be to do, and longed to do it; but had no more power to withdraw the veil than to dismiss the spectre at his side.

Oh cold, cold, rigid, dreadful Death, set up thine altar here, and dress it with such terrors as thou hast at thy command: for this is thy dominion! But of the loved, revered, and honoured head, thou canst not turn one hair to thy dread purposes, or make one feature odious. It is not that the hand is heavy and will fall down when released; it is not that the heart and pulse are still; but that the hand WAS open, generous, and true; the heart brave, warm, and tender; and the pulse a man's. Strike, Shadow, strike! And see his good deeds springing from the wound, to sow the world with life immortal!

No voice pronounced these words in Scrooge's ears, and yet he heard them when he looked upon the bed. He thought, if this man could be raised up now, what would be his foremost thoughts? Avarice, hard dealing, griping cares? They have brought him to a rich end, truly! He lay, in the dark empty house, with not a man, a woman, or a child, to say he was kind to me in this or that, and for the memory of one kind word I will be kind to him. A cat was tearing at the door, and there was a sound of gnawing rats beneath the hearth-stone. What *they* wanted in the room of death, and why they were so restless and disturbed, Scrooge did not dare to think.

Spirit, this is a fearful place. In leaving it, I shall not leave its lesson, trust me. Let us go!

I understand you, and I would do it, if I could. But I have not the power, Spirit. I have not the power.

Still the Ghost pointed with an unmoved finger to the head.

Again it seemed to look upon him.

If there is any person in the town, who feels emotion caused by this man's death, show that person to me, Spirit, I beseech you!

The Phantom spread its dark robe before him for a moment, like a wing; and withdrawing it, revealed a room by daylight, where a mother and her children were.
She was expecting some one, and with anxious eagerness; for she walked up and down the room; started at every sound; looked out from the window; glanced at the clock; tried, but in vain, to work with her needle; and could hardly bear the voices of the children in their play.
At length the long-expected knock was heard. She hurried to the door, and met her husband; a man whose face was care-worn and depressed, though he was young. There was a remarkable expression in it now; a kind of serious delight of which he felt ashamed, and which he struggled to repress.
He sat down to the dinner that had been hoarding for him by the fire; and when she asked him faintly what news (which was not until after a long silence), he appeared embarrassed how to answer.

Is it good, or bad?

Bad.

We are quite ruined?

No. There is hope yet, Caroline.

If he relents there is! Nothing is past hope, if such a miracle has happened.

He is past relenting. He is dead.

She was a mild and patient creature if her face spoke truth; but she was thankful in her soul to hear it, and she said so, with clasped hands. She prayed forgiveness the next moment, and was sorry; but the first was the emotion of her heart.

"What the half-drunken woman, whom I told you of last night, said to me when I tried to see him and obtain a week's delay; and what I thought was a mere excuse to avoid me; turns out to have been quite true. He was not only very ill, but dying, then."

"To whom will our debt be transferred?"

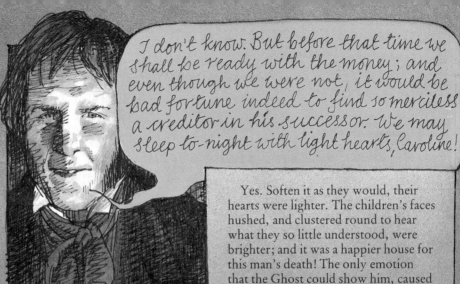

"I don't know. But before that time we shall be ready with the money; and even though we were not, it would be bad fortune indeed to find so merciless a creditor in his successor. We may sleep to-night with light hearts, Caroline!"

Yes. Soften it as they would, their hearts were lighter. The children's faces hushed, and clustered round to hear what they so little understood, were brighter; and it was a happier house for this man's death! The only emotion that the Ghost could show him, caused by the event, was one of pleasure.

"Let me see some tenderness connected with a death, or that dark chamber, Spirit, which we left just now, will be for ever present to me."

The Ghost conducted him through several streets familiar to his feet; and as they went along, Scrooge looked here and there to find himself, but nowhere was he to be seen. They entered poor Bob Cratchit's house; the dwelling he had visited before; and found the mother and the children seated round the fire.

Quiet. Very quiet. The noisy little Cratchits were as still as statues in one corner, and sat looking up at Peter, who had a book before him. The mother and her daughters were engaged in sewing. But surely they were very quiet!

"'And He took a child, and set him in the midst of them.'"

Where had Scrooge heard these words? He had not dreamed them. The boy must have read them out, as he and the Spirit crossed the threshold. Why did he not go on?

The mother laid her work upon the table, and put her hand up to her face.

"The colour hurts my eyes."

The colour? Ah, poor Tiny Tim!

"They're better now again. It makes them weak by candle-light; and I wouldn't show weak eyes to your father when he comes home, for the world. It must be near his time."

"Past it rather. But I think he's walked a little slower than he used, these few last evenings, Mother."

They were very quiet again. At last she said, and in a steady cheerful voice, that only faultered once:

"I have known him walk with—I have known him walk with Tiny Tim upon his shoulder, very fast indeed."

"And so have I, often."

"And so have I!"

"But he was very light to carry and his father loved him so, that it was no trouble—no trouble"

"And there is your father at the door!"

She hurried out to meet him; and little Bob in his comforter—he had need of it, poor fellow—came in. His tea was ready for him on the hob, and they all tried who should help him to it most. Then the two young Cratchits got upon his knees and laid, each child a little cheek, against his face, as if they said, "Don't mind it father. Don't be grieved!"

Bob was very cheerful with them, and spoke pleasantly to all the family. He looked at the work upon the table, and praised the industry and speed of Mrs. Cratchit and the girls. They would be done long before Sunday, he said.

"Sunday! You went to-day then Robert?"

"Yes, my dear. I wish you could have gone. It would have done you good to see how green a place it is. But you'll see it often. I promised him that I would walk there on a Sunday."

"My little little child! My little child!"

He broke down all at once. He couldn't help it. If he could have helped it, he and his child would have been farther apart perhaps than they were.

He left the room, and went up stairs into the room above, which was lighted cheerfully, and hung with Christmas. There was a chair set close beside the child, and there were signs of some one having been there, lately. Poor Bob sat down in it, and when he had thought a little and composed himself, he kissed the little face. He was reconciled to what had happened, and went down again quite happy.

They drew about the fire, and talked; the girls and mother working still. Bob told them of the extraordinary kindness of Mr. Scrooge's nephew, whom he had scarcely seen but once, and who, meeting him in the street that day, and seeing that he look a little—"just a little down you know" said Bob, inquired what had happened to distress him.

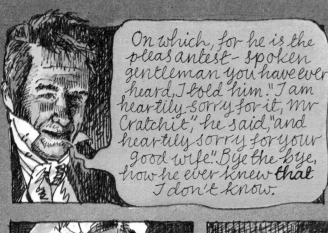

On which, for he is the pleasantest-spoken gentleman you have ever heard, I told him. "I am heartily sorry for it, Mr Cratchit," he said, "and heartily sorry for your good wife." Bye the bye, how he ever knew **that** I don't know.

Knew what, my dear?

Why, that you were a good wife.

Everybody knows that!

Very well observed, my boy! I hope they do. "Heartily sorry," he said, "for your good wife. If I can be of service to you in any way" he said, giving me his card, "that's where I live. Pray come to me." Now, it wasn't for the sake of anything he might be able to do for us, so much as for his kind way, that this was quite delightful. It really seemed as if he had known our Tiny Tim, and felt with us.

I'm sure he's a good soul!

You would be surer of it, my dear, if you saw and spoke to him. I shouldn't be at all surprised, mark what I say, if he got Peter a better situation.

Only hear that, Peter.

And then, Peter will be keeping company with some one, and setting up for himself

Get along with you!

It's just as likely as not, one of these days; though there's plenty of time for that, my dear. But however and whenever we part from one another, I am sure we shall none of us forget poor Tiny Tim—shall we— or this first parting there was among us?

Never, Father!

And I know, I know, my dears, that when we recollect how patient and how mild he was; although he was a little, little child; we shall not quarrel easily among ourselves, and forget poor Tiny Tim in doing it.

I am very happy!

No, never father!

'No, never father!'

Mrs. Cratchit kissed him, his daughters kissed him, the two young Cratchits kissed him, and Peter and himself shook hands. Spirit of Tiny Tim, thy childish essence was from God!

Spectre, something informs me that our parting moment is at hand. I know it but I know not how. Tell me what man that was whom we saw lying dead?

The Ghost of Christmas Yet To Come conveyed him, as before— though at a different time, he thought: indeed, there seemed no order in these latter visions, save that they were in the Future—into the resorts of business men, but showed him not himself. Indeed, the Spirit did not stay for anything, but went straight on, as to the end just now desired, until besought by Scrooge to tarry for a moment.

This court through which we hurry now, is where my place of occupation is, and has been for a length of time.

I see the house. Let me behold what I shall be, in days to come

The Spirit stopped; the hand was pointed elsewhere.

The house is yonder. Why do you point away?

The inexorable finger underwent no change.

Scrooge hastened to the window of his office, and looked in. It was an office still, but not his. The furniture was not the same, and the figure in the chair was not himself. The Phantom pointed as before.

He joined it once again, and wondering why and whither he had gone, accompanied it until they reached an iron gate. He paused to look round before entering.

A churchyard. Here, then, the wretched man whose name he had now to learn, lay underneath the ground. It was a worthy place. Walled in by houses; overrun by grass and weeds, the growth of vegetation's death, not life; choked up with too much burying; fat with repleted appetite. A worthy place!

The Spirit stood among the graves, and pointed down to One. He advanced towards it trembling. The Phantom was exactly as it had been, but he dreaded that he saw new meaning in its solemn shape.

Before I draw nearer to that stone to which you point, answer me one question. Are these the shadows of the things that Will be, or are they shadows of the things that May be, only?

Still the Ghost pointed downward to the grave by which it stood.

STAVE V

——

THE END OF IT

Yes! and the bedpost was his own. The bed was his own, the room was his own. Best and happiest of all, the Time before him was his own, to make amends in!

He was so fluttered and so glowing with his good intentions, that his broken voice would scarcely answer to his call. He had been sobbing violently in his conflict with the Spirit, and his face was wet with tears.

I will live in the Past, the Present, and the Future! The Spirits of all Three shall strive within me. Oh Jacob Marley! Heaven, and the Christmas Time be praised for this! I say it on my knees, Old Jacob; on my knees!

They are not torn down, they are not torn down, rings and all. They are here: I am here: the shadows of the things that would have been, may be dispelled. They will be. I know they will!

His hands were busy with his garments all this time: turning them inside out, putting them on upside down, tearing them, mislaying them, making them parties to every kind of extravagance.

He had frisked into the sitting-room, and was now standing there: perfectly winded.

There's the saucepan that the gruel was in!

There's the door by which the ghost of Jacob Marley entered!

There's the corner where the Ghost of Christmas Present sat!

There's the window where I saw the wandering spirits. It's all right, it's all true, it all happened. Ha ha ha!

I don't know what to do! I am as light as a feather, I am as happy as an angel, I am as merry as a schoolboy. I am as giddy as a drunken man. A merry Christmas to everybody! A happy New Year to all the world! Hallo here! Whoop! Hallo!

Really, for a man who had been out of practice for so many years, it was a splendid laugh, a most illustrious laugh. The father of a long, long, line of brilliant laughs!

I don't know what day of the month it is! I don't know how long I've been among the Spirits. I don't know anything. I'm quite a baby. Never mind. I don't care. I'd rather be a baby. Hallo! Whoop! Hallo here!

He was checked in his transports by the churches ringing out the lustiest peals he had ever heard. Clash, clang, hammer, ding, dong, bell. Bell, dong, ding, hammer, clang, clash! Oh, glorious, glorious!

Running to the window, he opened it, and put out his head. No fog, no mist; clear, bright, jovial, stirring, cold; cold, piping for the blood to dance to; Golden sunlight; Heavenly sky; sweet fresh air; merry bells. Oh, glorious. Glorious!

What's to-day?

. . . calling downwards to a boy in Sunday clothes, who perhaps had loitered in to look about him.

Eh?

What's to-day my fine fellow?

To-day! why, CHRISTMAS DAY

It's Christmas Day! I haven't missed it. The Spirits have done it all in one night. They can do anything they like. Of course they can. Of course they can.

Hallo my fine fellow! Do you know the Poulterer's, in the next street but one, at the corner?

I should hope I did,

An intelligent boy! A remarkable boy! Do you know whether they've sold the prize Turkey that was hanging up there? Not the little prize Turkey: the big one?

What, the one as big as me?

What a delightful boy. It's a pleasure to talk to him. Yes, my buck!

It's hanging there now.

Is it? Go and buy it.

Walk-ER!

No, no, I am in earnest. Go and buy it, and tell 'em to bring it here, that I may give them the direction where to take it. Come back with the man, and I'll give you a shilling. Come back with him in less than five minutes and I'll give you half-a-crown!

The boy was off like a shot. He must have had a steady hand at a trigger who could have got a shot off half so fast.

The hand in which he wrote the address was not a steady one, but write it he did, somehow, and went down stairs to open the street door, ready for the coming of the poulterer's man. As he stood there, waiting his arrival, the knocker caught his eye.

I'll send it to Bob Cratchit's. He sha'n't know who sends it. It's twice the size of Tiny Tim. Joe Miller never made such a joke as sending it to Bob's will be!

I shall love it, as long as I live! I scarcely ever looked at it before. What an honest expression it has on its face. It's a wonderful knocker!

Here's the Turkey. Hallo! Whoop! How are you! Merry Christmas!

It *was* a Turkey! He never could have stood upon his legs, that bird. He would have snapped 'em short off in a minute, like sticks of sealing-wax.

Why, it's impossible to carry that to Camden Town. You must have a cab.

The chuckle with which he said this, and the chuckle with which he paid for the Turkey, and the chuckle with which he paid for the cab, and the chuckle with which he recompensed the boy, were only to be exceeded by the chuckle with which he sat down breathless in his chair again, and chuckled till he cried.

Shaving was not an easy task, for his hand continued to shake very much; and shaving requires attention, even when you don't dance while you are at it. But if he had cut the end of his nose off, he would have put a piece of sticking-plaister over it, and been quite satisfied.

He dressed himself "all in his best," and at last got out into the streets. The people were by this time pouring forth, as he had seen them with the Ghost of Christmas Present; and walking with his hands behind him, Scrooge regarded every one with a delighted smile. He looked so irresistibly pleasant, in a word, that three or four good-humoured fellows said, "Good morning, sir! A merry Christmas to you!" And Scrooge said often afterwards, that of all the blithe sounds he had ever heard, those were the blithest in his ears.

He had not gone far, when coming on towards him he beheld the portly gentleman, who had walked into his counting-house the day before and said, "Scrooge and Marley's, I believe?" It sent a pang across his heart to think how this old gentleman would look upon him when they met; but he knew what path lay straight before him, and he took it.

He passed the door a dozen times, before he had the courage to go up and knock. But he made a dash, and did it:

Yes, sir.

Is your master at home, my dear?

Where is he, my love?

He's in the dining-room, sir, along with mistress. I'll show you up stairs, if you please.

Thank'ee. He knows me, I'll go in here, my dear.

He turned it gently, and sidled his face in, round the door. They were looking at the table (which was spread out in great array); for these young housekeepers are always nervous on such points, and like to see everything is right.

Fred!

Dear heart alive, how his niece by marriage started! Scrooge had forgotten, for the moment, about her sitting in the corner with the footstool, or he wouldn't have done it, on any account.

Why bless my soul! Who's that?

It's I. Your uncle Scrooge. I have come to dinner. Will you let me in, Fred?

Let him in! It is a mercy he didn't shake his arm off. He was at home in five minutes. Nothing could be heartier. His niece looked just the same. So did Topper when *he* came. So did the plump sister, when *she* came. So did every one when *they* came. Wonderful party, wonderful games, wonderful unanimity, won-der-ful happiness!

But he was early at the office next morning. Oh he was early there. If he could only be there first, and catch Bob Cratchit coming late! That was the thing he had set his heart upon.

And he did it; yes he did! The clock struck nine. No Bob. A quarter past. No Bob. He was full eighteen minutes and a half, behind his time. Scrooge sat with his door wide open, that he might see him come into the Tank.

His hat was off, before he opened the door; his comforter too. He was on his stool in a jiffy; driving away with his pen, as if he were trying to overtake nine o'clock.

Hallo! What do you mean by coming here at this time of day?

I'm very sorry, sir, I am behind my time.

You are? Yes. I think you are. Step this way, if you please.

It's only once a year, sir. It shall not be repeated. I was making rather merry yesterday, sir.

Now, I'll tell you what, my friend, I am not going to stand this sort of thing any longer. And therefore,

. . . he continued, leaping from his stool, and giving Bob such a dig in the waistcoat that he staggered back into the Tank again:

and therefore I am about to raise your salary!

Bob trembled, and got a little nearer to the ruler. He had a momentary idea of knocking Scrooge down with it; holding him; and calling to the people in the court for help and a strait-waistcoat.

A merry Christmas, Bob! A merrier Christmas, Bob, my good fellow, than I have given you, for many a year! I'll raise your salary, and endeavour to assist your struggling family, and we will discuss your affairs this very afternoon, over a Christmas bowl of smoking bishop, Bob! Make up the fires, and buy another coal-scuttle before you dot another i, Bob Cratchit!

Scrooge was better than his word. He did it all,
and infinitely more; and to Tiny Tim, who did
NOT die, he was a second father. He became as
good a friend, as good a master, and as good a
man, as the good old city, or any other good old
city, town, or borough, in the good old world.
Some people laughed to see the alteration in him,
but he let them laugh, and little heeded them; for
he was wise enough to know that nothing ever
happened on this globe, for good, at which some
people did not have their fill of laughter in the
outset; and knowing that such as these would be
blind anyway, he thought it quite as well that they
should wrinkle up their eyes in grins, as have the
malady in less attractive forms. His own heart
laughed: and that was quite enough for him.

He had no further intercourse with Spirits, but
lived upon the Total Abstinence Principle, ever
afterwards; and it was always said of him, that he
knew how to keep Christmas well, if any man alive
possessed the knowledge. May that be truly said of
us, and all of us! And so, as Tiny Tim observed,
God Bless Us, Every One!

The End